Corporate Governance

Institute of Public Enterprise

Corporate Governance

A Global Perspective

R.K. Mishra
Stuart Locke
D. Geeta Rani

ACADEMIC FOUNDATION
NEW DELHI

www.academicfoundation.com

First published in 2012
by

ACADEMIC FOUNDATION
4772-73 / 23 Bharat Ram Road, (23 Ansari Road),
Darya Ganj, New Delhi - 110 002 (India).
Phones : 23245001 / 02 / 03 / 04.
Fax : +91-11-23245005.
E-mail : books@academicfoundation.com
www. Academicfoundation.com

In association with

Institute of Public Enterprise, Hyderabad

Corporate Governance: A Global Perspective
by R.K. Mishra, Stuart Locke and D. Geeta Rani

ISBN 13: 9788171889341
ISBN 10: 8171889344

Typeset by Italics India, New Delhi.
Printed and bound in India.

Contents

About the Authors

R.K. Mishra, Senior Professor and Director, Institute of Public Enterprise (IPE), Hyderabad, did his PhD from University of Rajasthan. A Visiting Fellow at London Business School (UK), he also studied for International Teachers programme at SDA Bocconi, Milan. Dr Mishra taught at the University of Bradford, and was a Visiting Professor at Maison Des Sciences De L' Hommes, Paris and Faculty of Economics, University of Ljubljana, Slovenia. He is a member of the UN Task Force on International Standards of Excellence in Public Administration and Education. He is special invite on OECD Working Group on Privatization and Corporate Governance of SOEs and Asian Network of Corporate Governance. He is Non-Executive Director on some of the public and private enterprise boards in India. He has considerable experience of teaching and guiding research for doctoral degree in management, economics, public administration and commerce. His areas of interest include: corporate governance, international management, international finance, public-private partnership and restructuring and environmental administration.

Stuart Locke is Director of the Institute for Business Research at the University of Waikato, New Zealand and Chairperson of Department of Finance, which is ranked as number one for research in the country. Dr Locke has a background in finance, economics and chartered accountancy. His current research interests are in corporate governance in mature and emerging markets across the spectrum from small businesses, cooperatives, voluntary, state sector and listed public companies. Stuart continues to publish widely in academic journals, participates regularly in media events, public speaking at conventions and is a Board member of his local Chamber of Commerce. Stuart also has a small thoroughbred horse breeding and training business based in Cambridge, New Zealand.

D. Geeta Rani is working as Research Fellow, Waikato University, New Zealand and also Visiting Professor at the Institute of Public Enterprise, Hyderabad. Apart from teaching, she is also involved in research projects like Performance Appraisal of Andhra Pradesh-State Level Public Enterprises and Corporate Governance Public and Private Enterprises. She taught at undergraduate, graduate and postgraduate levels in the North-East African Universities, like, Addis Ababa University and Debub University in Ethiopia; Asmara University and Asmara Commercial College in Asmara, Eritrea, for a period of six years.

Preface

Corporate governance will be the guidepost for determining the growth, quality of services rendered and accountability to the society at large during the 21st century. It is an integrative tool and philosophy to guide businesses—local, national, regional and global. It will provide an effective connect between businesses and politics, people and businesses, present and future, performance and sustainability, and operations and innovations.

More and more liberalisation will result into more and more independence for businesses. Corporate governance will act as a radar to avoid any clash between markets and businesses. Instead of a warring world, corporate governance will ensure a harmonious society in search of shared common future and a better understanding. Businesses and society will not be at daggers drawn but shaking hands in the common pursuit of value addition without endangering peace.

The present volume, based on an intensive research of corporate governance practices in various countries, makes an attempt to discern the art and science of corporate governance. Besides highlighting the specifics of corporate governance in these countries, the volume brings out the areas which required greater attention for an intensive application of corporate governance and the possible gains that are likely to occur as a result of holistic application of this vital philosophy.

Functioning of Boards

> Board effectiveness can be judged by performance against appropriate benchmarks and accountability is measured by the degree to which boards respond to the needs of those they are there to serve. The two go together to the extent that, the more accountable a company is the more its standards of performance are set objectively from outside the enterprise.
>
> —Sir Adrian Cadbury[1]

The primary focus of this chapter is to throw light on the functioning style and performance of boards and discuss the issues relating to it with references to popular corporate cases. The cases of Swissair (now SWISS) and General Motors are discussed at length. Besides, the three conceptual-based models relating to the boards' performance are also presented.

While boards have previously been regarded as passive (Mace, 1986), the growing power of investors and the media have to a larger extent pressured boards to play a more active role in company affairs (Coles *et al.*, 2001; Judge and Reinhardt, 1997). The demands made on directors have grown significantly and the issues with which they have to deal with have widened by a great extent. Boards can no longer enjoy the luxury of passivity (Lorsch and Khurana, 1999). They need to be active players in shaping the companies. Directors have no choice but to perform their roles seriously (Cadbury, 2002). Boards' performance is therefore an important area of research.

1.1 Board Structure

Board structure is a foundation for an effective board, focussing on the background interests, affiliations and position of members. It is concerned

---

1. Sir Adrian Cadbury, Chairman of the UK Committee on the Financial Aspects of Corporate Governance, which published its *Report and Code of Best Practice* in December 1992. His book, *Corporate Governance and Chairmanship—A Personal View* (2002), has been translated into Japanese, Chinese and Italian. In 2005, he was awarded the Laureate Medal for Corporate Governance.

with balances of power and is at the heart of board performance and accountability. In recent times, one of the primary approaches to improve governance effectiveness is changing the board structure. These changes often focussed on reducing the size of the board, and removing or reducing geographic parameters in board composition. In addition, organisations focussed on governance models and the competencies of board members.

Board structure distinguishes between those directors who hold management positions in the company and those who do not. Those with management positions are referred to as executive directors and those without are called non-executive directors in Britain and outside directors in USA. Not all non-executive directors are the same. There is a difference between the non-executive director and the independent non-executive director. As per the Cadbury Report (1992), '"Independent" directors are defined as persons who "apart from directors' fees and shareholdings [are] independent of the management and free from any business or other relationships which could materially interfere with the exercise of the independent judgment."'

The responsibility of the board is to govern the company, while the managers' task is to run its business. The work of board is corporate governance and that of the executive organisation is management (Tricker, 1984).

1.2 The Board and Management Differentiated

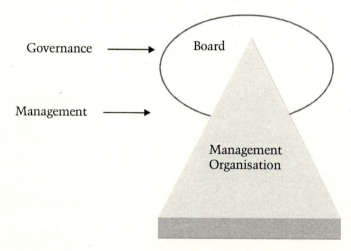

Basically there are four alternative board structures:

- The all-executive board structure in which every director is also a managerial employee of the business. In India, many small private and family firms have this structure. There is no outsider representation in the top management team in this model.
- The majority executive board on which the outside directors are in the minority.
- The majority outside board with a majority of outside, non-executive directors.
- The two-tier board in which there are no common members between the board and the executive management team. This model is more popular in Germany.

1.3 A Theory-based Review on Board Performance

The three conceptual models (Wong and Van, 2008) for board performance are presented below:

1.3.1 The Structure Model

Pfeffer (1983) provided the basic rationale for expecting a direct relationship between board structure and board role performance. The governance theories of agency, stewardship and resource dependence can be used to develop the propositions in terms of the board roles of monitoring, service, strategy, and resource provision.

Monitoring: The propositions for the relationship between board structure and board monitoring role come from the agency perspective. Agency theorists adopt a control approach aimed at cutting down the self-interests of managers (agents) that may negatively impact shareholders' (principals) wealth (Eisenhardt, 1989). A control approach stresses discipline (Sundaramurthy and Lewis, 2003). As noted by Fama (1980: 294), 'the board is the "ultimate internal monitor...whose most important role is to scrutinise the highest decision makers within the firm."'

Structurally, agency proponents thus argue that an impartial assessment of managers will occur more readily if the board is independent of executive management. Since the insider directors are subordinates of the CEO, they will be either unwilling or in a very difficult position to perform a monitoring role. On the other hand, as outsider directors are not part of the organisation's management team, they are less subjected to the same potential conflicts of interest that are likely to affect the judgments of insider directors (Kosnik, 1987).

Independence is, however, not only a structural attribute, but also a psychological trait that gives rise to corresponding behaviours. Board structure may therefore be related to, but is not an adequate proxy for independence (Cadbury, 2002; Dalton *et al.*, 1999). The presence of independent board members does not imply that they have inherently higher standards of integrity than their executive colleagues. It is simply that it is easier for them to take an objective view of whatever matters are under review. They stand further back from the action; they bring outside standards on the issues and their interests are less directly at stake (Cadbury, 2002). Nevertheless, both insider and outsider directors have the same legal responsibilities in most jurisdictions. These include a duty of care and diligence to all shareholders.

Agency proponents such as Jensen (1993) argued that a small board is more effective for monitoring role. When the boards get larger, they are less likely to function effectively and it becomes easier for the CEO to control the board. Thus, under the agency theory, it is proposed that: board size is negatively related to board monitoring role.

Service: Board service role is advocated under the competing theories of agency and stewardship. In terms of the agency theory's board structure, Fama and Jensen (1983) noted that outsider directors may facilitate effective evaluation of management proposals by providing valuable advice. A small board size should be more beneficial for effective functioning. As noted by Firstenberg and Malkiel (1994: 34), a small board size of eight or fewer members 'engenders focus, participation, and genuine interaction and debate' for directors to advise management on company issues. Thus, under the agency perspective, it is proposed that: the proportion of outsider directors is positively related to board service role.

Strategy: Both the agency and resource dependence theories cover strategy as a board role. The two theories are similar in supporting outsider-dominated structures. Agency theorists argue that outsider directors, in view of their industry exposure, are more likely to suggest company strategies (Baysinger and Hoskisson, 1990). In contrast, while insider directors are likely to have better company information than outsiders, they may be reluctant to propose radical strategies as this may conflict with the CEO's plan or it may seem that they are stealing the CEO's limelight (Johnson et al., 1996). Resource dependence proponents see the advantages of having outsider directors in a board's link with the external environment for strategic information (Stiles and Taylor, 2000). With this information, directors may be actively involved in the strategic arena by initiating their own analyses or suggesting alternatives (Zahra and Pearce, 1989).

Hence, under both the agency and resource dependence perspectives, it is proposed that: the proportion of outsider directors is positively related to board strategy role.

Resource provision: Resource dependence theory provides the theoretical foundation for directors' resource role (Daily et al., 2003). Boards are important boundary spanners that secure resources for a company (Pfeffer and Salancik, 1978). Outsider directors are crucial in securing essential resources for the firm. They can bring in more knowledge, efforts and debate to the board (Conger et al., 2001). Outsider-dominated boards tend to attract more scarce resources (Provan, 1980). By attracting or co-opting prominent members of the community to serve on their boards, companies are better placed to attract sources of funds.

Board size is often taken as a measure of an organisation's ability to form environmental links to secure critical resources (Goodstein et al., 1994). A larger board is associated with a firm's ability to extract critical resources such as amount of budget, external funding and leverage from the environment (Pfeffer, 1972; Provan, 1980). Thus, under the resource dependence theory, it is proposed that: the proportion of outsider directors is positively related to board resource provision role.

1.3.2 The Process Model

The theoretical basis for the process model is derived from social psychology research that analyses interactions among group members (Smith et al., 1994). As a board is essentially a group at the apex of a company's decision control structure (Fama and Jensen, 1963), researchers have therefore hypothesised that an in-depth understanding of group process is important (Bettenhausen, 1991; Pierce, 1994). Pierce (1994) for example reasoned that much of the director's output happens at board level, and therefore research should emphasise not so much on the competencies of an individual director but at the level of the group. In his opinion, it is the team working together rather than the individual director's effectiveness which is of significance, and therefore issues regarding the extent of interaction, synergy and complementarily should be considered. Effectiveness of the board is likely to depend greatly on the socio-psychological processes, especially those related to group participation, interaction, exchange of information and critical discussion (Butler, 1981; Jackson, 1992; Milliken and Vollrath, 1991).

The process model will be explained in terms of the individual board process variables of effort norms, cognitive conflict and use of skills (Forbes and Milliken, 1999).

Effort norms: Effort norm is a group-level construct that refers to the group's shared belief on the level of effort each individual is expected to contribute towards a task (Wageman, 1995). As directors only meet periodically, there is always a possibility of process losses (Steiner, 1972). This is the situation whereby the lack of interaction may result in the board not reaching its full potential. There is also the chance of 'social loafing' whereby individuals in the group fail to give their maximum effort to the task, perhaps thinking that they can rely on the others to do the group's work (Williams *et al.*, 1981).

Some researchers thus reasoned that directors who devote sufficient time to their duties and seek out information they need are better able to perform their roles (Lorsch and MacIver, 1989). Other researchers have gone a step further. They argued that effective usage of time during meetings is more critical. Vafeas (1999) noted that the quality of board meetings is an important area for further research. Boards that spend similar amount of time can exhibit different levels of effort (Monks and Minow, 2004). Thus, boards that have high-effort behaviour among members should be better able to perform their roles.

Cognitive conflict: In cognitive conflict, open debate of different views in groups could lead to faster completion of tasks and more effective use of resources (Schwenk and Valacich, 1994; Tjosvold *et al.,* 1992). Cognitive conflict within groups also encourages people to develop new ideas and approaches, hence enhancing group learning and assessment of situations (Jehn and Mannix, 2001).

The presence of disagreement and criticism from the board may require CEOs to explain, justify and possibly modify their positions on important issues. It serves to remind management of the power and role of the board and of the importance of considering shareholder's interests. This will improve the board's performance of its monitoring role.

In addition, the different views of directors should result in better guidance and counsel to the CEO and top management (Milliken and Vollrath, 1991). Cognitive conflict results in consideration of more alternatives and a more careful evaluation of alternatives processes that could contribute to the quality of strategic role of boards (Eisenhardt *et al.,* 1997; Jackson, 1992). Finally, with cognitive conflict, firms may be able to obtain more valuable information (Amason, 1996). This serves to reduce the transaction costs of dealing with uncertainties of the environment, thereby enhancing the resource provision role of boards (Conger *et al.,* 2001).

Use of skills: Boards must tap and apply a variety of skills to function effectively in today's business environment. Directors need to use two types of skills to perform effectively. One type of skills is functional skills and the other is firm-specific skills (Ancona and Caldwell, 1988; Nonaka, 1994). Functional skills pertain to the domains of businesses, including strategic thinking, analytical thinking and result-oriented outlook (Dulewicz *et al.,* 1995). Boards, as the apex of a firm's decision-making structure (Fama and Jensen, 1983), must have directors with such functional skills.

If boards want to provide good service to CEOs/top managers, they must be able to combine their knowledge of various functional areas and apply that knowledge to firm-specific issues (Forbes and Milliken, 1999). Similarly, if boards are to perform their monitoring role effectively, they must integrate their knowledge of the firm's internal affairs with their expertise in areas such as law and strategy (Carpenter and Westphal, 2001; Forbes and Milliken, 1999).

Boards as elite, strategic-issue processing groups must have members who possess skills that they could utilise in information gathering and strategic evaluation (Ancona and Caldwell, 1988). Directors value strategically relevant experience as it will improve strategic skills.

While skills may be present, the actual use of skills is of utmost significance. Anecdotal evidence from corporate failures has shown that boards with directors of excellent skills sets do not use them (Sonnenfeld, 2002). In addition, the possibility of 'social loafing' whereby individuals in the group fail to use their skills to the task provide further argument that the presence of skills does not automatically lead to the use of skills (Williams *et al.,* 1981).

1.3.3 The Mediation Model

The mediation model is a combination of structure and process models. It posits that board structure will affect process that in turn influence performance (that is, board structure, board process and board role performance). In essence, board structure has no direct impact on board's role performance (Cohen and Bailey, 1997; Gladstein, 1984; Hackman and Morris, 1975). In this approach, the structural board characteristics will affect process before results appear. Despite the intrinsic benefit of mediation models, there is limited empirical attention (Stewart and Barrick, 2000). The reason is possibly due to the lack of access to primary data from directors. The development of mediation propositions is explained in terms of the three board process variables of effort norms, cognitive conflict and use of skills.

Effort norms: The presence of outsider directors will boost the level of effort norms as such directors view their roles differently from those of the insider directors. In contrast, the insider directors are more likely to see their directors' duties as an extension of their management functions. Thus, with the presence of a separate chairman and outsider directors, insider directors (including CEOs) may be coerced into performing better. Consequently, the level of effort norms within the board rises (Forbes and Milliken, 1999).

Large boards may have difficulty in enhancing or even maintaining board effort norms. According to group dynamics theory, if a group grows too large, communication among directors become increasingly difficult; directors would find it harder to get to know each other and only a fraction of the board would participate in board discussions. If a director fails to prepare for a board meeting or to participate, the chances are that the lapse would go completely unnoticed (Gladstein, 1984; Goodstein et al., 1994; Shaw, 1981). This is the situation of 'social loafing' that usually exists in large groups (Latane et al., 1979; Williams et al., 1981). Social loafing refers to the decrease in group effort as the total number of people in the group increases. Large boards tend to be more diverse, more contentious and more fragmented than smaller boards (Dalton et al., 1999). Thus, a larger board would likely be associated with a lower level of effort norms within the board.

Cognitive conflict: The presence of outsider directors is likely to enhance the level of cognitive conflict in the board. This is because this group of directors is likely to share significantly fewer experiences with management. They are more likely to think freely with regard to the firm's goals and the range of alternatives available to them (Forbes and Milliken, 1999). Similarly, a larger board is likely to possess an abundance of differing perspectives. This will enhance the level of cognitive conflict in boards.

Use of skills: Outsider directors are often lawyers, financial representatives, top management of other firms, public affairs or marketing specialists, government officials and community leaders who bring with them important expertise, experience and skills (Hillman and Dalziel, 2003). Board size is often taken to represent an organisation's ability to link itself to the external environment for resources (Goodstein et al., 1994). Larger boards are likely to possess more skills for use at their disposal in decision-making (Forbes and Milliken, 1999).

1.4 Passive Board: A Case of Swissair

Effective corporate governance can lead to managerial excellence but managerial ethical excellence does not always exist without effective corporate governance. Embedded in both effective corporate governance and managerial excellence is the 'righteous of decisions' or the ethical decision-making process (Nwabueze and Mileski, 2008).

Swissair was started in 1931 when the two main Swiss airlines (Balair and Ad Astra Aero) merged to become Swissair. The company was Switzerland's national airline for 71 years from 1931 to 2002. For most of the Swissair's history, it was financially sound and stable. Because of its financial stability, it was 'renowned as a flying bank and it came to be regarded as a Switzerland's national symbol' (Steger and Krapf, 2002). However, Swissair had become a case study in failure. The main reason attributed for the failure of the Swissair is the interference of the national politics with the corporate governance of the company by eroding the corporate boundaries.

Swissair, considered as national pride, had a great deal of government control (owning 30 per cent of the stock) over certain aspects of the decision-making process (Ibid). Infact, at that time airline industry was undergoing major structural change worldwide. Airline strategy in the early 1990s had become one of alliances/partnership/joint venture relationships to expand routes for firms. An airline needed to partner at least with other airline to insure that its passenger would have access to destinations (Domke-Domonte, 2000). Airlines were now required to have seamless itineraries for passengers. With the changing times in the airline business, Swissair faced a choice between national pride manifest through tight government influence in decision-making or survival.

Swissair chose to engage in a 'Hunter Strategy' aimed at growing through acquisition rather than alliances (Ibid). This decision to acquire was driven primarily by the political need for control of this corporataion which represented the Swiss national pride. These processes did not recognise the economic facet of the industry or the European Union. The political and social facets of the Swiss society were driving managers into the years of poor decisions, made by political appointees who were incompetent and mostly absentee managers, who had little experience in the air transport industry (Teahan, 2002).

An example of this decision-making process for Swissair is manifest in the behaviour of the Swissair CEO at the time. Philippe Bruggisser, who emphasised a strategy of acquisition of stakes in different airlines; while outsiders openly questioned the value of these investment that were both experiencing financial difficulties and operating in lower market segments. Even board members thought Bruggisser was playing a lonely power game. However, the board failed to challenge the CEO's decisions because Swiss politics and society supported the national symbol (Ibid).

Further, the responsibility of corporate governance of Swissair was 'split in accordance with Swiss law'. For example, the day-to-day business was left to executive management but the board, which comprised the 'who's who of Switzerland', had ultimate responsibility for leading the company (Ibid). In a study done in the 1980s, the conclusion was that Switzerland was run by elite of 300 people from industry, banks, and trade associations (Ibid). And, as such, board members of corporations were often invited by their friends or chosen as a result of their political and banking connection. In addition, Swiss law required the majority of board members to be Swiss nationals as residents.

As a result of the legal requirements, some people held up to a dozen boards' seats in various companies, which led to the CEO of one company being the chairman of the board in another and vice-versa (Ibid). For example Swissair board chairman Eric Honegger, was also the director of Union Bank of Switzerland (UBS), the main bank of Swissair. UBS's chairman of the board, Robert Studer, was a Swissair board member. Financial Committee member, Vreni Spoerry-Toneatti, and deputy chairman, Tomas Schmidheiny, were also directors at Credit Suisse (CS). In turn, Rainer E.Gut, CS chairman and mentor of Lukas Muhlemann, sat on the Swissair board (Ibid).

With all these political and social interconnections, the management of Swissair, although legal in its composition, lacked appropriate checks and separations of powers between management and board. This created a situation where the questioning of decisions would have been a threat to the entire corporate board governance system of Switzerland. Therefore, questioning the ethics or even the economics of a decision would have been considered anti-Swiss.

The Swissair case shows a good example of how appropriate norms were not embedded in the various levels. The government with an equity holding of 30 per cent decided who the CEO was and how he was to conduct the business of Swissair congruent with the political agenda of the Swiss government and people. At an individual level, Philippe Bruggisser, the appointed COO of Swissair was made CEO of the company. He lacked the integrity to communicate to the government, board members and public the risks of the 'hunting' strategy which eventually led to the company to drown in debt that could not be paid until the government bailed it out (Ibid).

This dominance of political norms led to the board membership to reflect political affiliation rather than competence and experience in the aviation industry. Also, due to the split in corporate governance structure required under Swiss law, the board and management behaved as if there were a split in responsibility that got further 'muddled' by the difference between the business operations at Swissair and the clear functioning of the Swiss government. As a result of the compliance with political and social norms, economic norms and ethical norms were ignored, and thus, corporate failed.

At the corporate governance system level, the lack of accuracy in the auditing of Swissair's finances, PricewaterhouseCoopers (PWC)[2] (the auditors) led to four years of identical accounting statements which never reported the risk associated with the different holding (Steger and Krapf, 2002). As such, the political norm of Swissair as a national airline representing the pride of Swiss people, pressured auditors to fail to use due care in auditing financial statements. Further, the lack of questioning from the board confirmed that politics outweighed any other considerations.

Now the issue to address is how to develop, sustain and incorporate appropriate ethical, political, social and economic norms effectively into the daily decision-making process within the corporate governance structure?

Recommendations forwarded (Nwabueze and Mileski, 2008) to the members of the corporate governance structures as a result of the Swissair failure experience are as follows:

---

2. PricewaterhouseCoopers (trading as PwC) is a global professional services firm headquartered in London, United Kingdom. It is the world's largest professional services firm measured by revenues and one of the 'Big Four' accountancy firms.

1. Board of directors, CEOs and members of the executive management teams of companies need to be given clear messages about their expectations, their roles and responsibilities as the leaders of the organisation. Their scopes of authority must be defined in corporate bylaws, regulations and codes of conduct. They must be made to understand that they are 'servant leaders' and are obligated to serve the interest of the company stakeholders first and foremost. Executive management compensation should not translate into bloated executive pay packages, exorbitant stock option and fringe benefits. They should not benefit from insider information.

2. Executive management teams of companies also have obligations to the community in which it operates. Good corporate governance, which stems from the top, demands that officials steer companies towards being social conscious. Companies must embrace social equity and political awareness.

3. Good corporate governance dictates that the executive management team of companies should advocate labour practices that are fair, just and equitable. Corporations have an obligation to promote employees based upon their talents and skills. They also need to provide the employees with opportunities to enhance their skills and knowledge so that the workers can continue to meet the needs of business.

4. Good corporate governance also dictates that companies should produce quality and safe products. Products should be free from defects and should not cause harm directly or indirectly. Corporations should have utmost consideration for all rights of consumers and efforts must be made to obtain constant feedback about products that are introduced in the market. The process would enable the corporations to ensure that customer needs have been met.

1.5 Case of General Motors (GM)

Businessmen go down with their business because they like the old way so well they cannot bring themselves to change. One sees them all about—men who do not know that yesterday is past, and who woke up this morning with their last year's as a formula that when a man begins to think that he had at last found his method better begin a most searching examination of himself to see whether some part of his brain has gone to sleep.

—Henry Ford, *My Life and Work*, Doubleday, 1992.

The above quote of Henry ford has relevance to the General Motors case which is discussed as below.

In 20 years GM had gone from being a golden corporate success to being what *Fortune* magazine called a corporate 'dinosaur'. What went wrong?

The history of GM is an instructive story in how success can breed failure; how being the biggest and the best can lead to arrogance and an inability to adapt. GM was the premier car company in the world for so long that it failed to see the need for change. The company was so used to being leader that it couldn't contemplate following others. It was this mindset, this overwhelming belief that it was GM's divine right to be the most successful automobile company on earth that condemned the company to two decades of disaster. When GM did finally see the need to adapt, it did so with wild ineptitude, spending tens of billions in the 1980s for little reward.

As we review what went wrong at GM, and why; let us keep in mind our corporate 'tripod' of shareholders, directors, and management:

- Which group should have been responsible for seeing that GM adapted to a new competitive environment? All three?

- Or some other group, less intimately involved in GM and less beholden to its culture: suppliers, consumers, employees, the government?

- Given that it is in none of these groups' interests to see GM fail, and given the company's enormous resources to compete, why did no one (or at least no one in a position to do anything about it) see GM's decline coming?

- And why couldn't anyone head the crisis off before billions of dollars were wasted and tens of thousands of jobs lost?

GM was not alone in its failure to reposition itself for a new competitive environment. Ford displayed equal hubris in the face of the Japanese and suffered just as badly; Chrysler was only saved from bankruptcy by the intervention of billions of dollars in federal loan guarantees. However, both companies, being smaller, were able to respond to their respective crises with more rapidity. GM, by contrast, became living proof of the old boxing maxim: the bigger they are, the harder they fall.

1.5.1 Governance at GM: What went Wrong?

One episode sums up most of what was wrong with GM. The story concerns the Chevrolet Corvair, built in 1959. Even in the testing stage, Chevrolet's engineers noted some alarming safety defects, particularly the car's tendency to spin out of control when taking turns at speed. The president of Chevrolet wished to add a stabiliser bar to the vehicle, at a cost of $15 per car. He was overruled by the finance department, which claimed that the bar was an unnecessary cost. The Corvair rapidly gained a reputation as a lethal vehicle, but rather than admitting to the Corvair's faults and making changes, GM continued to market the dangerous car. In a sop to the critics, GM spent $1 million on safety studies.

General Motors was subjected to embarrassing congressional hearings led by Senators Abraham Ribicoff and Edward Kennedy. Chairman Frederic G. Donner was unable to recall GM's earnings from the year before, and had to ask an aide to come up with the $1.7 billion figure. Kennedy said that $1 million spent on safety out of such enormous profits was a meaningless gesture.

The main source of GM's nemesis turned out to be a young consumer advocate named Ralph Nader. Nader exposed the safety defects of the Corvair in a book entitled *Unsafe At Any Speed (1965)*. Instead of responding to the allegations, GM assailed Nader. The company hired private investigators to tail Nader, and produce whatever dirt they could. Rumors were spread that the consumer advocate was a homosexual and anti—Semitic. Ultimately, GM's president James Roche publicly apologised to Nader and admitted the defects in the Corvair. A stabiliser bar was finally added to the car in 1964, but by then Corvair's name was already damaged beyond repair.

1.5.2 GM's Lack of Vision in 1970s

At the peak of GM's power in the 1950s and 1960s Americans liked their cars big and showy. Power was vital, fuel efficiency irrelevant! When the Japanese showed up in the late 1960s and early 1970s, with their small, non-gas guzzling vehicles 'shit-boxes,' as they were known in Detroit, GM paid no attention. If there was a market in America for small cars, ran the reasoning, GM would already have cornered it. Rather, the company pledged to continue the lines that had always made money, the big, wide and heavy cars that could carry a family in comfort and the rich in luxury.

General Motors could be forgiven for its lack of vision in 1970. It was quite true that small cars did not sell in America, and the Japanese competition at this time was terrible, producing badly designed, badly made cars. But by 1980, Japan was making good small cars and Americans were buying them. GM's market share dwindled year after year as a result. This was not just a failure to guess where the new markets might be, it was a failure to adapt to a current market that was right before GM's eyes.

In retrospect, the 1970s can be identified as the decade when the American car industry should have changed its ways. Three factors combined to reshape the competitive environment:

1. ever-improving Japanese quality and design;
2. two oil crises that drove up the price of gas; and
3. federal regulations demanding better fuel efficiency and safety standards.

Infact, these factors were related. It was the oil crises that awoke the Federal government to the need for fuel efficiency; and it was Detroit's reluctance to treat quality and reliability as important issues that allowed the Japanese a huge headstart in that field.

In 1973, in response to America's support for Israel in the Yom Kippur war, the Organization of the Petroleum Exporting Countries (OPEC) agreed to impose an oil embargo on the West. As America and Europe scrambled to step up the search for oil in the North Sea, Alaska and the Gulf of Mexico, Western leaders also looked for ways to avoid being put at the mercy of OPEC again. One solution was to use less oil.

The oil crisis of 1973 or the energy crisis as it came to be called was a shock to Americans, who were used to paying about 30 cents a gallon for gas. Overnight, it was a dollar! People found themselves lining up all day for a commodity that had been almost as readily available as water. Suddenly, driving a car that only ran 10 miles to the gallon was no longer affordable. The move to smaller, lighter, more efficient cars was lightning fast. There was one group in a position to respond: the Japanese.

At the time of the 1973 oil crisis, Japanese cars accounted for about 10 per cent of the car market, compared with the 80 per cent share commanded by the Big Three (Chrysler, Ford and General Motors). Japanese automakers were still finding their feet in the early 1970s; they were not proficient in body design or engine production. Moreover, they had little idea about the market, producing cars in designs and colors that failed to appeal to Americans. But the Japanese response time was incredibly quick. Sensing a massive market for smaller, cheaper cars, Toyota and Honda worked at producing just that. They focussed on quality, efficiency, and reliability—issues that Detroit, with its massive guaranteed market share, had ignored.

1.5.3 GM's Bureaucratic Practices *versus* Japanese Lean and Flexible Practices

Japanese management practices, in contrast to GM's bureaucracy, were lean and highly flexible. They had none of the burdensome committee structures that crippled Detroit, none of the rigid hierarchies, and none of the acrimonious labour relations. The result was an altogether more efficient operation. As late as 1981, a GM internal study found that the Japanese could build a car for $1,800 less than it cost GM.

The Japanese were not overwhelmed by GM's institutional culture. Rather, the Japanese stressed innovation and customer service. Manufacturers and designers, labour and management, worked in teams with the lowliest assembly line workers, all seeking ways to make jobs easier and products better. At the same time, Japanese firms guaranteed their workers employment for life, engendering a loyalty to the company that was matched only by a loyalty to the customer. As a result, quality was built into the system. In Detroit, cars were pulled from the assembly line to correct defects or were sent to the market on the basis that discontented customers could send them back. In Japan, cars were built right the first time. Even in 1993, Japanese companies manufactured nine out of the top 10 quality-ranked vehicles, according to one survey. Japan was able to respond to consumer trends in a fraction of the time that it took the Big Three! As Americans moved toward smaller cars, the Japanese were there. As customers increasingly sought quality and reliability, the Japanese were there again. Even today, Japanese automakers are able to get a new model to the market a year quicker than their American counterparts. In the 1970s, this meant that Japan was able to get a massive headstart in the race to build small, efficient cars.

A second oil crisis in 1979, prompted by the overthrow of the Shah of Iran, merely accelerated the Japanese invasion. By 1980, the Japanese had raised their market share to 20 per cent, double to what it had been in 1970. In less than a decade, the Japanese had made quantum leaps in design and styling, and the small car market had become far more than a niche. But GM continued to underestimate the threat.

The Big Three's response to new federal regulations was to lobby for loopholes. In 1975, Congress passed the Corporate Average Fuel Economy (CAFE) law, which established increasingly stringent fuel efficiency standards for US cars. The intention was to double car mileage by 1985. The law encouraged smaller cars, since automakers were bound only by the average that their fleet recorded. Larger cars could underperform the CAFE standard as long as smaller cars could make up the difference. The CAFE law grew progressively weaker as Congress approved loophole after loophole. By 1986, GM had failed to meet the standards for four years in a row, but had paid no fines thanks to laws lowering the mileage requirements, or approving new methods of measurement that allowed GM to record higher fuel efficiency. In 1986, an attorney for Ralph Nader's Public Citizen consumer group told the Wall Street Journal, 'If all the [CAFE] statute is designed to do is ratify what GM and Ford wants to do on their own, there isn't much point to the statute.' Detroit also resisted efforts to improve safety standards. In April 1971, listening devices in the White House (made famous by the Watergate scandal) recorded Ford executive Lee Iacocca telling Richard Nixon that a federal law mandating airbags would cost US automakers crippling sums of money. He told Nixon that airbags represented a possible $4 billion annual cost to Ford, 'and you can see that safety has really killed all of our business.' Iacocca's pitching was successful in getting Nixon delay the federal laws mandating airbags.

Safety features such as airbags actually represented a competitive advantage for the Big Three; they were way ahead of the Japanese on safety technology. But they failed to anticipate increasing consumer demand for safety features, stressing the paramount importance of protecting the earnings column.

Detroit responded to new CAFE and safety standards by arguing that efficiency and safety standards were low among consumers' priorities compared to comfort and reliability. The automakers argued that they would provide more efficient engines and safety features just as soon as buyers demanded them. As we shall see in our discussion of the import restraints of the 1980s, the Big Three were very quick to abandon this free market position.

As small cars became increasingly popular, GM tried half-heartedly to compete. In 1970, it introduced its 'import buster', the Vega. The car was a lemon. It failed to meet any of its projections for weight, length, or price, and arrived at the market costing $300 more than the VW Bug. It was also riddled with mechanical defects. The car was outsold by the Ford Pinto in its first year, and was cancelled the next in the wake of a violent strike at the Vega plant. GM didn't mind. Executives resisted the opportunity to improve the Vega, believing that its failure merely proved that the small car market was ephemeral and a distraction.

By the late 1970s, when it was clear that small cars had arrived to stay, GM was still confident of its leadership. In a momentous high-cost decision, the company planned to shift away from heavy, gas-guzzling, rear-wheel-drive cars to more efficient front-wheel versions. The generation of 'X-cars', due to hit the streets in 1980 would show that GM's engineering was still the best there was.

The X-cars were disastrous. GM underestimated the huge changes that were necessary to switch from rear-wheel to front-wheel drives, and failed fully to re-engineer engines and transmissions. The result was that X-cars achieved a reputation for being shoddily made and unreliable. In 1981, GM unveiled the J-car project, another car series that was meant to send the Japanese packing. GM president F. James McDonald called the J-cars a $5 billion 'roll of the dice'. The J-cars suffered from the same cost-cutting problems as the X-cars, borrowing unsuitable engine and transmission designs from earlier models. The result was that the J-cars, like the X-cars, were panned both by the automotive press and the buying public. Indeed in 1981-82, GM recalled more cars than it produced. The X-cars also looked bad, hardly surprising since GM didn't bother with consumer market research until 1985. By contrast, the Japanese had made huge strides in styling, creating glossy paints and friendly interiors with appealing trim. They had developed features like internal trunk and gas cap releases, things that appealed to the driver as a 'user.' Detroit was still relying on decorative gimmicks like a chrome strip.

1.5.4 The 1980s: GM Thinks of Upgradation and Competition

The X-cars were meant to show the world that GM still led in automotive engineering, but they only showed how out of touch the automaker had become. In 1980, GM lost over $700 million, its first loss since 1921, as its sales dropped 26 per cent. But the scale of GM's problems was overshadowed by the crises threatening Ford and Chrysler. In 1979, Ford recorded a $1.5 billion loss, followed by losses totalling a further $1.75 billion over the next two years. This volume of red ink was almost enough to leave Ford bankrupt. 1979 was an even worse year for Chrysler. Iacocca, travelling to Washington as Chrysler's new CEO, told the Federal government that without a massive loan guarantee, the company would fold with the loss of tens of thousands of jobs. The next year, 1980, the government approved $1.5 billion in loan guarantees. The loans covered Chrysler's $1.7 billion loss, and allowed the company to survive.

It wasn't just Chrysler that received help from the government. All three members of the Detroit trio joined to lobby for protection from the Japanese. In other words, Detroit sought to keep the Japanese out of the United States rather than compete with them. In 1981, after months of negotiation with both the UAW and the Federal government, Japan agreed voluntarily to limit the number of cars it would ship to the US each year. The first year's limit was set at 1.68 million vehicles significantly reducing the Japanese threat. Detroit had negotiated itself a breathing space; indeed the uncompetitive market allowed the Big Three to enjoy record profits over the next few years. It was a golden opportunity to take charge of the auto market, improve efficiency and quality to Japanese levels, and compete fairly and squarely with the Japanese. But the hard-won lull proved brief especially for GM.

Ford and Chrysler's perilously close journey to the brink of collapse forced them to rethink. Clearly, they could no longer run their companies as they once had. The world had moved on, and they had to move on too if they were to survive. As a result, the two automakers showed some brave developments through the decade: Chrysler with the reintroduction of the convertible and in the production of minivans, Ford with a new aerodynamic design. As a result, Ford and Chrysler made it through the 1980s. Both companies had mixed results through the decade, but both were vastly better positioned to compete in 1990s than they had been 10 years earlier.

GM was not driven to change by the same fiscal crises that beset its Detroit counterparts. In 1980, GM was still a massively wealthy corporation, protected by its size and its financial strength. Not that GM went untouched by the changes made at Ford and Chrysler; it too saw the need to upgrade and compete. In 1981, GM appointed a new chairman and CEO who was determined to drag GM into the 21st century, Roger Bonham Smith.

1.5.5 Smith's Era in General Motors

Roger Smith had a consuming vision of the GM of the future. He saw the car as not just a mechanical object, but an electromechanical one, in which on board computers and circuitry were as important as the actual engine. He saw cars manufactured in 'lights out' factories, where the only employees were people supervising the robots and computers. Smith also envisioned a world in which high-tech smoothed the process of buying a car. The customer would reel off his order—tinted glass, automatic transmission, color blue, power windows—to a salesman who would tap the particulars into a computer. The information would be relayed to factory robots that could custom-build every vehicle. The consumer would no longer be forced to choose between competing models, since every car could be tailor-made.

Clearly, Smith was thinking of long term. He had a vision of the industry as it might develop in the 21st century. But he was determined to put GM on the fast track towards that future, and to block the Japanese from using their superiority in microelectronics to dominate the car market as they had the consumer electronics market. With a cast-iron balance sheet and mountains of cash, Smith was determined to remake GM into the world's strongest automaker.

Over the next decade, GM spent nearly $90 billion reforming itself. By most accounts, this money was all but wasted. GM lost market share throughout the 1980s, and became a high-cost, inefficient producer. The company's continued decline set the scene for the massive downsizing of 1991, and the ouster of Robert Stempel in 1992. Why did the 1980s prove so disastrous for GM? An examination of Smith's strategy reveals three main themes:

1. reforming GM's bureaucracy;

2. purchasing advanced technology; and

3. attempting to instill an entrepreneurial spirit in the company.

1.5.6 Organisational Reform

The CEO, Roger Smith, was acutely aware of GM's bloated, blundering organisation. He knew that GM would have to become leaner and meaner if it wished to compete. In 1984, Smith set out to reorganise totally the outdated GM structure.

Through the 1960s, as the men from finance had increased their control over the separate divisions, GM had become more centralised. Alfred Sloan's rule of 'centralised policy and decentralised administration' was being eroded by the demands from the fourteenth floor (GM's Detroit Headquarters). This problem was compounded in the 1970s by the onslaught of federal efficiency and safety regulations that limited design possibilities.

Also, all car bodies were made by a single division Fisher Body and assembled by another GM Assembly. These two divisions were able to impose their own authority over the designers and engineers at Chevy and Pontiac, etc. The result was that Sloan's structure of five semi-autonomous divisions had become an anachronism. The extent of the problem became apparent during the 1970s, when GM experimented with 'badge engineering'. Under this scheme, divisions shared as many parts as possible to keep costs down, while small stylistic changes were meant to identify a particular car as a Pontiac or an Oldsmobile. 'Badge engineering' was not a success since it resulted in cars that looked too much alike.

But although GM was becoming increasingly centralised, each division maintained its own design and marketing operations, so that resources were duplicated across GM. The company was organised the wrong way. A number of design centres produced a range of similar cars.

Smith wished to accomplish two goals: decentralise authority back to the manufacturing divisions and streamline the company's resources so that the divisions didn't duplicate each other's work.

Smith reorganised GM into two main groups. Chevrolet-Pontiac-Canada (CPC) would design, manufacture, and market small cars. Buick-Oldsmobile-Cadillac (BOC) would take charge of the big ones. The regrouping eliminated two whole divisions: Fisher Body and GM Assembly in a move that eliminated thousands of jobs and created thousands of others. It was a wholesale shift of personnel in which reporting structures were realigned and channels of communication redirected. The reorganisation might have been a good idea in theory, but in practice it created chaos. As Fortune put it, 'The shakeup froze GM in its tracks for 18 months.' The problem was that while the old structure had been dismantled, a new structure had not been constructed in its place. The result was an organisation in which no one knew who was responsible for what! Suppliers complained that they could never find the right representative, or when they did, he or she soon changed jobs. In the mêlée, new layers of management were created to try and sort out the mess. Indeed, CPC wound up adding 8,000 people following the restructuring.

In 1985, CPC produced 3.5 million cars a year roughly the same as Toyota. But CPC employed 160,000 people in contrast to Toyota's 60,000.

General Motors became more, not less, inefficient, causing more people to be hired. In 1983, the total GM workforce was 691,000. By 1985, it had climbed to 811,000. The confusion led to chaos in GM's basic manufacturing. In one absurd instance, it became efficient for a Chevrolet plant to build Cadillacs, while Buick assembled Pontiacs. One GM observer told Fortune that GM started producing 17 ignition systems where three would have been enough, and 40 types of catalytic converter instead of four. Even as late as 1992, GM produced more than a dozen separate caps for windshield washer fluid bottles! Smith's reorganisation seemed to have exactly the wrong effect. Rather than chasing the Japanese dream of leanness and efficiency, the plan had made GM more confused and cumbersome.

1.5.7 GM-10

The failure of the reorganisation was most acutely felt in Smith's other big shake-up, the GM-10 programme. One academic called GM-10 'the biggest catastrophe in American industrial history'.

GM-10's aim, was to streamline the resources of the five divisions to create a consistent, non-duplicative car line. Starting in 1982, GM set out to replace all existing mid-sized cars produced by Chevrolet, Pontiac, Oldsmobile and Buick. Under GM-10, each division would manufacture a coupe, a sedan, and a station wagon. The plan called for seven plants, each to assemble a quarter of a million of the new cars, which would account for 21 per cent of the US car market a bigger market share than Ford's. According to Fortune, 'It would be the largest new-model program ever, the ultimate expression of GM's ability to capitalise on its enormous economies of scale. But GM couldn't pull it off. The world's largest corporation choked.' The 1984 reorganisation played havoc with the management of GM-10: people working on the project were moved; responsibilities shifted or were left undefined; the programme manager in charge of GM-10 was replaced, as was his successor; responsibility for the programme was moved to CPC; finally, and most gallingly, GM was forced to change the styling of GM-10 cars so they didn't appear to be replicas of the Ford Taurus, introduced in 1986. As GM-10 suffered setback after setback, GM pulled back from the grand vision that had initiated the programme. First, GM downsized the project, dropping the station wagon arid cutting back the plants involved from seven to four. Then GM found that it couldn't afford to produce all eight GM-10 cars simultaneously, so it rolled the cars out to market over two years, two-doors before four-doors. But even in this, GM guessed wrong. Baby boomers who wanted coupés in 1980 now wanted family-size sedans.

Ford, for instance, never introduced a two-door Taurus, yet in 1988, GM was rolling out four brand new two-door coupés. In 1990, eight years after the GM-10 programme was launched, the final cars hit the showrooms. They were a disaster. In 1989, GM lost over $2,000 on every GM-10 car it produced. In 1979, Oldsmobile had sold 518,000 models of a car, scheduled for replacement under the GM-10 programme. Twelve years later, in 1991, Oldsmobile sold only 87,500 models of the new GM-10 version when asked by Fortune, why GM-10 was such a catastrophe, Roger Smith replied, 'I don't know. It's a mysterious thing.'

1.5.8 Look Alikes

Other errors compounded the manufacturing problems. In attempting to unify the disparate sections of the five divisions, GM endeavoured to create a corporate 'look' so that consumers could identify a GM vehicle at a glance. GM took this plan too far and created a line of identical-looking cars. GM shrank its luxury cars to such an extent that they no longer looked different from their cheaper counterparts a $9,000 Pontiac ended up looking similar to $25,000 Cadillac.

The results were disastrous for GM's luxury end, traditionally the company's most profitable business. GM resorted to cosmetic changes, such as adding a three inch fender extension to one Cadillac model to make it appear longer. The irony was plain to all. Once, GM had cornered the large car market. Indeed, during the 1970s it seemed that those were the only cars GM made well; now the company couldn't even seem to do that right.

1.5.9 Purchase of New Technology

If there is one characteristic of Roger Smith that came to dominate his tenure as chairman, it was his love of technology. To Smith, GM's future lay with high-tech, and he was determined that GM should be the leader. In his 10-year tenure as CEO, Smith spent over $50 billion on technology projects. As Bob Eaton, chief of GM's advanced engineering, put it, 'When you told Roger about new technology, he'd get excited and ask, "Where do I sign?"'

The list of GM's high-technology projects through the 1980s is a long one:

- When Roger Smith was appointed chairman, GM had 300 robots. Smith made a pledge to acquire 14,000 by 1990. To fulfill this promise, Smith engaged in a 1981 joint venture with the Japanese robot manufacturer, Fujitsu-Fanuc. GMF Robotics would build robots for the US market, with 70 per cent of the output earmarked for GM. Via this joint venture, GM became the largest manufacturer of robots in the world.

- Detroit also poured money into an acquisition binge of small-time European car manufacturers. GM bought 48 per cent of Lotus for $20 million and half of Saab for $600 million. The hope was that GM could exploit the advanced engineering of these companies.

- In 1983, Smith unveiled Saturn, the 'car of the future.' The plan was to reinvent the way GM made small and mid-sized cars. Saturn would be built in new plants, employing the newest technology and the most productive management practices, arid sold in standalone showrooms. Quality would be the watchword of the new vehicles. Saturn held out the promise that GM could manufacture small cars as well as the Japanese.

- Smith also spent money to learn directly from the Japanese. In 1983 he formed New United Motor Manufacturing Inc. (NUMMI), a joint venture with Toyota. NUMMI was set up in an idle GM factory in Fremont, California, and set out to build Chevy Novas, using American labour and Japanese management.

- In 1985, GM offered $5.2 billion to purchase Hughes Aircraft, an aerospace manufacturer. Smith hoped that Hughes's space-age engineering could be used to juice up GM's cars.

- In 1984, GM bought Electronic Data Systems (EDS) for $2.55 billion. The Texas concern, headed by Ross Perot, was fully bought out by GM, yet remained independent within the company, trading under a separate GM 'E' stock. Smith hoped that EDS would speed up GM's huge data-processing operation, and put GM on the cutting edge of information technology. The purchase of EDS made GM the world's largest data-processing company.

Smith didn't just pursue high-tech. GM bought two major mortgage companies that overnight turned GM into America's largest home-mortgage holder.

Smith's plan was to use technology to make GM responsive to niche markets. Rather than employing a blanket strategy, in which GM produced 'a car for every purse and purpose'. Smith intended GM to cover niches as they appeared. As consumer trends developed, GM would respond, bringing the right car rapidly to the market.

The high-technology dream never materialised; nor did Smith's 'rapid response' to niche markets. GM was so big that scale economies didn't kick in until large numbers of cars were sold. GM needed to sell over 100,000 cars of a new model to make its development profitable. The Japanese made money selling models in volumes of 40,000 or less. Nor could GM speed up its production time. The C-car line, due to hit the showrooms in the Fall of 1984, wasn't ready until December 1985. Other lines failed to satisfy their target markets. A good example concerns the Pontiac Fiero, a zippy two-door sports car, aimed particularly at young females. GM spotted the market and dominated it, selling over 100,000 Fieros in both 1984 and 1985. Encouraged by initial sales, GM continued to manufacture and market the car as if there were no tomorrow and no threat of competition. Both came, and GM was not ready to face either. For instance, during Fiero's development, to keep costs down, GM had eliminated power steering. As it turned out, however, power steering became a popular feature with women since it makes a car so much easier to park. The Japanese picked up on the trend, GM didn't. Toyota shipped its MR-2 with retrofitted power steering, and ate into the Fiero's market. As Fiero's sales sunk, so GM found it couldn't afford to compete in the market. The MR-2 and Mazda's Miata are still on sale today, unlike the Fiero cancelled in 1988. General Motors found that the new technology created more problems than it solved. Typical of the problem were those experienced by the Hamtramck plant in Michigan. The plant was opened in 1985-86 at a cost of $600 million, and was to be a showcase for GM's brave new manufacturing world. Hamtranck boasted nearly 2,000 computers on its assembly line, requiring 400 workers to be trained for a year before the plant opened.

GM engineers were having a devil of a time de-bugging the hundreds of advanced machines and laser-guided devices. No sooner did the robots in the body shop weld sheet metal properly than the new modular painting robots commenced spraying one another. If GM had tried to introduce one or two glitzy automation projects instead of dozens and dozens, the [Hamtranck] plant might have opened smoothly. GM's software and engineering expertise, under extreme deadline pressure, just wasn't sufficient for the job.

Despite the advanced machinery, Hamtranck never operated at more than 50 per cent capacity. The Wall Street Journal commented in 1986 that the plant 'instead of a showcase, looks more like a basket case.' Just 25 miles away, Mazda opened its own plant for a quarter of the cost of Hamtranck. With 1,500 fewer employees, the Mazda plant made just as many cars, of better quality. The results of the technology improvements did not justify their huge cost. In a 1986 management conference report, executive vice-president of finance F. Alan Smith pointed out that GM projected to spend $34.7 billion between 1986 and 1989. That sum, he argued, was equal to the total market capitalisation of Nissan and Toyota combined. Theoretically, GM could buy out both companies, increasing its worldwide market share to 40 per cent. What was GM's $34 billion going to buy them that would generate that kind of sales increase?

1.5.10 Deteriorating Results

In actual fact, GM became only less competitive as the spending continued. Alan Smith's report pointed out the nasty numbers. In 1983, GM had the highest operating margins in the game—it earned 2 per cent more on sales than either Ford or Chrysler. By 1985, those two companies were both 3 per cent more efficient. Over the same two-year period, GM's sales increased 22 per cent, though earnings declined 35 per cent. And whereas, in 1980, GM could produce a car for $300 less than it cost Ford or Chrysler, by 1986, GM's costs were $300 more than both.

GM lagged its cross-town rivals by other measures:

• In 1985, GM's profit margin was 4.1 per cent, compared to 7.7 per cent for Chrysler.

- An investment in GM during 1983-1985 returned 16.2 per cent, compared to 22.9 per cent in Ford over the same period.

- According to GM's calculations it took the company 35 hours to assemble the average GM-10 car, compared with the 18 hours it took Ford workers to build a Taurus.

- In 1985, GM recorded 12 vehicles produced per employee, compared with 18 for both Ford and Chrysler.

- In 1986, GM achieved annual revenue of $100 billion. Yet in the same year, the company earned less money than its smaller rival, Ford. In 1986, in a booming economy that produced record auto sales, GM lost money.

Market share continued its depressing downward spiral: from 44.6 per cent in 1984 to 42.7 per cent in 1985 to 41.2 per cent in 1986. Each lost percentage point represented about $1 billion in annual revenue, and 6,000 jobs at GM and its suppliers.

In 1986, the chairman of the Chrysler Motors unit of Chrysler told the *Wall Street Journal*, 'There was a day when the gorilla said "jump" and you jumped, because GM was the pricing leader and the styling leader. They've lost that. They aren't the low-cost producer. The industry no longer marches to their tune.' GM said that the poor results could be expected as a result of its reorganisation, and predicted rapid recovery. In 1987 there could be no such complacency.

- Market share plummeted nearly five points to 36.6 per cent.

- Oldsmobile alone sold nearly 400,000 fewer cars in 1987 than it had the year before.

The skid resulted from a combination of problems:

- GM's costs were still huge. GM's production cost of the 1985 S-car line was twice that of Isuzu for a similar model.

- Those who had bought GM in 1981-82 and had been disappointed by the quality and reliability of the X-cars had not come back to GM next time round.

- GM's shrunken Cadillacs, and the 'look-alike' problem damaged the higher-end divisions.

- GM's smaller line of A-cars came to the market in 1985 just as gas prices headed downwards again, revitalising the large car market. GM continued to market its older models, damaging sales of the new models and causing confusion among customers.

- GM lagged the competition in styling. The 1985 Ford Taurus revolutionised the sales of 'aero'-look cars, even as GM was still producing boxy, square-shouldered vehicles. Meanwhile, Chrysler took a huge headstart in the minivan market.

- Smith wanted GM to develop cars more quickly, but in the effort to rush new models to the market, it failed to concentrate on quality. Most GM models produced through the 1980s were not as good as the vehicles they replaced. GM still retained the production capacity to serve a 50 per cent share of the US market, despite the fact that its share was less than 40 per cent and slipping. The result was that GM operated fearfully under capacity, with six car factories even running at half capacity. The fixed costs of running auto plants at anything less than full capacity were huge.

- GM remained stuck in the past in other ways, as discussed in a 1986 Wall Street Journal report. The article discussed a 53-year old GM plant in Ohio that turned out 19,000 car brakes daily, shipping the parts for inclusion in every GM car from Chevy to Cadillac. The plant typified the massive vertical integration that had once made GM the most powerful company on earth. But in 1986, GM spent 15 per cent more on manufacturing its own brake parts than it would cost to buy them from an outside supplier. Ford and Chrysler, by contrast, purchased their brakes from suppliers as far away as Brazil, and saved money.

1.5.11 Smith's Saturn at GM

Like Smith's other projects, Saturn was hugely ambitious. Saturn had to sell 500,000 cars a year over the long haul to be profitable, as much as Nissan sold in the US each year.

A Wall Street Journal article explained how Saturn's ambition might be its downfall:

Everything at Saturn is new: the car, the plant, the workforce, the dealer network and the manufacturing process. Not even Toyota Motor Corp., everyone's candidate for the world's best automaker, tackles more than two new items on any single project.

The very size of the undertaking meant that GM was unable to complete it cheaply. Moreover, it did not get as much "bang for the buck" as did its chief competitor, Honda.

- Honda's US factories cost $600 million, employed 3,000 workers, and turned out 300,000 cars a year.

- GM's new Saturn plant cost $5 billion, employed 6,000 workers and would turn but, at most, 500,000 cars a year.

- Saturn was launched in the Fall of 1990 in a $100 million blitz of advertising and publicity. The opening months proved far from auspicious.

- GM hoped Saturn would sell 150,000 in its first year. In the first nine months of production, Saturn built 24,000 cars and sold 15,000 of them.

- Six months after opening, Saturn was operating at half-speed, and selling only half of what it produced. One manager told the Wall Street Journal that the plant made cars at full speed for maybe a few hours, 'then we run into a snag'.

- Despite its emphasis on quality, the division has not delivered. In Saturn's first months, some 35-40 per cent of the car's plastic panels were sent back with defects.

Despite the glitches, Saturn was very popular with its buyers, the only problem being there weren't very many of them. Saturn opened just as the US was slipping into a recession—inhospitable circumstances for the launching of a new car line. Saturn also proved to be cannibalistic—41 per cent of Saturn owners already owned a GM vehicle.

1.5.12 Japan's Two-Pronged Strategy

Just as GM was making a terrible mess of reinventing itself, the Japanese were plotting their return. Anyone who thought that the import restriction would hold Japan at bay for long was sorely mistaken.

Japan had adopted a two-pronged strategy. In the first place, it circumvented the import restrictions by building plants in mainland America rather than shipping them from Japan. In this respect, the voluntary restraint helped the United States—Honda, Toyota and Nissan invested billions of dollars and created tens of thousands of jobs—but it didn't help Detroit. The Japanese, more than ever before, were competing in the Big Three's backyard.

- In 1980, Honda announced that it would open its first US assembly plant in Ohio.

- In 1986, Toyota opened a factory in Kentucky.

- In 1989, Honda opened a second plant, and

- Subaru and Isuzu announced that they too would open US-based operations.

Second, the Japanese targeted the luxury car market. Since they were limited to a number of vehicles they could export, it made sense for the Japanese to export higher-priced vehicles that carried a greater profit margin per car. Hence, the arrival of Acura in 1986 and Lexus and Infiniti in 1989. In 1992, these three divisions sold over $3.5 billion worth of automobiles. While this was money made partly at the expense of the leading European luxury car makers: Mercedes, Volvo, BMW and Jaguar, it also heavily dented Cadillac's performance.

General Motors found it was not merely being outclassed in the small car market, but in the expensive, classier range as well. GM remained dominant in the luxury car market. Cadillac was positioned at first, fourth and seventh in the top 10 selling luxury cars in 1992 but the Japanese had nabbed spots third and sixth. Japan did not dominate the big car market as it did the small, but it was a serious competitor in a market GM had once owned. All of this contributed to GM's ever-dropping market share. It was not technology that made the Japanese better competitors, it was their superior, participatory management.

Differences lay in:

- Japan's automakers made do with 5 levels of management; GM had 14.

- NUMMI, run with GM labour under Toyota managers, produced the low-cost, best quality cars in GM. Yen for dollar, it spent less but earned more.

- GM's own quality audit found that the Honda and Nissan plants in the American South produced cars with one-fifth as many defects as did GM's. In other words, the difference between Japanese and American quality was not labour. The Japanese could beat the United States in the United States.

The Japanese success was encouraged partly by the US automakers. The voluntary restraint agreement (VRA) forced the Japanese to raise their prices by as much as $2,000 a vehicle. It presented a perfect opportunity for Detroit to exploit their price advantage and recapture market share. Instead, the Big Three raised their own prices, creating a short-term boom in profits. The VRA merely raised the cost of cars for consumers, and did nothing to restore American competitiveness.

1.5.13 Labour Relations at GM

Labour relations had never been good at GM, dating back to violent strikes in Flint, Michigan, in the 1930s. But even as the Japanese showed the way in creating a friendly working environment, relations between GM management and labour grew ever worse.

Seeing the need to cut costs, GM signed a new contract with the United Auto Workers (UAW) in 1982. Management stressed 'shared sacrifice' to get through difficult times, and wrung a $2.5 billion concession out of the union in the form of a freeze of the cost of living adjustment (COLA). The very same day, GM's proxy statement was mailed to shareholders. One of the items under consideration was a new bonus scheme, awarding 5 million shares to 600 senior executives. In the firestorm of criticism that resulted, Smith cut his own pay and that of other bonus-eligible executives by $135 a month, the same deduction as the UAW had agreed to take. The notion that millionaire Roger Smith (who had taken an 18.8 per cent rise in base pay the year before) and a $12-an-hour machinist taking the same pay cut entailed 'shared sacrifice' was, of course, non-sensical. Smith only fanned the flames of the controversy.

To develop better relations with the UAW, GM began a profit-sharing programme for blue-collar workers. In 1985, GM workers were paid $384 as part of the programme, compared with the $1,200 Ford workers were paid under a similar scheme.

Roger Smith regarded labour as opposition, to be replaced by machines wherever possible. In negotiations with the UAW, Smith said, 'Every time you ask for another dollar in wages, a thousand more robots start looking more practical.' In 1986, Smith initiated an aggressive cost-cutting drive, which included the closure of 13 plants and 25,000 white-collar layoff. The next year he promised to cut a further $10 billion out of GM's costs.

1.5.14 The 1980s: Smith's Strategy Fails

Clearly, Smith's strategy failed. GM ended up spending tens of billions of dollars for little or no reward. Despite the high technology, GM became less, not more, efficient. Its cars found no favour with the public. Its market share dropped. When its competitors burgeoned in a booming auto market, GM lost money.

General Motors suffered throughout the 1980s because it failed to address its basic problems with sufficient alacrity or aggression. The Chrysler and Ford crises, and the relentless Japanese onslaught, should have shown GM that it needed to compete, that it could not take a 50 per cent market share for granted any longer. The massive vertical integration that had served GM so well for so long was out of date.

At the time of the voluntary restraint agreement in 1981, the Japanese had shown that they could produce high quality cars in a fraction of the time it took GM. To stay in step, GM needed to show that it too could efficiently produce a well made car. Given the breathing space afforded by the import restraint, GM could have committed itself to streamlining operations, and cutting away the layers of the organisation that stood between the makers of the automobile and their customers.

The import agreement brought record profits to the Big Three. But the windfall was wasted. GM didn't put the money back into its core operations, upgrading their operations to Japanese standards. GM didn't reinvest the money in ways that would lower the cost, and improve the quality of cars that went to the showrooms. GM failed in the 1980s because it tried to solve problems without addressing their fundamental, underlying causes. Its problem was not that it was short of technology; it was that it was a badly organised, insular, backward-looking, and inefficient producer of motor vehicles. Smith's obsession with technology made no impact on GM's ability to compete.

Its failure was also a failure of leadership. Smith failed to realise that GM's most important commodity was its people. GM could not become a 21st century automaker without the company's employees, its engineers, machinists, and assembly-line workers coming along for the ride. But Smith treated labour as a problem to be limited, not as a resource to be nurtured. Indeed, with all his talk of a 'lights out' factory and robot automation, one could be forgiven for thinking that Smith wanted to dispose of labour altogether. How could Smith hope that GM's employees would pursue his vision, if all it promised them was the sack?

1.5.15 And the Board Played on...

Where was the GM's board of directors when Smith's strategy started to fall apart at the seams in 1986? The answer to this question is important because the ultimate problem and solution for GM lay in the realm of corporate governance. It is a truism of the corporate system that management must have sufficient freedom to take risks and experiment. Inevitably, not every risk taking venture succeeds. Plenty of companies adopt strategies that ultimately prove to be costly mistakes. It is at this point that governance becomes important. It is the board's job to see that management has adopted a sound strategy and executes it competently; and it is the board's responsibility to replace management when it fails in these duties. In turn, the board is beholden directly to shareholders, and indirectly to stakeholders such as consumers, suppliers and employees.

As we saw earlier in the discussion of the Corvair episode, GM did not appreciate outside critics. This same view dominated board management relations through the 1980s. As *Fortune* put it:

> Roger Smith kept the board on a very short leash. He withheld key financial data and budget allocation proposals until the day before meetings and sometimes distributed them minutes before the participants convened. The monthly sessions were rigidly structured

and Smith adjourned them promptly at five minutes to noon, leaving little room for discussion. Circumstances and personality enabled Roger Smith to exercise his iron control. Quick to anger, he was intolerant of criticism. Few directors had the ability or desire to take him on.

One outside director told the *Wall Street Journal* that board meetings 'were like ceremonial events, with no real information.'

Smith was able to exert control via the board committees. Increasingly, the full board became just a ratifying council for the work of the various committees. This allowed Smith to keep loyalists on key committees. The make-up of the board allowed Smith to exercise such control. In 1989, three members of the board (excluding Smith) were GM executives who reported directly to Smith. Among the 11 non-executive directors, four had little or no business experience—Anne Armstrong, former ambassador to the Court of St. James (UK); Thomas E. Everhart and Marvin L. Goldberger, both academics; and the Reverend Leon H. Sullivan. Of the eight remaining directors, two were retired and a third ran GM's chief Detroit bank.

The non-executive directors were paid average fees of $45,000 a year and received a new GM car for their own use every quarter. But these material benefits paled in comparison to the prestige conveyed by sitting on the board of General Motors. Doron Levin speculates on the motivations of one outside director, Edmund T. Pratt, chairman emeritus of Pfizer Inc.:

> Ed Pratt had served on numerous corporate boards of directors. None of the posts, including his chairmanship of Pfizer, one of the nation's leading pharmaceutical firms, carried as much prestige or clout as his GM director's seat. In Pratt's eyes, GM was an American institution, the country's dominant single business force. Hell, GM was America! For a businessman such as himself association with the nation's premier corporation was an immense honor.

But the honour he felt belonging to the GM board did not inspire Pratt to commit much personal wealth to the company. In 1988, Pratt owned 100 GM shares, despite having been on the board for 11 years. In other words, he had purchased about nine shares each year he was a director. Pratt was not alone. Five other outside directors owned 500 shares, and three owned 200 shares.

This was the group responsible for probing, challenging, and, if necessary, changing Smith's strategy. Yet, for many critical years it did nothing of the sort. GM's directors let themselves be browbeaten by the CEO's personality, and blinded by the honour of serving on the board. They had too much to gain—and too little to lose—from the status quo to shake it up. Thus, the GM story is one not just of management failure, but also one of the failures of the board.

In the rarefied atmosphere of the fourteenth floor, GM executives were cut off not only from the vast body of GM's employees but also from the board of directors and the shareholders the board was meant to represent. Management was accountable to no one. The truth of this statement will be made clear when we examine the courtship, brief marriage, and messy divorce between GM and Texas billionaire, and later presidential candidate, Ross Perot. The Perot episode shows how completely the governance structure had collapsed at GM, and how unwilling the board was to challenge management, no matter what the circumstances.

1.5.16 General Motors and Ross Perot

Roger Smith was more frustrated by GM's hidebound culture. He was frustrated and confused at his company's inability to turn its operations around. He felt burdened by GM's insular, backward-looking culture, and he tried hard to break it. Smith liked to explain his vision in the form of an allegory: a GM manager clinging to a tree stump, unwilling to swim across a fast-moving river. Smith's job, as he saw it, was to convince the manager to let go and swim hard, aiming for some unknown spot on the other side. The tree stump was GM's old way of doing business, the river was the fast-moving marketplace, the unknown place on the opposite shore where the swimmer ended up was GM in the next century. In Smith's view, GM could no longer cling to the past, it had to swim for it. The question was, how could he persuade GM to let go of the stump?

Smith did not believe incremental, evolutionary changes would work. Rather, GM would need to be revolutionised. Programmes such as Saturn, NUMMI, and the purchase of Hughes were ways of wrenching GM dramatically from the past and forcing it into the future. Ross Perot and his company, Electronic Data Systems (EDS), seemed to present an ideal opportunity. On the one hand, GM was held back by outmoded data processing and computing methods—how could GM be lean and responsive without modernising its paper-driven bureaucracy?, and on the other hand, EDS was headed by a feisty, no-nonsense Texan entrepreneur who could lend some zip to GM's stodgy style. Smith liked successful entrepreneurs; they represented everything that GM wasn't. That was why Smith wasn't content just to hire EDS, but wanted rather to buy it and make it part of GM. Smith hoped that some of what had made EDS successful would rub off on the GM giant.

Roger Smith and Ross Perot were perfect for each other. Smith sought an aggressive entrepreneur, not beholden to GM and ready to speak his mind. Perot was lured by the challenge of lending his services to such a giant corporation, and, born with a strong patriotic streak; he liked the idea of helping out America's most established company.

General Motors was assiduous in its pursuit of EDS, seeking to overcome Perot's reluctance to sell the company he had spent his life building. The essence of the agreement appeared paradoxical: GM would pay $2.55 billion to buy EDS, yet EDS would remain independent inside the parent company, managed by EDS executives, setting its own compensation practices, and answerable only to Roger Smith and the GM board. In other words, within the button-down establishment of GM would exist a group of autonomous, non-conformist, Texan rebels.

The deal worked as follows:

- GM issued promissory notes to EDS executives that their new ownership in 'E' stock would not be worth less than $125 in seven years that is, if, in seven years, 'E' traded at only $100, GM would make up the $25 difference. It was a way of guaranteeing EDS officers a wonderful return on their holdings in EDS as well as creating an incentive for them to stay for seven years.

- Ross Perot would receive $1 billion for his interest in EDS and 43 per cent of the newly created 'E' stock. Perot instantly became GM's largest individual shareholder, and one of the largest overall, owning 0.8 per cent of the stock, or 11 million Class E shares. By contrast, Smith had acquired 26,500 GM shares in a 36-year career.

- EDS was guaranteed long-term, fixed-price contracts for its wolk on GM. The contracts guaranteed EDS $2.6 billion of new business, a sum that was 33 times EDS's current earnings.

- To merge EDS with GM's own data processing operation, 10,000 GM employees would be transferred to EDS.

No sooner had the vows been exchanged than the problems began. The new couple started fighting before the honeymoon had even started! As EDS's senior executives arrived in Detroit, they were given a glacial reception indeed; many GM-ers seemed not to have been briefed about EDS's arrival at all. One account of the merger tells how some senior EDS executives were introduced to Alex Cunningham, executive vice-president of North American operations. Cunningham uttered not a word to his visitors before showing them out of his office.

General Motors executives were not the only ones to oppose the arrival of EDS. For the 10,000 GM data processors who would be transferred to EDS, the move meant an end to the strict hierarchy and chain of command they were used to. Instead, they were told to accept lower pay, lower benefits, and more job risk under EDS management. GM employees wondered how EDS could be owned by GM and yet be in charge. Some of the data workers applied to the UAW for affiliation, a move that had upset EDS's tradition-free labour relations.

Meanwhile, Ken Riedlinger, EDS's most senior officer in Detroit, was receiving hate mail and obscene phone calls, and was finding his car tires slashed almost daily. Ultimately, he quit. Perot himself received a cold shoulder. On arriving for his first meeting of the board of directors, he found that he had been placed on the public policy committee, the least influential of any of the board committees. Perot believed that the holder of 11 million shares should be closer to the beating heart of GM's decision-making, on the finance or executive committees. Perot's irritation, however, was minor compared to the fundamental difficulties of getting GM and EDS to work together.

The agreement that EDS would have a monopoly over GM's data processing business soon broke down. GM, because of its size, was used to being able to bully its suppliers. EDS, by contrast, charged premium prices for the vast numbers of computers and processors it wished GM to purchase. The data processing department felt it should be receiving discounts. EDS replied that if GM wanted a 21st century computer system, then it needed to pay what it cost. Anyway, advanced systems would help lower costs for GM in the long term. By the same token, EDS was astonished by examples of spectacular inefficiency and money wasting inside GM, but felt they weren't given the opportunity to cure them. EDS felt its efforts were being sabotaged by their own client.

The result was constant bickering over pricing and contract terms, so that it was not until April 1986, nearly two years after the merger, that GM and EDS finalised a pricing agreement for EDS's services. The compromise settled little—just months later, Perot considered suing GM for its failure to sign long-term contracts with EDS. Increasingly, EDS-ers found themselves appealing to Perot, and GM-ers to Smith for their help in defending their turf: the two chief executives found that their main role in the merger was as peacemakers.

Another increasingly bitter bone of contention concerned compensation. GM employees were used to climbing up an utterly predictable career ladder, with guaranteed annual salary increases, regular bonuses, a generous package of benefits, and a secure retirement. Compensation at GM was utterly risk-free and never spectacular. Roger Smith certainly made a lot of money—more than most executives in the country—but even Smith's pay paled in comparison to the fortunes amassed by EDS's senior officers. EDS was a place where spectacular fortunes could be made in a relatively short time. Base salaries and benefits were far smaller than GM's but the possible rewards via stock options and performance grants were the stuff that dreams are made of.

Perot loved incentives: if his people performed, he rewarded them lavishly. For instance, his number two, Mort Myerson, was promised a salary equal to 1 per cent of EDS's 1984 profits. The sky was the limit. Perot believed that this motivated not just his top employees, but everyone in the company, since even the lowliest worker could see that hard work and success were rewarded with wealth. Perot believed that such a system was essential to the success of EDS.

Compensation soon became a thorny problem. The nature of the original merger agreement meant that, even as relations between the two companies grew worse and worse, EDS-ers continued to expect huge rewards. But GM dragged its feet on the lavish stock bonuses promised in the merger agreement. Under EDS's pre-merger stock incentive plan, shares were due to have been distributed late in 1984. Following the merger, the award was postponed until early 1985. By mid-summer no decision had been reached, despite Perot's frequent reminders to Smith. Perot became annoyed. Not only did he regard the stock awards as his prime means of employee motivation, but they had been categorically guaranteed in the GM-EDS merger agreement.

The cause of delay was Roger Smith. He felt insulted by how much wealth was already being transferred to EDS's employees and the proposed grants were far richer than the grants made to any GM executive, including Smith. GM had already made EDS's top executives multimillionaires— Perot was worth nearly a billion, Myerson a hundred million—and Smith couldn't justify any extra largesse. By GM's calculations, the award would cost GM a further $300 million—paid to people already vastly wealthy thanks to GM. In Smith's view, the payouts were obscene. In Perot's view, that was the way EDS had always worked and, under the merger agreement, would continue to work.

Finally, Smith told Perot that he was vetoing the grants, and he travelled to Dallas to explain why to the top EDS officers. The meeting was not a success. According to Levin's (1985) account, Tom Walter, EDS's CFO, told Smith that he was overstating the cost to GM of the stock grants because he was working from a false set of numbers. Levin writes:

> Walter didn't get a chance to finish his point.
>
> People in the room later would remember Smith's angry explosion as being wondrous and terrifying at the same time: wondrous for the extreme colors and sounds it brought to the room, terrifying because none of them had ever seen someone lose his temper so completely in a business meeting...
>
> 'Don't tell me my numbers aren't correct,' Smith sputtered. His already ruddy expression flushed a furious scarlet. His voice rose almost to choking, and he slammed his briefing book on the table.

Inadvertently, Walter had delivered the most humiliating insult possible to a GM financial executive. Smith might have endured accusations of being a poor marketer or manager. Telling a GM finance man he had 'bad numbers' was invitation to a brawl.

'I didn't come here to be insulted,' Smith shouted. By this time flecks of saliva had formed at the corners of his mouth. The EDS officers stared in disbelief as the chairman of the world's biggest and most powerful company lost it.

The outburst was the first step down a slippery slope that led to Perot's separation from GM. Despite all the problems involved with integrating EDS into GM, and despite all the petty rows and disagreements and frustrations, Perot had always believed that the merger would work. He had expected difficulties, and he had expected it to be hard to merge a small, lean, entrepreneurial company with a vast, old, and bureaucratic one. But ultimately, Perot had believed it could be done. He felt that he and EDS had something that could help GM. Following Smith's outburst, he began to doubt it. He began to doubt that Roger Smith was a man with whom he could do business or that GM could overcome its culture. Perot thought he had been brought on board to shake GM up a little. Now he wasn't so sure it could be done. Was Smith really ready to do what it would take? Was he going to talk about revitalising GM, or was he actually going to do it?

But Perot was more than just the man who had created EDS. He was also GM's largest shareholder, with tens of millions of dollars tied up in the company's performance. And as grave as EDS's problems with its new corporate parent might be, Perot was first and foremost a member of the GM board of directors.

Perot was concerned that even as GM's massive capital spending programme was failing to solve the company's fundamental problems, Smith was intent on spending big bucks to acquire Hughes Aircraft. To Perot, the purchase was simply money down the drain at a time when GM was taking bigger and bigger hits to its market share. Perot's increasing dissatisfaction at GM and its management reached a climax at a board meeting held in November 1985. One of the items of the agenda was for final board approval to buy Hughes Aircraft for $5.2 billion. To Perot, the planned purchase represented everything that was wrong with the way GM was being run—big, thoughtless spending with no regard for the company's most basic problems. In a dramatic speech to the board, Perot explained his opposition.

First, he outlined where he thought GM had gone wrong. He explained that the company was 'procedures oriented, not results oriented' and that business matters that should be decided in minutes took days or weeks shuttling up the hierarchy in a series of unproductive meetings. Also, 'senior management is too isolated from the people,' Perot concluded. Perot told the board that he had attended a Cadillac dealers' conference where the common complaint had been that it was impossible to sell Cadillacs when they were riddled with defects. Perot had asked the dealers why the problems were so pervasive: the answer was 'GM doesn't give people the responsibility and authority to get things done and the GM system avoids individual accountability.'

Perot asked the directors why they should approve a $5 billion purchase for space-age engineering when GM couldn't even build a reliable car. He argued that throwing money at the problem was not going to solve it: 'The experiences of our successful competitors demonstrate that people plus the intelligent application of capital are the keys.' Whether Perot meant it to be or not, this was a sharp dig at Smith's entire strategy.

Perot did not just attack management; he also went after the board. He called for the board to become a genuine decision-making body, not a silent ratifying counsel: 'We must change the format of board meetings from passive sessions with little two-way communication to active participatory sessions that allow us to discuss real issues and resolve real problems.' Months earlier, Perot had sought approval from Smith for meetings of the outside directors alone. He felt the board would be better able to assert its independence if it was freed from the counterweight of the executive board members. Smith refused Perot's request.

Perot reminded the directors of their duty to represent the stockholders:

> They own this company. We must make it clear that the management serves at the pleasure of the shareholders... The managers of mature corporations with no concentration of owners have gotten themselves into the position of effectively selecting the board members who will represent the stockholders.

When it came to a vote on the Hughes purchase, Perot's was the lone dissenting vote. It was the first such dissension in the GM board room since the 1920s.

Relations could not help but deteriorate. Perot and Smith continued to haggle over compensation and bonus formulae, an issue that Perot believed was none of GM's business. Meanwhile, Perot forbade GM to audit EDS's balance sheet. In a series of increasingly combative letters to Smith, Perot demanded that EDS be left to run its business independently the way the merger agreement intended. In a letter of May 19, 1986, Perot accused the automaker of trying to 'GM-ize EDS.' Of course, the entire point of the merger had been to 'EDS-ize GM.'

In background interviews with the *Wall Street Journal* in the spring and early summer of 1986, Perot explained where the EDS-GM merger had gone wrong. He went far beyond the difficulties of combining the two companies; instead, he discussed why GM was failing in the marketplace. '"Until we nuke the GM system," he said, "we'll never tap the full potential of our people."' He was even more critical of Roger Smith than before, saying that, '"he talks a good game" about turning GM around but that he failed to understand how to do it.' Perot criticised management for its obsessive attention to executive perks and bonuses and even demanded that GM scrap its executive dining rooms! Perot believed the trappings of power interfered with management's ability to see the company in an honest light.

Perot reserved further ire for the board: 'Is the board a rubber stamp for Roger? Hell, no! We'd have to upgrade it to be a rubber stamp.' Perot believed that the board knew nothing of GM's fundamental problems. Each outside director received the latest GM model every three months what would they know about reliability? Perot bought his own cars, and sometimes visited showrooms incognito, trying to discern problems. He came across GM dealers who were now selling Japanese cars to stay competitive. How could the directors, receiving a new car every 90 days, hope to know anything about problems like these?

The *Wall Street Journal* published Perot's comments much watered down in an article entitled 'Groping Giant'. The article showed how GM, despite its pricey automation drive, was more inefficient than its rivals and losing market share as a result. 'Poised for the 21st Century?' asked the Journal, the first paper to criticise Smith's highly lauded strategy. The criticisms were backed by the poor performance of the year. The rest of the financial media pricked up its ears, and Perot was willing to talk. In a series of interviews, Perot continued to assail GM, telling *Business Week* that 'revitalising General Motors is like teaching an elephant to tap dance.'

As the battle between Perot and Smith became ever more public, so the chances of reaching an understanding became ever more slim. Smith was infuriated by Perot's public ridicule of GM; senior executives were distressed by the lack of respect Perot showed for what had for so long been the most respected company in the world. The marriage between GM and EDS had broken down irreparably, and divorce became the only option.

Perot's lieutenants and GM's counsel negotiated a buyout of Perot's holding in GM. On December 1, 1986, the board agreed to pay Perot $742.8 million for his stake in GM. The buyout offered $61.90 for shares that were then trading at about $33. In return, both GM and Perot agreed that neither side would criticise the other, on penalty of $7.5 million. In other words, if Perot continued his attacks on GM, he would have to return $7.5 million to GM. The buyout was so preferential to Perot that he could not believe the board approved it. He thought the price was so great that the directors could not but oppose Smith. Perot was dumbstruck that not one director dissented from the decision to send him packing with so much of GM shareholders' money. In court testimony two years later, Perot said, 'My attitude all the way was no one will ever sign this agreement on the GM side, it's not businesslike. I underestimated the desire on the GM board to get rid of me.'

Perot was concerned the press would report that he had bribed GM, that he had offered the deal as the price of his silence. He was determined to show that GM had initiated the deal. So he offered the money back. He put the money in escrow and gave the GM's board two weeks to rethink the decision to buy him out. If, after two weeks, the board of directors thought that ridding GM of Ross Perot was in the shareholders' best interest, he would take the money. If not, Perot would pay the money back and continue to work at GM. In a press conference held immediately after he signed the buyout agreement, Perot told reporters, 'Is spending all this money the highest and best use of GM's capital?... I want to give the directors a chance to do the right thing. It is incomprehensible to me that they would want to spend $750 million on this. I am hopeful that people will suddenly get a laser like focus on what needs to be done and do it.' Following the announcement of the buyout, and Perot's press conference, GM's stock declined $3, and EDS stock lost $4.50.

Ross Perot's involvement in GM caused almost immeasurable bad publicity for GM. Roger Smith and his fellow board members were painted as corporate villains. One group particularly incensed was, unsurprisingly, the shareholders! One sizeable shareholder, the State of Wisconsin Investment Board (SWIB), wrote a letter to GM directors saying the buyout 'severely undermines the confidence we have in the board and in the officials of General Motors.' SWIB was prepared to back up its letter with a shareholder resolution or a lawsuit, but one phone call from GM to the governor of Wisconsin threatening to shut down some planned developments in the state, quickly put an end to the protest.

This is indicative of the governance structure at GM. Roger Smith ran his company unchallenged by either the board or the shareholders the board was meant to represent. Smith wanted to revitalise the company, but it had to be done his way!

To conclude, we made an attempt in this chapter to draw insights into the concepts and issues relating to the board's functioning and performance by linking to the corporate failure cases of Swissair and General Motors.

References

Amason, A. (1996). "Distinguishing the Effects of Functional and Dysfunctional Conflict on Strategic Decision Making: Resolving a Paradox for Top Management Teams", *Academy of Management Journal* 39(1): 123-48.

Barrick, M.R., G.L. Stewart, M.J. Neubert and M.K. Mount (1998). "Relating Member Ability and Personality to Work-team Processes and Team Effectiveness", *Journal of Applied Psychology* 83: 377-91.

Baysinger, B. and R. Hoskisson (1990). "The Composition of Boards of Directors and Strategic Control: Effects on Corporate Strategy", *Academy of Management Review* 15(1): 72-87.

Bettenhausen, K. (1991). "Five Years of Group Research: What we have Learned and What Needs to be Addressed", *Journal of Management* 17(2): 345-81.

Butler, R. (1981). "Innovations in Organisations: Appropriateness of Perspectives from Small Group Studies for Strategy Formulation", *Human Relations* 34(9): 763-88.

Cadbury, A. (1992). *Report of the Committee on the Financial Aspects of Corporate Governance: The Code of Best Practice (Cadbury Code)*. London: Gee & Company.

————. (2002). *Corporate Governance and Chairmanship: A Personnel View*. New York: Oxford University Press.

Conger, J., E. Lawler and D. Finegold (2001). *Corporate Boards: Strategies for Adding Value at the Top*. San Francisco, C.A.: Jossey-Bass.

Daily, C., D. Dalton and A. Cannella (2003). "Corporate Governance: Decades of Dialogue and Data", *Academy of Management Review* 28(3): 371-82.

Dalton, D., C. Daily, J. Johnson and A. Ellstrand (1999). "Number of Directors and Financial Performance: A Meta-Analysis", *Academy of Management Journal* 42(6): 674-86.

Eisenhardt, K. (1989). "Agency Theory: An Assessment and Review", *Academy of Management Review* 14(1): 57-74.

Eisenhardt, K., J. Kahwajy and L. Bourgeois (1997). "How Management Teams can have a Good Fight", *Harvard Business Review* 75(4): 77-85.

Fama, E. (1980), "Agency Problems and the Theory of the Firm", *Journal of Political Economy* 88(2).

Fama, E.F. and M.C. Jensen (1983). "Separation of Ownership and Control", *Journal of Law and Economics* 26: 327-49.

Forbes, D.P. and F. Miliken (1999). "Cognition and Corporate Governance: Understanding Board of Directors as Strategic Decision-Making Groups", *Academy of Management Review* 3: 489-505.

Gladstein, D.L. (1984). "Groups in Context: A Model of Task Group Effectiveness", *Administrative Science Quarterly* 29(4): 499-507.

Hillman, A. J. and T. Dalziel (2003). "Boards of Directors and Firm Performance: Integrating Agency and Resource Dependence Perspectives", *Academy of Management Review* 28: 383-96.

Jackson, S. (1992). "Consequences of Group Composition for the Interpersonal Dynamics of Strategic Issue Processing", in J. Dutton, A. Huff and P. Shrivastava (eds.), *Advances in Strategic Management*. Vol. 8. Greenwich, CT: JAI Press. pp.345-82.

Jehn, K. and E. Mannix (2001). "The Dynamic Nature of Conflict: A Longitudinal Study of Intragroup Conflict and Group Performance", *Academy of Management Journal* 44(2): 238-51.

Jensen, M. (1993). "The Modern Industrial Revolution, Exit, and the Failure of Internal Control Systems", *Journal of Finance* 48(3): 831-80.

Johnson, J., C. Daily and A. Ellstrand (1996). "Boards of Directors: A Review and Research Agenda", *Journal of Management* 22(3): 409-38.

Kosnik, A. (1987), "Greenmail: A Study of Board Performance in Corporate Governance", *Administrative Science Quarterly* 32(2): 163-85.

Lorsch, J. and E. MacIver (1989). *Pawns or Potentates? The Reality of America's Corporate Boards*. Boston, MA: Harvard Business School Press.

Milliken, F. and D. Vollrath (1991). "Strategic Decision-Making Tasks and Group Effectiveness: Insights from Theory and Research on Small Group Performance", *Human Relations* 44(12): 1-25.

Monks, A. and N. Minow (2004). *Corporate Governance*. Maiden, MA: Blackwell Publishers.

Pfeffer, U. (1983) in L.L. Cummings and B.M. Staw (eds.), *Research in Organisational Behavior*. Vol. 5. Greenwich, CT: JAI Press. pp.299-357.

Pfeffer, U. and G. Salancik (1978). *The External Control of Organisations: A Resource-Dependence Perspective*. New York: Harper & Row.

Pierce, C. (1994), "The Competencies of Future Company Directors", in T. Clarke and E. Monkhouse (eds.), *Rethinking the Company*. London: Pitman Publishing.

Provan, U. (1980). "Board Power and Organisational Effectiveness among Human Service Agencies", *Academy of Management Journal* 23(2): 221-36.

Schwenk, C. and U. Valacich (1994). "Effects of Devil's Advocacy and Dialectical Inquiry on Individuals Versus Groups", *Organisational Behavior and Human Decision Processes* 59(2): 210-22.

Smith, K.G., K.A. Smith, U. Olian, H. Sims, D. O'Bannon and J. Scully (1994). "Top Management Team Demography and Process: The Role of Social Integration and Communication", *Administrative Science Quarterly* 39(3): 412-38.

Steiner, I. (1972). *Group Process and Productivity*. New York: Academic Press.

Stiles, P. and B. Taylor (2000). *Boards at Work*. Oxford University Press.

Sundaramurthy, C. and M. Lewis (2003). "Control and Collaboration: Paradoxes of Governance", *Academy of Management Review* 28(3): 397-415.

Tjosvold, D., V. Dann and C. Wong (1992), "Managing Conflict between Departments to Serve Customers", *Human Relations* 45(10): 1035-54.

Tricker, B. (1984). *Corporate Governance*. Oxford: Blackwell Publishing Limited.

Tricker, R.I. (1984). *Corporate Governance: Practices, Procedures and Powers in British Companies and their Boards of Directors*. Aldershot, U.K.: Gower Press.

Tjosvold, D., V. Dann and C. Wong (1992) "Managing Conflict between Departments to Serve Customers", *Human Relations* 45(10): 1035-54.

Useem, M. (2003). "Corporate Governance is Directors Making Decisions: Reforming the Outward Foundations for Inside Decision Making", *Journal of Management and Governance* 7: 241-53.

Vafeas, N. (1999). "Board Meeting Frequency and firm Performance", *Journal of Financial Economics* 53(1): 113-42.

Wageman, R. (1995). "Interdependence and Group Effectiveness", *Administrative Science Quarterly* 40(2): 145-80.

Williams, K., S. Harkins and B. Latane (1981). "Identifiability as a Deterrent to Social Loafing: Two Cheering Experiments", *Journal of Personality and Social Psychology* 40(2): 303-11.

Wong, C.H. and David Van (2008). "Three Conceptual Models of Board Role Performance", *Journal of Corporate Governance* 8(3): 317-329.

Zahra, S.A. and J.A. Pearce (1989). "Board of Directors and Corporate Financial Performance: A Review and Integrative Model", *Journal of Management* 15: 291-334.

2 | Board of Directors

> Directors as individuals have a responsibility to contribute actively, thoughtfully, and responsibly to the debate, but not to be individual super-managers... The board role, then, requires that directors assume personal responsibility to behave so that the group as a group exercise authority and the group as a group bears accountability for the behavior of the entire company.
>
> —Carver and Oliver, 2002: 28.

Most of the countries today, anticipate the boards to demonstrate greater independence from management and more effectively carry out their oversight role. New or revised governance codes and exchange regulations—such as the Sarbanes-Oxley Act in the US, the Combined Code in UK, Singapore's Code of Corporate Governance, India's listing requirement of clause 49, New Zealand SEC listing guidelines and similar initiatives in Europe, Asia-Pacific and South Africa underscore board's responsibilities to shareholders.

Central to these reforms is the concept of a corporate board that includes active, knowledgeable independent directors. A common theme throughout the newly updated governance codes and guidelines is the call for increased representation by truly independent directors. Increasingly, governments or stock exchanges are defining independence and setting minimum standards for independent membership on boards. The aim of these initiatives is to prevent future scandals and rebuild investor confidence.

2.1 The Role of a Chairman

The chairman's primary role is to ensure that the board is effective in its tasks of setting and implementing the company's direction and strategy. The chairman is appointed by the board and has the same legal duties as other directors. The position may be full or part-time. The role is often combined with that of managing director; chief executive in smaller companies. However, the joint role is considered inappropriate for public companies listed on the Stock Exchange.

The main features of the role of chairman are as follows:

- providing leadership to the board;
- taking responsibility for the board's composition and development;
- ensuring that the board receives proper information;
- planning and conducting board meetings effectively;
- getting all directors involved in the board's work;
- ensuring that the board focusses on its key tasks;
- engaging the board in assessing and improving its performance;
- overseeing the induction and development of directors; and
- supporting the chief executive/managing director.

2.2 The Role of a Managing Director/Chief Executive

The managing director or chief executive is the most senior full-time executive of the company (except when there is an executive chairman). The role of managing director (MD) and chief executive officer (CEO) are virtually the same. (The latter title originally comes from the United States.)

An MD is responsible for the performance of the company, as dictated by the board's overall strategy. He or she reports to the chairman or board of directors. The MD's responsibilities include:

- formulating and successfully implementing company policy;
- directing strategy towards the profitable growth and operation of the company;
- developing strategic operating plans that reflect the longer-term objectives and priorities established by the board;
- maintaining an ongoing dialogue with the chairman of the board;
- putting in place adequate operational planning and financial control systems;
- ensuring that the operating objectives and standards of performance are not only understood but owned by the management and other employees;

- closely monitoring the operating and financial results against plans and budgets;
- taking remedial action where necessary and informing the board of significant changes maintaining the operational performance of the company;
- monitoring the actions of the functional board directors;
- assuming full accountability to the board for all company operations;
- representing the company to major customers and professional associations; and
- building and maintaining an effective executive team.

2.3 Separation of the Roles of Chairman and Managing Director

The chairman is the person who leads and runs the board, whereas the MD leads and runs the company. The recommendation that the roles of chairman and MD should be separated first came to prominence in the code of best practice set out in the Cadbury Report. This has been a contentious issue; however, the figures show that although there are still joint role holders there is in general a high level of compliance, particularly among larger listed companies. According to Deloitte and Touche's (2007) research findings, only three FTSE 100 companies and eight FTSE 250 companies had a combined role.

2.4 Forces Behind the Setting Up of Codes for the Independent Directors

One can categorise the forces behind setting up code for independent directors into two categories. First, external forces and Second, internal forces.

2.4.1 External Forces

The role of the stakeholders/creditors in pressurising the companies to improve the governance, threatening those that fail to adhere to global governance standards with higher rates or reduced access to capital markets is growing in the present times. It is evident from the fact that the credit rating agencies have begun to factor corporate governance in addition to the financial health into their evaluations. Companies with weak governance policies are also being punished with higher premiums for liability insurance for corporate officers and directors.

Shareholders also are more willing to challenge the management than in the past. In the US, corporate annual meetings have grown from friendly forums to opportunities for investors to grill management on everything from director's terms to management decisions, to choosing an auditor. Investors in other regions also have become more aggressive. In France for instance, Eurotunnel group's shareholders, angry over the company's high debt and poor performance, ousted the entire board of directors. Likewise, in Asia, where domestic and foreign investors traditionally have not challenged management, it is more common today that they are being more argumentative now. Investor activists in Japan, for example, have been successful in winning greater access to information about management salaries and benefits. In Malaysia, the Minority Shareholder Watchdog Group is producing a ranking of Malaysian companies based on their corporate governance practices.

There are some instances where the directors also face new levels of personal accountability for failing to live upto their fiduciary responsibility. For example, the Korean Parliament passed a bill in 2003, allowing class action lawsuits by shareholders for the first time. More investors and other stakeholders have been willing to pursue legal remedies in response to corporate mismanagement or self-dealing. Lawsuits, once exceedingly rare in Europe and Asia, are growing in number. For example, the April 2004 'Study of Cases against Directors in Singapore', commissioned by insurance broker Jardine Lloyd Thompson (JLT), found that not only is the number of lawsuits against directors of Singapore companies are on the rise, directors have also lost about 70 per cent of the time.

Finally, reforms are mandated in new government codes and regulations or through stock exchange listing requirements. In its 2004 governance issue, *McKinsey Quarterly* points out that new governance codes have been developed in nearly every G8 country during the past two years, setting off reviews and the creation of new codes in many other countries. In fact today China, Hong Kong, India, Indonesia, Malaysia, the

Philippines, Singapore, South Korea, Taiwan and Thailand all require directors to be independent. On the contrary, in 1997, only Hong Kong, Malaysia and Singapore required directors to be independent.

2.4.2 Internal Forces

Many companies are recognising the benefits of adopting global corporate governance best practices, including those that improve the effectiveness and independence of the board of directors. These companies value independent voices on the board for their role in improving the companies' long-term performance, enhancing the share price over time, lowering the cost of capital and increasing access to capital markets and foreign investment. First and foremost, independent directors—who are not just outsiders to the company, but are also free of personal and business connections to management. Hence, they increase the confidence of the stakeholders. Investors, customers, suppliers, employees and lenders will feel confident that appropriate checks and balances are in place, that financial reporting is sound and that the best interests of the company are of paramount importance.

2.5 Independent Directors

The questions relating to the roles, responsibilities and implications of outside/independent directors are at the top of any discussion on corporate governance today. Defining an independent/outside director is really a big issue. Some of the key questions which apply to the new, outsider directors include: what should the independent/outside directors know and ask about the company and the board that are considering them? What sensitivities does a new, outside director have to be aware of?

An effective board can ensure that prudent and effective controls are in place and that risks are assessed accurately and managed appropriately. The Board helps set the company's strategic goals and ensures that the necessary financial and human resources are in place. In the United States and many Western countries, one of the primary responsibilities is to hire and be willing to fire, if necessary the CEO. Independent directors are essential in completing all of these responsibilities. Independent directors can be defined as an individual who has no current or recent materialistic relationship with the company. Broadly speaking the following criteria can be added to the definition of independent director:

- Is not a partner, shareholder or officer of an organisation that has a relationship with the company;
- Has not been an employee of the company for at least five years;
- Has not been an employee of the present or former auditor for five years;
- Does not receive significant consulting fees from the company; and
- Has no family member in the above categories: is also subject to the five-year provision.

Increasingly, governments and stock exchanges are establishing new governance codes that put formal definitions to the notion of independence, with the goal of increasing the number of directors who are free from conflicts.

Singapore's Corporate Governance Committee (CGC) defines an independent director as one who has no relationships with the company or its affiliates that could interfere, or reasonably be perceived to interfere, with the exercise of the director's independent business judgment with a view to attaining the best interests of the company. Australia takes a similar approach, and requires companies to assess the independence of directors and disclose any directors considered to be independent in the annual report. The Malaysia code looks to ensure that there is no relationship with management or a significant shareholder. The French code discourages the swapping of the board seats between companies.

According to the Toronto Stock Exchange's (TSE's) Dey Report of 1994 'The Principal objective of the direction and management of a business is to enhance shareholder value, which includes balancing gain with risk in order to ensure the financial viability of the business.' The report proposed guidelines for improved corporate governance, highlighting the importance of independent directors on a board: 'The board of directors of every corporation should be constituted with a majority of individuals who qualify as unrelated directors. If the corporation has a significant shareholder and a majority of unrelated directors, the board should include a number of directors who do not have interests in or relationships with either the corporation or the significant shareholder and who fairly reflect the investment in the corporation by shareholders other than the significant shareholder.' An unrelated director is a director who is independent of management and free from any interest and any business or other relationship which could, or reasonably be perceived to, materially interfere with the director's ability to act with a view to the best interests of the corporation. The ultimate responsibility for determining who is an unrelated director lies with the board.

The Dey Report gives the following example of who may not be considered an unrelated director: 'A director who provides services to the company, for example legal or financial services, would generally not be regarded as an unrelated director because the dependence of the adviser/director upon management of the company as a client could, or could be perceived to interfere with the director's ability to objectively assess, for example, the performance of management.'

2.6 Case in Point: Warren Buffet on Boards

In his 2002 report to Berkshire Hathaway shareholders, the most successful investor of all time (and a director of several companies, including Coca-Cola and the Washington Post), wrote about the failures of corporate boards:

> In theory, corporate boards should have prevented this deterioration of conduct... [In 1993] I said that directors 'should behave as if there was a single absentee owner, whose long-term interest they should try to further in all proper ways.' This means that directors must get rid of a manager who is mediocre or worse, no matter how likeable he may be. Directors must react as did the chorus-girl bride of an 85-year old multimillionaire when he asked whether she would love him if he lost his money. 'Of course,' the young beauty replied, 'I would miss you, but I would still love you,' ...

> Why have intelligent and decent directors failed so miserably? The answer lies not in inadequate laws—it's always been clear that directors are obligated to represent the interests of shareholders—but rather in what I'd call 'boardroom atmosphere.'

> Over a span of 40 years, I have been on 19 public-company boards (excluding Berkshire's) and have interacted with perhaps 250 directors. Most of them were 'independent' as defined by today's

rules. But, the great majority of these directors lacked at least one of the three qualities I value. As a result, their contribution to shareholder well-being was minimal at best and, too often, negative. These people, decent and intelligent though they were, simply did not know enough about business and/or care enough about shareholders to question foolish acquisitions or egregious compensation. My own behaviour, I must ruefully add, frequently fell short as well: Too often I was silent when management made proposals that I judged to be counter to the interests of shareholders. In those cases, collegiality trumped independence. (Monks and Minow, 2004).

It is interesting to note that the key role of independent director is to help and act as a check on the management/executives and it is troubling to acknowledge that directors are often chosen by that same management. A truly independent director must scrutinise and question corporate activities and management proposals objectively. The Dey report states that 'This creates the sometimes awkward anomaly of directors being required to exercise critical judgment of those executives to whom they owe their position.'

It is important to reflect on the following issues:

• Under such circumstances (consider the above paragraph) is it possible for the independent directors to remain truly independent and be bold enough to express and question the management?

• Are they free of concern about how the management would perceive their actions?

• Does the outside position held by the independent director make a difference in raising the tone?

• Why would an individual who is unrelated to a company join the board as an independent director?

> One major concern expressed about the independent directors in the literature is that they may not be willing to use their power to the fuller extent. 'Independence' can also mean 'indifference'.

In fact, it is a common belief that without appropriate independent directors, a board can barely make a more valuable contribution than the company's management already does. Inside directors are not in a position to express their independent opinions about the activities of the company or management and as officers; their loyalty is to the CEO. Evidently, as directors, they have a fiduciary duty to shareholders. In general, it is impossible for officers to fulfill that fiduciary duty because it is difficult for an officer to challenge the CEO on management policies.

However, the obvious attraction of the fully unrelated or independent director should be examined closely as well. While independence is a valued quality, a corporation clearly wants directors who are also committed and knowledgeable, both generally and about the company particularly. Outsiders' interests in a company can help justify the liability risk and the time needed to serve as a director. Independent/outside directors can also provide a window on corporate affairs that will help the director to perform effectively.

The role of the independent director is significant in case of the audit committee and other committees. The listing requirements of various stock exchanges insist that the committees (audit, nomination and so on) should be headed by the independent directors. For instance, as per Indian SEBI Clause 49, a qualified and independent audit committee shall be set up under the chairmanship of an independent director with minimum three directors as members of which two-thirds shall be independent. Likewise, as per New Zealand SEC guidelines on audit committee, each publicly owned company should establish an audit committee of the board which should comprise all non-executive directors, a majority of whom are independent and a chairperson who is independent and who is not the chairperson of the board.

Independent directors are instrumental in providing the objectivity and continuity necessary for a company to grow and prosper. They help the corporation to plan its long-term strategy and meet regularly to review its implementation which is highly advantageous. Having independent directors on boards will also give the corporation access to talent and specialised knowledge that might otherwise be very expensive. 'A board of directors is the cheapest form of consultancy,' says John M. Nash, President of the National Association of Corporate Directors (NACD), Washington, D.C.

2.7 The Board and Management

The independent directors should be briefed about the corporate developments regularly by either the chairman or CEO or member of management. A good practice is that the directors should have access to managers as well as the CEO. This would be a somewhat controversial proposition, particularly for CEOs who deal with the issue only when directors seek management's input on the CEO's performance. The full involvement of a broader management team should be positive if directors are sensitive to management's responsibilities (Barry, 1999). In fact, there are some boards who also invite the appropriate managers to speak about the current issues. The managers from the key areas such as research, development, marketing and sales are also invited to strategic planning meetings, which are scheduled at least once a year. The intention is this would allow directors to become familiar with the managers and enable meaningful relationships to develop. Likewise, the relationship between the board and the CFO is one of the most important. As a director's independence increases, so does their distance from the business and from information provided by management. The key provider of that information is usually the CFO, who will have to respect the dual reporting lines to the CEO and directors. This delicate situation requires either a cohesive management team or a brave CFO. Many CEOs welcome the CFO's full and timely disclosure. Others believe that independent directors should be told only positive news so management appears to be in control and doing a great job. A CFO who fears a CEO fails to find a way to deliver to the board and ends up in disaster.

The separation of the functions of ownership and management has led to a growing role for board of directors (BoD). The board is becoming a body that acts in the interest of major shareholders and controls the activities of management. The boards of the companies with separated functions have proportionally twice as many outside and independent directors. Based on an Independent Directors Association study completed on 2007, there are 256 independent directors in major 100 companies. Board committees are established in 85 per cent of the surveyed companies. The average board has 9 members, the range being from 4 to 16. The share of independent non-executive directors (INEDS) is about 28 per cent. Among independent directors in the larger companies there is a trend towards increased representation of foreigners among INEDs, from 40 per cent in 2006 to 52 per cent in 2007, which can be explained by initial public offerings (IPOs) recently held in foreign markets, mostly in London.

Experienced Western board practitioners who have worked with the top Russian executives and board members would observe the drive to improve governance in Russia. Forward-thinking companies are searching for ways of improving board's effectiveness and further improving their reputation. Directors have looked to improve their skill sets and companies have sought to improve the way their boards operate so that they can add more value. While a number of these companies need to meet standards set in countries in which they propose to list, there is a growing trend for leading Russian companies to get better value from their board. They also understand that high levels of governance need to add value far beyond the box-ticking exercise that one sees with codes of governance such as Sarbanes-Oxley and the United Kingdom's Combined Code.

The degree of board independence has also been linked to firm performance. Independence is not just a function of the proportion of inside *versus* outside directors, but also includes whether the board has dual leadership (CEO is also chairman) and the degree of director share ownership. Boards with dual leadership are considered less independent, as are boards with heavy share ownership. Song and Windram (2004) found that independent boards promote audit committee's effectiveness in financial reporting, and that director share ownership and multiple directorships undermine effectiveness. Anderson *et al.* (2004) found that independent audit committees had a lower cost of debt financing. In contrast, Mak and Roush (2000) found that boards with dual leadership, that is relatively less independent boards, were associated with more growth opportunities. The authors suggest that firms with greater agency problems, attributable to low inside share ownership and significant growth opportunities are likely to choose boards that are more effective at mitigating the associated agency problems. Again, we see mixed results in terms of BoD independence and firm performance, especially in relation to dual leadership, leading one to question the utility of studying single board characteristics in relation to firm performance.

2.8 Satyam Case: An Issue of Corporate Governance Failure

Corporate governance had drawn the attention and came under prickly focus in December 2008 at India's well-known software company Satyam. This happened when the $1.6 billion infrastructure proposal was moved by Ramalinga Raju, the founder and chairman of Satyam Computers which was subsequently approved by the board of directors. The proposal was to buy—Maytas Infrastructure and Maytas Properties, which were owned by Raju's sons. These firms were unlisted. However, the plan was rolled back after a major shareholder insurgence. Moved by this event, the majority equity holders started raising questions about the propriety of the board to approve a 'related party transaction'.

Clearly, this is the case of corporate governance issue and corporate governance collapse.

2.8.1 How Many Boards?

As per the literature, the independent directors can sit on as many boards as they feel capable of serving effectively. A company which is about to hire an independent director or a director considering joining a board, should take the following into account:

- A 'professional director' could well serve on more boards than a director who maintains active outside business interests.

- Will the directors also sit on committees (almost always a requirement of outside directors)? If so, how many and which ones?

- Where is the company in its corporate development? A company that has just become public and is still experiencing growing pains will typically require more attention than a more stable company with a controlling shareholder.

- Whether the company is in crisis or is likely to experience one. The likelihood of crises and director involvement is typically greater in smaller companies where management issues and significant departures from the business plan are regular events. However, the crises that occur in larger companies tend to be significant and time-consuming when they do arise (financial crises, high-profile management or board issues and the like).

2.9 Case of Compaq Computers

Ben Rosen, a venture capitalist with a significant stake in Compaq, served as the non-executive chairman of the company's board. After the stock price of the company plummeted, matched by Compaq's first–ever quarterly loss, a major disagreement developed between management and the board as to how the company should address the crisis. The board believed the company needed a fundamental shift in strategy, and the company's Co-founder and CEO Rod Canion was forced to resign. The result was vastly increased earnings over the next year and a doubling of the stock price. In testimony to the House of Representatives, Rosen described the criteria for a strong board.

1. An outside, independent chairman: All directors, with the exception of the CEO, should be outsiders.
2. Board members who all have meaningful ownership in the company, making them natural allies of the shareholder owners.
3. Key committees that exclude the CEO.
4. Boards that are relatively small, to increase their effectiveness. In addition, reciprocal directorships should be discouraged, if not eliminated.

Compaq had such a board, which was vital as the company faced a difficult period: Compaq Computers after a period of meteoric and profitable growth, ran into serious difficulties engendered by fundamental shifts in the marketplace. Their historical recipe for success was out of tune with the new needs of customers. For the first time, the board and management differed on the fundamental direction of the company. Because the board was composed of all-outside directors (except CEO), had a non-CEO chairman, and was small (seven members), it was able to act dispassionately and entirely in the interest of the corporation. The board moved promptly, and the rest, as they say is history.

As noted earlier, 10 years later Compaq faced the same problem and came up with the same solution—replacing the CEO. Is this an evidence that the board is successful? Or, that it made mistakes in allowing the problems to get to that point? (Monks and Minow).

2.9.1 Role of an Independent Director

In the case of Satyam Computers scandal one of the most debated issues was relating to the role of independent directors. There is a consensus that the independent directors on Indian boards are seldom empowered and this leads to ineffective board functioning. In India, in most of the cases the chairman plays a dominant role in deciding the line and length of the strategic discussion that should take place and also how to utilise the competencies of the independent directors most effectively.

Freedom of expression: Independent directors need to be more involved in board meetings since their role demands a contribution to risk management—they must ask the right questions, seek answers from the executives and evaluate those answers in relation to the strategy of the company. According to Deepak Satwalekar (2009),[1] 'I think it is independent director who has to decide how independent he or she wishes to be. And I think the more independent one wishes to be, one should be able to commit time. And if one is unwilling to commit time, I don't think one is entitled to ask questions of the board or even be on the board.' Truly engaged directors will know and understand the business of the company, and with their wide experience they should be able to evaluate whether management overlooked any risks in its strategy. If taken in the true spirit of governance, this does not necessarily mean doubting management, but raising questions so that the board is able to think through to take the right decisions. The role of the independent directors is not to question the management, but to challenge it; challenge the strategic assumptions, challenge the business scenarios being sketched.

One of the reasons given for this hesitancy on the part of the independent directors to voice their opinions has been the board culture in India. As Vaghul (2009) explains: 'We seem to be operating under a cultural constraint where it is very difficult for the independent director to disagree with the chairman, particularly since directors frequently owe their appointment to the chairman.' Boards constituting family and friends are a common sight in India and, more often than not, directors are only present at the meetings for compliance sake. Consequently, there is a natural

---

1.   Deepak M. Satwalekar, Independent Director, Infosys Technologies Ltd., Bangalore, Karnataka. Sector: Technology/Technical & System Software.

reluctance on their part to dissent from the views of the chairman. Furthermore, board directorships are very often offered to retired individuals, for whom the compensation is very important and therefore this affects the quality of their engagement with the board. This is also a compelling reason for having non-executive independent chairmen. However, as Bharat Doshi (2009), Mahindra & Mahindra explains: 'If an independent director finds that he or she is the only person dissenting every time and finds no support from the chairman or the board, he or she should walk away.' At the end of the day, independent directors are professionals, with personal reputations to protect and if they feel their views are going unheard on a board, it is better for them to step down. If they feel there is information that shareholders should be aware of and is being withheld, they should report it. In no way should that be considered a breach of trust. Deepak Satwalekar (2009) explains: 'While this is important and may be necessary to fulfill the role and responsibility as an independent director, "cultural constraints" will not let this happen, unless there is a liability attached for not reporting, when one was aware of something amiss. In India, people step off the board for "personal reasons".' To enable true governance in this area, independent directors' hands need strengthening.

The chairman should be instrumental in empowering the independent directors and also in ensuring the culture of silence is replaced with constructive criticism. The point to be emphasised is not whether the chairman has relationships with the directors, but whether the right individuals have been chosen to be on the board. A good nomination committee, led by non-executive chairman and comprising only independent directors, will also provide continuity on the board when new members are required. Another means of ensuring clarity of role would be to issue letter of appointment to independent directors clearly spelling out expectations and responsibilities. In recent time, especially since the recent financial crisis, the qualifications of independent directors have come into focus. In many cases, while boards often comprise people with stature and extensive experience, not all of them necessarily understand the business of the company. In the US, there is a strong feeling that the absence of people with financial expertise in the boardrooms of financial institutions was a major contributing factor to the economic crisis. Julie Daum (2009) explains: 'Everybody does not need to understand every aspect of a business, but boards need people who have a real feel for the business and have the guts to raise their hands and ask the intelligent questions. In US, the boards in majority are moving towards this model-building board with leadership and real expertise relevant to that business.'

According to Kiran Karnik (2009),[2] the former president, NASSCOM: 'Sometimes the need for domain knowledge can be overstated. Directors need not be experts, it is more important for them to look at strategy and to make sure that the systems processes are right'. Furthermore, the composition of the board should be such that every member complements the other. Therefore, a combination of different age groups and different backgrounds can be beneficial, as long as each director is capable of contributing to the strategy.

2.9.2 Should the Independent Directors be Centre-Stormed?

The independent directors are always victimised for any corporate scandal or lapses. There is a mindset among stakeholders to hold them responsible for the shortcomings of the board—a mindset that is quite unfair. The board cannot ultimately shirk responsibility, as the lion's share of that responsibility lies with the management of the company. According to a corporate leader, it will be very difficult to prevent corporate fraud unless the management is held responsible and has values and ethics. One cannot get away from those. Today, most boards are spending enormous amounts of time on compliance. This needs to be changed. Boards should not spend the majority of their time looking over the shoulders of management, but should refocus their attention on strategy.

2.10 Independent Director: New Zealand Context

Independence of mind is a basic requirement for directors. Each should endeavour to have an independent perspective when making

---

2. Kiran Karnik held the office of President of NASSCOM, the premier trade body and the Chamber of Commerce for the IT software and services industry in India, till January 2008. During his tenure at NASSCOM, industry exports grew almost eight times and NASSCOM became a globally-known and respected brand. Mr Karnik has been recognised as the guiding force for the Indian IT industry, especially for his leadership of the industry during the outsourcing backlash in the US and elsewhere.

judgments and decisions on matters before the board. This means a director puts the interests of the entity ahead of all other interests, including any separate management interests and those of individual shareholders (except as permitted by law). Directors with an independent perspective are more likely to constructively challenge each other and executives—and thereby increase the board's effectiveness.

Securities and Exchange Commission (SEC) views that there would be practical constraints in New Zealand if too high a level of formal independence is required of boards. With New Zealand's relatively small pool of qualified and experienced directors, there would be a risk in seeking independence at the cost of all. Else it will lead to missed opportunities to appoint directors who can contribute to the success of entities. SEC considers the underlying issues relating to director independence can be addressed by:

- Directors having an independent perspective in their decision-making.

- A non-executive director being formally classified as independent only where he or she does not represent a substantial shareholder and where the board is satisfied that he or she has no other direct or indirect interest or relationship that could reasonably influence their judgement and decision-making as a director.

- The chairperson of a publicly-owned entity being independent.

- In every issuer, the board including independent director's representation.

- Boards of publicly-owned entities comprising:
  - a majority of non-executive directors; and
  - a minimum one-third of independent directors.

- Boards taking care to meet all disclosure obligations concerning directors and their interests, including information about the directors, and identify which directors are independent.

2.11 Independent Director: Indian Context

Kumar Mangalam Birla Committee,[3] appointed by SEBI to formulate guidelines of good corporate governance in listed companies in India, was of the opinion that the touchstone of independence is the absence of material pecuniary relationships or transactions with the company. Accordingly, the Committee defined Independent Directors as follows:

> Independent Directors are directors who apart from receiving director's remuneration do not have any other material pecuniary relationship or transactions with the company, its promoters, its management or its subsidiaries, which in the judgment of the Board may affect their Independence of Judgment.

Independent directors are defined by clause 49 of the listing agreement of SEBI as follows: The expression 'independent director' shall mean a non-executive director of the company who:

(a) apart from receiving director's remuneration, does not have any material pecuniary relationships or transactions with the company, its promoters, its directors, its senior management or its holding company, its subsidiaries and associates which may affect independence of the director;

(b) is not related to promoters or persons occupying management positions at the board level or at one level below the board;

(c) has not been an executive of the company in the immediately preceding three financial years;

(d) is not a partner or an executive or was not partner or an executive during preceding three years, of any of the following:

   (i) the statutory audit firm or the internal audit firm that is associated with the company; and

   (ii) the legal firm(s) and consulting firm(s) that have a material association with the company.

---

3.   In 1999, Securities and Exchange Board of India (SEBI) had set up a committee under Shri Kumar Mangalam Birla, member SEBI Board, to promote and raise the standards of good corporate governance. The report submitted by the committee is the first formal and comprehensive attempt to evolve a 'Code of Corporate Governance', in the context of prevailing conditions of governance in Indian companies, as well as the state of capital markets.

(e) is not a material supplier, service provider or customer or a lessor or lessee of the company, which may affect independence of the director; and

(f) is not a substantial shareholder of the company i.e., owning two per cent or more of the block of voting shares.

Independent directors are considered both as a safeguard and source of competitive advantage. In view of their independence, experience and expertise, they are required to perform the following functions:

(i)   balance the often conflicting interests of the stakeholders;

(ii)   facilitate withstanding and countering pressures from owners;

(iii) fulfill a useful role in succession planning;

(iv)   act as a coach, mentor and sounding board for their full time colleagues; and

(v)   provide independent judgment and wider perspectives.

2.12 Non-Executive Director

2.12.1 The Role of a Non-Executive Director

UK context: Essentially the non-executive director's role is to provide a creative contribution to the board by providing objective criticism.

The 1992 Cadbury Report initiated a debate about the main functions and responsibilities of non-executive directors. Today, it is widely accepted that non-executive directors have an important contribution to make to the proper running of companies and, therefore, more widely to the economy at large. As the Cadbury Report said, they 'should bring an independent judgement to bear on issues of strategy, performance and resources including key appointments and standards of conduct.'

There is no legal distinction between executive and non-executive directors. As a consequence, in the UK unitary board structure non-executive directors have the same legal duties, responsibilities and potential liabilities as in the growing number of private companies, including executive counterparts. Clearly, it is appreciated that non-executive directors cannot give the same continuous attention to the business of the company. However, it is important that they show the same commitment to its success as their executive colleagues.

All directors should be capable of seeing company and business issues in a broad perspective. Nonetheless, non-executive directors are usually chosen because they have a breadth of experience, are of an appropriate calibre and have particular personal qualities. Additionally, they may have some specialist expertise or, perhaps, key contacts in related industries or the city.

Not all non-executive directors are the same. There is a difference between the non-executive director and the independent non-executive director. Independent directors are defined in the Cadbury Report as persons who 'apart from directors' fees and shareholdings [are] independent of the management and free from any business or other relationships which could materially interfere with the exercise of the independent judgement'. The Cadbury Committee (1992), Hampel Committee (1998) and Higgs Committee (2003) Reports, some of whose recommendations are included in the revised Combined Code, stress that the board should include independent non-executive directors of sufficient calibre and number for their views to carry significant weight in the board's deliberations.

The Combined Code, which effectively codifies the main features of the Cadbury, Hampel and Higgs Reports for listed companies, advises that the balance of executive and non-executive directors should be such that no individual or small group of individuals can dominate the board's decision-making. Non-executive directors should comprise not less than half the board.

While much of the comment and discussion on non-executive directors tends to focus on listed companies, it is important to note that they can also make a valuable, *albeit* somewhat different, contribution to private companies. Indeed, there are a growing number of private companies, including relatively small ones, that are now actively searching for the 'right' non-executive director.

Non-executive directors are expected to focus on board matters and not stray into 'executive direction', thus providing an independent view of the company that is removed from its day-to-day running. Chairmen and chief executives should use their non-executive directors to provide general counsel—and a different perspective—on matters of concern. They should also seek their guidance on particular issues before they are raised at board meetings. Indeed, some of the main specialist roles of a non-executive director will be carried out in a board subcommittee, especially in listed companies.

2.13 Key Responsibilities of Non-Executive Directors (NEDs)

- *Strategic direction:* As an 'outsider', the NED may have a clearer or wider view of external factors affecting the company and its business environment than the executive directors. The normal role of the NED in strategy formation is therefore to provide a creative and informed contribution and to act as a constructive critic in looking at the objectives and plans devised by the MD and his or her executive team.

- *Monitoring:* NEDs should take responsibility for monitoring the performance of executive management, especially with regard to the progress made towards achieving the determined company strategy and objectives.

- *Communication:* The company's and board's effectiveness can benefit from outside contacts and opinions. An important function for NEDs, therefore, can be to help connect the business and board with networks of potentially useful people and organisations. In some cases the NED will be called upon to represent the company externally.

- *Audit:* It is the duty of the whole board to ensure that the company accounts properly to its shareholders by presenting a true and fair reflection of its actions and financial performance and that the necessary internal control systems are put into place and monitored regularly and rigorously. NEDs have an important part to play in fulfilling this responsibility, whether or not a formal audit committee (composed of NEDs) of the board has been constituted.

2.14 Seven General Duties of Directors: Institute of Directors (IoD), UK

- to act within the powers of the company;
- to promote the success of the company for the benefit of its members as a whole, paying due regard in decision-making to:
  - likely long-term consequences;
  - employees' interests;
  - the need to foster relationships with suppliers, customers and others;
  - the impact of operations on the community and the environment;
  - the need to maintain high standards of business conduct and to act fairly between members of the company;
- the need to exercise independent judgment;
- the need to exercise reasonable care, skill and diligence;
- the need to avoid conflicts of interest;
- the need not to accepts benefits from third parties;
- the need to declare, where applicable, any interest in a transaction or arrangement with the company.

New Zealand context: Non-executive directors, with no other interests to hinder their judgment in the interests of the entity, can contribute a particularly independent perspective to board decisions. Increasingly, international practice has been to establish criteria for defining some independent directors of listed entities, and to require or encourage a majority of such directors on the board. Recent studies indicate, however, that board effectiveness is not always enhanced by director's formal independence if this is given too much weight in contrast to the independence of mind, and the skills, knowledge, experience, and time that a director can contribute to the entity. Independent representation is an important contributor to board effectiveness, but only when considered along with the other attributes sought in a non-executive director.

2.15 Cases Evidencing the Unethical Practices
of the Boards

2.15.1 WorldCom

The share price of WorldCom which was $62 in 1999 fell to 7 cents in 2002 due to the unethical practices of the self-centred board members.

In his early business career, Bernard Ebbers acquired a reputation for being careful with business expenses and being skillful in making deals. By the end of 1984 Long Distance Discount Services (LDDS) had accumulated debts of about $1.5 million. Because he had proved himself as a shrewd businessman in running his motel chain, it was decided by the board of LDDS that it would be useful to ask Ebbers to take charge and, in 1985 he became CEO. Within a few months Ebbers was able to turn the company round and turn it into a profitable business.

Ebbers's stake was 14.5 per cent of share capital and he was one of the nine initial subscribers to the equity. In March 2004, he was charged with fraud, conspiracy and making false statements in connection with the accounting irregularities that led to WorldCom's collapse.

The consequences of the bankruptcy were severe for shareholders, who lost virtually all their investments, and many employees lost heir jobs. Creditors also lost out. However, the company did emerge from bankruptcy in May 2004 and was renamed MCI. In the late 1990s Ebbers' personal spending was beginning to climb. In July 1998 he bought a ranch in British Columbia for an estimated $66 million. He also acquired a yacht. In 1999 a private company in which he had a 65 per cent stake paid about $400 million for timberland in Alabama, Mississippi and Tennessee. In 2002 it was learned that WorldCom had made loans to Ebbers amounting to $341 million. Interest payable by Ebbers on these loans was about 2.16 per cent, which was lower than the cost to WorldCom of actually borrowing the money.

Why should the board of WorldCom adopt such a generous lending policy towards its CEO?

One possible explanation was a concern that Ebbers might be forced to sell large amounts of his shareholdings in WorldCom to resolve his personal financial problems and this could have a negative impact on WorldCom's share price.

Why did this Financially Strapped Telecom give its CEO such a Huge Gift?

WorldCom was worried that Ebbers, who speculated in tech companies, might have a margin call on the shares he owned in World-Com. If they were dumped in a forced sale, it could set off a panic that would further pummel the price of WorlCom stock. So the board loaned Ebbers the money to protect his personal holdings. This is capitalism at its finest. 'If the CEO's investments are successful, he wins. If they fail, the company loses' (New York Daily News, 25 March 2002: 3). At the beginning of April 2002, WorldCom was forced to announce that 3,700 US-based staff would be made redundant. At the end of April, Ebbers resigned and John Sidgmore was named as vice-chairman, president and chief executive officer.

Accounting Irregularities

The following were the irregularities in accounts as identified by the internal auditors.

- Overstating the Sales Commission.
- Capitalising (deferred expenditures) the operating expenses to stabilise the profit figures, i.e., instead of writing off the expense immediately in the profit-and-loss account (thereby reducing reported profit), WorldCom was capitalising some items and writing them off to the profit-and-loss account over a much longer period.

Analysis

It can be observed from the above case that the person who was the cause for turning around of the WorldCom also proved in the course of time as the main culprit, adversely impacting the performance of the WorldCom and thereby affecting all the stakeholders. For instance, livelihood of the employees, future of the investors, creating losses to the creditors, and threatening the future continuance of the organisation.

If only Ebbers was more ethical in his deeds:

- he would not have borrowed huge amounts of loans for a cost which was lower than the cost actually incurred by the WorldCom on its borrowings;
- he would not have been the cause for job loss of the 3,700 employees;
- he would not have been the cause of many investors who lost their investments;
- he would not have been the cause of the irregular reporting practices in accounting; and
- he would not have led WorldCom into bankruptcy.

Therefore, in the case of WorldCom ethics can be considered part of solution to prevent future bankruptcies.

Hence, it can be said that ethics does matter in the corporate governance.

2.15.2 Enron

The share price of Enron which was $90 during 2000 declined sharply to $1 towards the end of December, 2001.

Creative Accounting at Enron and
its Impact on the Accounting Profession

Transparency is an essential ingredient for a sound system of corporate governance. The USA has been dubbed the strongest capital market in the world, with the highest standards of integrity and ethicality. What went wrong? Both the audit function and the accounting function in Enron were fraudulent and opaque. However, Enron's collapse has had repercussions on the whole of the accounting and auditing profession, not just in the USA but worldwide. Enron's accounting was anything but transparent. Confidence in the company collapsed in 2001, when it became clear that their accounts were not only unreliable but fraudulent. Arthur Andersen, one of the Big Five (Deloitte Touche Tohmatsu, Pricewaterhouse-Coopers, Ernst & Young, KPMG), has now disappeared, partly as a result of its involvement in Enron's fraudulent accounting and auditing. However,

Enron was not Andersen's first major problem. They had already paid out millions of dollars in settlements following inaccurate and weak auditing on a number of companies including Sunbeam, Waste Management and Discovery Zone (*The Economist*, 15 November 2001). In 2000, Andersen collected $25 million for auditing Enron's books in addition to $27 million for consulting services. This seems excessive and demonstrates a notorious problem of conflicts of interest between the auditing and consultancy arms of accounting firms.

Examples of Enron's devious accounting are abound. The company recorded profits, for example, from a joint venture with Blockbuster Video that never materialised (*The Economist*, 7 February 2002). In 2002, Enron restated its accounts, a bad sign in itself and a process that reduced reported profits by $600 million (*The Economist*, 6 December 2001). Indeed, the process resulted in a cumulative profit reduction of $591 million and a rise in debt of $628 million for the financial statements from 1997 to 2000. This triggered an investigation by the SEC into the auditing work of Andersen, Enron's auditors. The difference between the profit figures was mainly attributable to the earlier omission of three off-balance sheet entities. Such profit inflation allowed the company to increase its earnings per share (EPS) figure. EPS is simply the total earnings figure divided by the number of shares. The company's exaggerated focus on its EPS was certainly a factor in its eventual decline. This is a common strategy and one which can lead to manipulation of accounting numbers in attempts to inflate the EPS figure (*The Economist*, 6 December 2001). The pressure on companies in the USA and elsewhere to increase their EPS year-on-year basis has been blamed for corporate short-termism. It also provides directors with an irresistible temptation to cheat the figures! Not only did the company clearly manipulate the accounting numbers to inflate the earnings figure, but it was found to have removed substantial amounts of debt from its accounts by setting up a number of off-balance sheet entities. Such special purpose entities are non-consolidated, off-balance sheet vehicles that have some legitimate uses, such as the financing of a research and development partnership with another company. However, they can also be used to hide a company's liabilities from the balance sheet, in order to make the financial statements look much better than they really are (*The Economist*, 2 May 2002). This was certainly the case for Enron. It meant that significant liabilities did not have to be disclosed on Enron's financial statements, as they were almost attributable to another legal entity (but not quite). To anyone, this is an obvious example of fraudulent, premeditated and unethical management. Furthermore, about 28 per cent of Enron's EPS was shown to have come from gains on sales of securitised assets to third parties connected to Enron (Ibid).

All this begs the question, 'Why did Enron's auditor allow this type of activity?.' They had to have been aware of it. Perhaps Andersen considered the transactions were relatively too small to be considered material. However, this is becoming less of a reasonable excuse (Ibid). In December 2001 the chief executive of Andersen, Joseph Berardino, stated that the firm had made an error of judgment over one of the off-balance sheet entities created by Enron (*The Economist*, 20 December 2001). One 'special purpose' vehicle in particular, called Chewco, again created by Enron to offload liabilities for off-balance sheet financing purposes, was cited as being a chief culprit, as it did not provide Andersen with adequate information. Clearly, had Andersen had this additional information, they would have forced Enron to consolidate Chewco into their accounts. However, such ignorance on the part of Andersen may not be adequate support for its lack of action. According to Enron, Andersen had been carrying out a detailed audit of the main structured finance vehicles, which made the auditing firm guilty of acting too slowly and inadequately (Ibid).

Approach of Enron Board in Reaction to Whistle Blower

On August 22, 2001, Kenneth Lay, Enron's chairman, received a letter from an Enron accounting executive, Sherron Witkins, which contained these allegations:

> I am incredibly nervous that we will implode in a wave of accounting scandals. My eight years of Enron work history will be worth nothing on my resume, the business world will consider the past successes as nothing but an elaborate accounting hoax. Skilling is resigning for 'personal reasons' but I would think he wasn't having fun, looked down the road and knew this stuff was unfixed and would rather abandon ship now than resign in shame in two years. I realise that we have had a lot of smart people looking at this and a lot of accountants including AA & Co. have blessed the accounting treatment. None of that will protect Enron if these transactions are

ever disclosed in the bright light of day. Involve Jim Derrick and Rex Rogers to hire a law firm to investigate the condor and Raptor transactions to give Enron attorney-client privilege on the work product. (Can't use Vinson & Elkins [V&E] due to conflict—they provided some true sale opinions on some of the deals). Law firm to hire one of the big 6, but not Arthur Anderson or Pricewaterhouse-Coopers due to their conflicts of interest: AA & Co (Enron); PWC (LJM).

The following points present the actual timeline of what happened thereafter:

1. The Watkins letter triggered an investigation by Vinson & Elkins (not withstanding Watkins request not to use V&E), which began in August 2001 and ended with a verbal report on September 21 and a written report on October 15, 2001.

2. The V&E report concluded that the facts revealed in its preliminary investigation did not warrant a 'further widespread investigation by independent counsel or auditors', although it did not note that the 'bad cosmetics' of the Raptor related party transactions, coupled with the poor performance of the assets placed in the Raptor vehicles, created 'a serious risk of adverse publicity and litigation'.

3. On October 16, 2001, Enron publicly announced a $44 million after-tax charge against earning and a reduction of its shareholders equity by $1.2 billion.

4. On December 2, 2001, Enron Corporation, then the seventh largest publicly traded corporation in United States, declared bankruptcy.

The investigation of Enron by V&E is a good example of a bad decision by the Enron board. The board delegated the investigation to the general counsel of Enron, even though the complaints by Sherron Watkins the Whistle blower, involved top management at Enron, V&E LLP, the primary outside counsel for Enron, and the Enron general counsel had a consensus on a very limited investigation that did not involve obtaining an independent accountants' opinion on the work of Arthur Andersen, even though accounting issues were at the heart of Watkins's complaint and even though she had specifically requested that Arthur Andersen not be involved in the investigation. Indeed, Watkins also requested that V&E LLP not be involved in the investigation; Enron's general counsel also ignored this request. At the end of the very limited investigation, V&E LLP gave Enron a report that, in general, found no substance to Watkins's complaint. Later, a separate investigation completed shortly after Enron's bankruptcy by an independent board committee, using completely independent counsel, found significant substance to Watkins's complaint.

Therefore, the above two cases clearly indicate the missing link between the corporate governance and business ethics. Infact, corporate governance is meant to run companies ethically in a manner such that all stakeholders—creditors, distributors, customers, employees, society at large and governments are dealt in a fair manner. There was a belief at one time that the job of the management is to look after its shareholders alone. Now the whole concept of capitalism has changed and it has started adopting a much broader view for its own survival, that is why it has now become important that governance should look at all stakeholders and not just shareholders. Corporate governance is not something which regulators have to impose on a management but it should come from within. There is no point in making statutory provisions for enforcing ethical conduct. It is not that there is no broad regulatory framework in position now. It is very imperative that there should be a convergence between the corporate governance and business ethics, because ethics does matter in the corporate governance.

References

Cadbury, A. (1992). *Report of the Committee on the Financial Aspects of Corporate Governance: The Code of Best Practice (Cadbury Code).* London: Gee & Company.

Higgs, D. Report (2003). *Review of the Role and Effectiveness of Non-Executive Directors.* London: Department of Trade and Industry. Available at: *www.dti.gov.uk/cld/ non_exec_review/ pdfs/higgsreport.pdf* (Accessed January 2004).

Hampel, S.R. (1998). *Committee on Corporate Governance: Final Report.* London: Gee & Co. Ltd.

3 | Corporate Governance and Board Composition

One of the widely discussed issues in academic literature concerns how to appropriately structure the board of directors and to what extent the make up of the board of directors influences board actions or corporate performance. In this respect, issues relating to the board size, board composition, effectiveness and board leadership are presented and discussed in this chapter.

3.1 Size of the Board

Board size is one of the well-studied board characteristics from two different perspectives. First, the number of directors may influence the board's functioning and hence corporate performance. Yermack (1996) found a negative relationship between board size and firm market value, using a sample of large US public companies. Similar results were reported using European data. Eisenberg et al. (1998) studied small non-listed Finnish firms and found a negative correlation between firm's profitability and the size of the board. The study by Conyon and Peck (1998) showed inverse relationships between return on shareholders' equity and board size for five European countries.

There are some researchers who have analysed board of directors as decision-making groups and integrated the literature on group dynamics and workgroup effectiveness. Hence, board size can have both positive and negative effects on its performance. Expanding the number of directors provides an increased pool of expertise because larger boards are likely to have more knowledge and skills at their disposal. Besides, large boards may be able to draw on a variety of perspectives on corporate strategy and may reduce domination by CEO (Forbes and Milliken, 1999; Goodstein et al., 1994). However, increasing board size might significantly inhibit board processes due to potential group dynamics problems associated with large groups. Larger boards are more difficult to coordinate and may experience problems with communication and organisation. Furthermore, large boards may face decreased levels of motivation and participation and are prone to develop factions and coalitions. Finally, boards may have difficulties in further cohesiveness and may suffer from a diffusion of responsibility or 'social loafing' often found in large groups. Consequently, these group dynamic problems may hinder boards of directors in reaching a consensus on important decisions and may put a barrier on the ability of the board to control management (Judge and Zeithaml, 1992; Goodstein et al., 1994; Eisenberg et al., 1998; Forbes and Milliken, 1999; Golden and Zajac, 2001).

The number of directors is a relevant feature that can have much to do with board monitoring and control activity. Infact, the ability of the board to monitor can increase as more directors are added, the benefits can be outweighed by the costs in terms of the poorer communication and decision-making associated with larger groups (Lipton and Lorsch, 1992; Jensen, 1993), along with the fact that the CEO can be more likely to control the board of directors.

3.2 Board Composition

There are number of studies focussing on the role and proportion of inside, outside and independent directors. In general, two theories form the basis for the reliance on insider or outsider-dominated boards. Agency theory focusses on the conflicts of interest that occur among the shareholders (principals) and the managers (agents), stemming from the separation of ownership and control. Managers who gain control may have the potential to pursue actions that maximise their self-interest at the expense of the shareholders. The board of directors is one of the mechanisms designed to monitor these conflicts of interest (Jensen and Meckling, 1976; Fama and Jensen, 1983). Thus, from an agency perspective, boards should be able to act independent of management and therefore must include a preponderance of outside directors.

The opposite perspective is grounded in stewardship theory. According to Stewardship theory, managers are good stewards of company assets. Managers do not misappropriate corporate resources at any price because they have a range of non-financial motives, such as the intrinsic satisfaction of successful performance, the need for achievement and recognition etc. Reallocation of control from shareholders to management leads to maximisation of corporate profits and hence, shareholders return (Muth and Donaldson, 1998). Following this reasoning, the boards of directors dominated by insiders are preferable.

Academic research provides evidence that support both perspectives. The effect of outsider-dominated board on performance is indeed contradictory. Greater representation of outside directors on the board has a negative impact on firm's performance, as measured by Tobin's Q (Agrawal and Knoeber, 1996) and on market value added (MVA) (Coles et al., 2001). In contrast, Rosenstein and Wyatt (1990) found that a clearly identifiable announcement of the appointment of an outside director leads to an increase in shareholders' wealth. Also Baysinger and Butler (1985) reported that firms with higher proportions of independent directors ended up with superior performance records. Wagner et al. (1998) conclude that both greater insider and outsider representation can have a positive impact on performance, while others conclude that there is virtually no relationship between board composition and firm performance (Dalton et al., 1998; Hermalin and Weisbach, 2000).

Evidence suggests that board composition is also related to strategic decisions taken by the board and to the monitoring of management. Outsider-dominated boards are more involved in restructuring decisions (Johnson et al., 1993) and positively influence diversification strategies (Baysinger and Hoskisson, 1990). Similarly, higher insider representation has a negative effect on overall board involvement in the strategic decision-making process (Judge and Zeithaml, 1992). The presence of outside directors has a negative implication for the intensity of R&D (Baysinger and Hoskisson, 1990) and other entrepreneurial activities of the company (Short et al., 1999). The inclusion of insiders in the board may be useful because they have access to information relevant to outside directors in assessing both strategic initiatives and managerial performance (Fama and Jensen, 1983; Baysinger and Butler, 1985).

Barry J. Reiter (1994) suggested the following factors to be considered while deciding on the board's appropriate mix and size:

- Sufficient directors and expertise to allow the board to make a full contribution to corporate activities. Independent directors' expertise will help managers evaluate employees' and consultants' recommendations. It will also help the board itself assess management proposals and corporate performance.

- Sufficient independent directors to perform the functions normally assigned to board committees. These include questions on compensation.

- Effective discussion and decision-making. If, for some reason, a very large board is necessary, committees may be formed to achieve appropriate board's functionality.

Singapore requires boards to compromise at least one-third of independent directors, or explain why this is not achieved. The Sarbanes-Oxley Act in US requires a majority of independent directors, while Germany's supervisory boards are entirely independent. Boards in the UK, Switzerland and Canada are highly independent. Spanish, Italian and Asian boards typically include some independent directors, as well as non-executive directors who are not 'independent' by definition.

In United Kingdom the company's Articles of Association prescribes the way directors are to be appointed, and often a minimum and maximum number of directors. For companies with a full listing on the London Stock Exchange there will be further requirements under the combined code on corporate governance. (The code doesn't apply to alternative investment market (AIM)–listed companies and includes some concessions for smaller companies.)

The key for a successful productive board is to have a good balance. In other words, there should be a mix of independent non-executive directors and executive directors and, importantly, of skills and experience. According to the Combined Code at least 50 per cent of board members should be independent directors and that the roles of chairman and chief executive should be separated. Further, the chairman should not be a former chief executive. In case if the companies feel they have good reason to against these recommendations, they need to state their case in their annual reports. (comply or explain!).

The board will work best if non-executives have a variety of experiences, skills and backgrounds: diversity will have an added value to debate and decisions. When the board looks into the future as a part of the annual strategic review of the organisation, its members will think of the resources needed in the years ahead to deliver the agreed strategy in times that will certainly have changed. Also, the structure of the board should be mindful of this, and where there is a shortage of skills or experience for the new realities of the future, those skills should be identified and filled as a part of the succession planning of the board.

Non-executive directors are appointed through the nomination committee after a rigorous process that starts with a definition of the role and a description of the competencies and experience sought. The nomination committee recommends to the board, which will make the final decision on new appointments.

The chairman examines annually the board composition and its effectiveness. This is a valuable exercise that will give good feedback on how the board can operate more efficiently and add greater value to the organisation. In addition, the chairman will have individual annual discussions with directors on their contribution to the board and identify any training or development needs. The senior non-executive director will also talk to other directors on the chairman's performance in order to give feedback to him or her. The non-executive directors play an important part in assisting the chairman to fulfill his or her role by regularly and rigorously assessing the effectiveness of the board's processes and activities.

Things to consider while deciding on the board composition:

- The ratio of non-executive director to executive director should be considered. The future needs of the business should be given a thought. Consider the energy, experience, knowledge, skills and personal attributes of current and prospective directors; ensure that there is a proper process for appointing directors.
- The cohesion of the board and the chemistry between the directors when making new appointments should be considered.
- Make succession plans for members of the board and senior executives and update them regularly.
- Agree on the procedures for appointing the chairman and the chief executive.

- Appoint a nomination committee whose terms of reference ensure: the range of potential candidates is wide; and recommendations are made to the board only after a rigorous selection process.

- Assess the contribution of each director in an annual review. (The chairman should lead the review and arrange individual development programmes where necessary or, in cases of persistent unsatisfactory performance, ask the director to leave the company.)

- Provide new members with comprehensive induction programme.

3.3 Board Effectiveness Review: The Key Elements

3.3.1 Corporate Strategy

- The corporate strategy is clearly understood by the board, shareholders and employees.

- Corporate strategy is regularly reviewed and updated to ensure its continued appropriateness, support and effectiveness.

- Directors have collectively and individually brought their knowledge and experience to bear in the testing and development of group strategy.

- Strategic options are effectively and systematically evaluated.

- There is an effective and productive process for the review and updating of group strategy.

3.3.2 Business Principles

- Are owned and championed by the board.

- Are underpinned by a set of clear and comprehensive group policies, approved by the board.

- Are reviewed annually by the board and updated to ensure their continued appropriateness, support and effectiveness.

- Are explicit, unambiguous and practicable.

- Are championed by the executive management group; provide appropriate guidance and motivation to all staff.

- Are effectively communicated to shareholders and other stakeholders.

3.3.3 Internal Controls and Risk Management

- There is a clear and comprehensive framework of risk-based internal controls to implement the group policies adopted by the board and thereby manage significant risks.
- Significant risks are effectively identified and evaluated.
- The board effectively assesses and monitors the system of internal controls and the effectiveness with which risk is being managed.

3.3.4 Shareholders and Stakeholders

- The group strategy is effectively communicated to shareholders and other stakeholders.
- The board receives sufficient information about the views of shareholders and other stakeholders from relevant external sources.

3.3.5 Communications

- The timing, coverage and quality of shareholder and stakeholder communications are appropriate.
- The board communicates effectively with the executive management group. The organisation has the resources, skills and experience to manage the key risks and deliver the business plan.

3.3.6 Organisation and Culture

- The group culture encourages continuous improvement.
- Performance reporting is adequate and timely, and ensures prompt capture of adverse trends.
- Variances from budget are clearly identified and corrective actions are detailed. Management performance is regularly and thoroughly reviewed, and rewards or sanctions are executed promptly.

3.3.7 Succession, Development and Reward

- There is an appropriate succession management plan for all board and executive management group positions.
- Training and development are encouraged and are focussed on the delivery of the business plan.

- The range of rewards is suited to recruiting and retaining qualified, capable and high-quality staff.
- Rewards are structured to focus on short-, medium- and long-term performance.

3.3.8 Board Composition

- The present board membership and composition are optimal for the company, given its current needs.
- The range of skills, knowledge and experience is appropriate.
- The process for identifying and recruiting new board members is transparent and appropriate.

3.3.9 Board Induction and Training

- There is a comprehensive programme to provide new non-executive directors with an induction to the group.
- Directors are kept up to date with the latest developments.
- There is a comprehensive training programme for directors to refresh their knowledge and skills.

3.3.10 Delegation and Accountabilities

- The matters reserved for the board are appropriate.
- The present range of committees is capable of addressing all areas that should be reviewed on behalf of the board.
- The committee chairs report appropriate and timely information on their activities to the whole board.
- The board delegates appropriate authority to senior management.

3.3.11 Board Meetings

- The agenda includes only what is important.
- Agenda items and presentations are relevant and timely.
- The agenda allows the appropriate amount of time for the discussion of each item.
- The time allowed for each item is appropriately allocated to ensure proper consideration of key issues.

- The schedule of meetings, lunch and dinner allows adequate time for discussion, participation and reflection.
- Meetings are of high quality and are productive, with a full and open discussion of issues.

3.3.12 Secretarial Service

- Board papers are received in sufficient time.
- Board papers are sufficiently clear and concise.
- The minutes accurately reflect the substance or the discussions.
- Minutes are distributed in a timely manner.
- The board receives timely and comprehensive advice on matters of governance relevant to items on discussion.

3.4 Four Key Tasks of the Board

In the Institute of Directors' (IoD) publication: *Standards for the Board* (2001), four key tasks of the board are identified. They are presented as follows:

3.4.1 Develop and Maintain Vision, Mission and Values

- Determine and maintain the company's vision and mission to guide and set the pace for its current operations.
- Determine and maintain the values to be promoted throughout the company.
- Determine and maintain, and review, company goals.
- Determine and maintain company policies.

Note: Vision is a view of the future state of the company. The best visions give picture of the potential of the company and therefore, inspire people; a leader uses a 'vision' to describe to colleagues what the company can be and to urge them to achieve. Mission is a statement of what needs to be done in order to achieve the envisaged state. Values are a set.

3.4.2 Develop Strategy and Structure

- Review and evaluate present and future opportunities, threats and risks in the external environment, and current and future strengths, weaknesses and risks relating to the company.

- Determine strategic options, select those to be pursued and decide the means to implement and support them.

- Determine the business strategies and plans that underpin the corporate strategy.

- Ensure that the company's organisational structure and capabilities are appropriate for implementing the corporate strategy.

3.4.3 Delegate to Monitor Management

- Delegate authority to and monitor management, and evaluate the implementation of policies, strategies and business plans.

- Determine the monitoring criteria to be used by the board.

- Ensure that the internal controls are effective.

- Communicate with senior management.

3.4.4 Fulfill Responsibilities to Shareholders and Stakeholders

- Ensure that communications both to and from shareholders and stakeholders are effective.

- Understand and take into account the interest of shareholders and stakeholders.

- Monitor relations with shareholders and stakeholders by the gathering and evaluation of appropriate information.

- Promote the goodwill and support of shareholders and stakeholders.

3.5 Board Directorships

Number of the board directorship is yet another important issue which elicited much discussion and debate in recent times. The issue is about limiting the number of board directorships that an independent director should hold. This is directly linked to how involved independent directors need to be in order to do justice to their board role. According to Directors Database (2009), out of 6,871 individuals, 285 hold five or more independent directorships in listed companies in India, with one person holding 14 independent directorships. Furthermore, these 6,871 individuals are also on the boards of 13,284 unlisted organisations. There is an accepted formula among the corporate circles that, in order to be effective and fulfill responsibilities, independent directors need to spend at least 2-3 days preparing for a board meeting. And therefore, one view was that 3-5 boards would be the optimum number of directorships independent directors can handle, if they want to do a thorough job. On the other hand, while agreeing that directors should be willing to spend time between board meetings, there was a view that becoming prescriptive in limiting the number of directorships was not the only solution except possibly for full-time executives.

3.6 Tenure of Directorships

Independence of the directors has also been linked to the tenure of directorships with individual companies. In the UK, the governance code states that an individual can serve for up to nine years as an independent director (three terms of three years). After nine years, the Financial Reporting Council, which is the overarching governing body, deems the director 'not independent'. However, a board is entitled to argue its case that the director remains independent. True independence ceases to exist the day the independent director ingratiates himself with the CEO, so independence is more about an attitude of mind than a question of time served.

In the US, there is a big problem—there is hardly any turnover on listed boards. The retirement age for directors is 72 or 75 years, with the result that the average age in boardrooms is currently 64 years, many. boards comprising individuals who are retired and have been on the board for a long time. Julie Daum explains: 'This is a big problem that may have been put together when the business and the environment were very different, and new experience is missing.' In India, there is a related issue. While we are proud of our young demographic profile, this is not reflected in the composition of our boards. Chairman and nominations committees need to hire people who understand and can better represent that generation and its aspirations.

This has built the case for some degree of rotation on Indian boards, with support for a 6-9 year tenure especially given the Indian context where there is a tendency not to disagree publicly with 'friends on boards'. Kiran Karnik explains: 'Independent directors, over a period of time, build a certain relationship with the board and in India board meetings are seen as public discussions. While this is good and builds trust, I think independent directors must have a degree of skepticism, and for this, rotation is necessary.' Deepak Satwalekar adds: 'The key is in selecting people with the right attributes to begin with. If the nominations committee feels that age is beginning to tell on the performance of a director, then it should make the appropriate call, without waiting for six or nine years to elapse.'

3.7 UK Context: Board Composition and Performance

3.7.1 The Role and Structure of a Board of Directors

The first directors of a company are appointed at the time of its registration. Subsequent appointments are governed by the company's articles of association, which will prescribe the way directors are to be appointed and, often, a minimum and maximum number of directors. Typically the articles will provide for the board of directors to fill any casual vacancies or to appoint additional directors up to the maximum number specified by the articles.

For companies with a full listing on the London Stock Exchange, there will be further requirements under the Combined Code on Corporate Governance. (Note that the Code does not apply to AIM-listed companies and includes some concessions for smaller companies). Key to a successful, productive board is a good balance. There should be a mix of independent non-executive directors and executive directors and, importantly, a mix of skills and experience. The Combined Code states that at least 50 per cent of the members of the board should be independent directors and that the roles of chairman and chief executive should be separated. Further, it says that the chairman should not be a former chief executive. When companies believe they have a good reason to go against these recommendations, they need to state their case in their annual reports.

In the United Kingdom all directors have the same basic duties and liabilities whether they are executive (full-time employed) or non-executive. The existence of non-executive directors and the split of the roles of chief executive and chairman depend, to a certain extent, on the size and type of company.

The importance of non-executive directors in improving both accountability and company performance has long been recognised. The past five years have seen more than a 10 per cent increase in the number of non-executive positions on boards in FTSE 350 companies and a 20 per cent reduction in the number of executive directors. In many companies the role of the chairman will have changed from executive to non-executive.

As shown in Table 3.1, the average FTSE 350 board has 10 members—six non-executive directors (including the chairman) and four executive directors—which has been the case for the past three years. It is unlikely that we will see further significant increases in the number of non-executive directors in FTSE 350 companies.

The question of the independence of non-executive directors has been of increasing concern in the United Kingdom in recent years and is essentially considered an attitude of mind and a matter of personality. Different measures have been adopted by different organisations, institutions and associations to measure dependence. This has been a problem for companies in two main ways. First, they have had to deal with sometimes conflicting criteria; and second, a 'tick-box mentality' has arisen, with standardised checklists being used by analysts and commentators.

In relation to composition, there is concern that the limited range of appointees to boards, particularly non-executive directors and chief executives, has resulted in the boards of UK companies being less effective than they could be. While there is little support for notions of diversity for its own sake, there is strong recognition that traditional methods of recruitment of directors through personal contacts have tended to act as a barrier to expanding the diversity of boards. Since the publication of the original Combined Code in 1998, one of the principles has been that companies should have a 'formal and transparent procedure for the appointment of new directors to the board'. They must, unless 'the board is small', establish a nomination committee.

The stereotypical white, male, middle-class board remains the norm. According to a Deloitte and Touche (2007) research finding, the typical age of an executive director is between 45 and 55 with an average of 50 years.

For women directors the average age is 47. Non-executive directors are generally older, typically between 53 and 63 with an average of 58. Around 5 per cent of executive directors are under the age of 40.

Table 3.1

Average Number of Executive and Non-Executive Directors

Type of Company	Chairman	Executive Directors	Non-Executive Directors	Total
Largest 100 companies (FTSE 100)	1	4	7	12
Largest 101-350 companies listed on the stock exchange (FTSE 350)	1	4	5	10

In September 2007 only 4 per cent of executive directors in FTSE 350 companies were women. Only nine FTSE 350 companies were headed by a woman chief executive. This figure is in stark contrast to the 30 per cent of women managers. The percentage of women directors increases with the size of company. Women non-executive directors constitute 21 per cent in FTSE 350 companies (13 per cent in FTSE 100 companies and 8 per cent in FTSE 250 companies). There are only two women non-executive chairmen and three women deputy chairmen in the top 350 companies, which is fewer than in the previous year. The ethnic composition of boards shows even less diversity. Only 7 per cent of directors are not British, with just 1 per cent from ethnic minority groups.

3.7.2 Board Composition

- Determine and regularly review board composition and identify any need for changes in board membership (including the chairman) and the timing thereof.

- Identify any gaps or (undesirable) overlap between individual director's roles and responsibilities; plan and execute corrective action required.

- Select, appoint, induct, develop or remove board members or company secretary.

- Ensure regular and rigorous appraisal of the competence of all board members.

- Identify and select external advisers when in-house expertise is insufficient.

- Consider the ratio and number of executive and non-executive directors.

- Consider the energy, experience, knowledge, skills and personal attributes of current and prospective directors in relation to the future needs of the board as a whole, and develop specifications and processes for new appointments, as necessary.

- Consider the cohesion, dynamic tension and diversity of the board and its leadership by the chairman.

- Make and review succession plans for directors and the company secretary.

- Where necessary, remove incompetent or unsuitable directors or the company secretary, taking relevant legal, contractual, ethical, and commercial matters into account.

- Agree proper procedures for electing a chairman and appointing the managing director and other directors.

- Identify potential candidates for the board, make the selection and agree terms of appointment and remuneration.

- New appointments should be agreed by every board member. Provide new board members with a comprehensive induction to board processes and policies, inclusion to the company and their new role.

- Monitor and appraise each individual's performance, behaviour, knowledge, effectiveness and values rigorously and regularly.

- Identify development needs and training opportunities for existing and potential directors and the company secretary.

3.7.3 Matters Reserved to the Board

One of the board's foremost jobs is to decide the way it will work and to identify and agree the things that cannot be delegated. Following on from that, and cascading through the organisation, will be a delegation of powers—to the executive committee, the subsidiary boards where applicable, and the senior management.

In its guide to best boardroom practice, *The Effective Director* (2008), the IoD identifies the following key tasks of the board:

- to establish and maintain vision, mission and values;
- to decide the strategy and the structure;
- to delegate authority to management and monitor and evaluate the implementation of policies, strategies and business plans; and
- to account to shareholders and be responsible to stakeholders.

3.8 New Zealand Context: Board Composition and Performance

The board must guide the strategic direction of the entity, and direct and oversee management. Each director must have skills, knowledge and experience relevant to the affairs of the entity. Individual directors may bring particular attributes that complement those of other directors. An effective board requires a range and balance of relevant attributes among its members. Each director must be able and willing to commit the time and effort needed for the position.

It is important to recognise the contribution of executives: the skills and perspectives they have provide a sound basis for challenge by non-executive directors. Strong executive representation at board meetings or on boards promotes a constructive exchange between directors and executives that is necessary for boards to be effective. To maintain proper balance between executive and non-executive directors, it can be useful for the latter to meet regularly to share views and information without executives being present.

Efficiency and accountability are improved if the respective roles of the board and executives are well understood by all. This can be assisted by the adoption of a board charter that sets out the responsibilities of the board and its directors and that includes details of any delegations given by the board to management. Directors are entitled to seek independent advice. This may be necessary to fully inform themselves about an issue before the board, and to effectively contribute to board decisions.

The chairperson is critical in director-executive relations. The chairperson's role includes promoting cooperation, mediating between perspectives, and leading informed debate and decision-making by the board. The chairperson also has a pivotal role between the CEO and the board. Balance in the relationship between management and the board is particularly important in entities with public shareholders. This balance is facilitated if the roles of chairperson and chief executive (or equivalent) are clearly separated and if the chairperson is an independent director. We agree with respondents to the consultation that in general, the chief executive should not move on to become chairperson. Only in special circumstances should the roles be combined, e.g. where an individual has skills, knowledge and experience not otherwise available to the entity (and where these circumstances are fully explained to investors).

The optimum number of directors for any entity will depend on its size and the nature and complexity of its activities, as well as its requirement for independent directors. If a board is too large, decision-making becomes unwieldy; if too small, it may not achieve the necessary balance of skills, knowledge and experience needed by the entity. This balance is most important for issuers. The need to achieve the right mix, and to choose directors who can make an appropriate contribution, make director selection and nomination vitally important. Rigorous selection, nomination and appointment processes are needed to achieve this. A separate nomination committee can help to focus resources on this task, and also on succession planning.

Non-executive directors often do not have the advantage of prior knowledge of an entity. This makes it important that they clearly understand their expected roles within the entity. It will be of value for a new director if the board sets out its expectations of his or her role. To be individually effective, directors need to make themselves familiar with both the activities of the entity and their responsibilities as a director. Induction training and opportunities to attend directors' professional education can greatly assist this process.

Effectiveness can also be enhanced if the board and directors regularly assess their own performance and that of their individual members against pre-determined measures of the efficiency and effectiveness of board processes, and on the contributions of individual directors. The Commission would like to see each board develop its own review and report processes as an integral element of its focus on good governance.

3.8.1 New Zealand SEC Principle and Guidelines

Principle: There should be a balance of independence, skills, knowledge, experience, and perspectives among directors so that the board works effectively.

Guidelines: Every issuer's board should have an appropriate balance of executive and non-executive directors, and should include directors who meet formal criteria for 'independent directors'.

- All directors should, except as permitted by law and disclosed to shareholders, act in the best interests of the entity, ahead of other interests.

- Every board should have a formal charter that sets out the responsibilities and roles of the board and directors, including any formal delegations to management.

- The chairperson should be formally responsible for fostering a constructive governance culture and applying appropriate governance principles among directors and with management.

- The chairperson of a publicly-owned entity should be independent. No director of a publicly-owned entity should simultaneously hold the roles of board chairperson and chief executive (or equivalent). Only in exceptional circumstances should the chief executive go on to become the chairperson.

- Directors should be selected and appointed through rigorous, formal processes designed to give the board a range of relevant skills and experience.

- Directors should be selected and appointed only when the board is satisfied that they will commit the time needed to be fully effective in their role.

- The board should set out in writing its specific expectations of non-executive directors (including those who are independent).

- The board should allocate time and resources in encouraging directors to acquire and retain a sound understanding of their responsibilities, and this should include appropriate induction training for new appointees.

- The board should have rigorous, formal processes for evaluating its performance, along with that of board committees and individual directors. The chairperson should be responsible to lead these processes.

- Annual reports of all entities should include information about each director, identify which directors are independent, and include information on the board's appointment, training and evaluation processes.

Table 3.2 presents the details of the Board Composition and Board Committees of New Zealand listed companies on New Zealand Stock Market (NZSX).

Table 3.2

Board Composition of Top Listed New Zealand Companies

No.	Company	BoD-Actual	ED	ID	NED	Chairman	Chairman's Appointment
1.	Air New Zealand	7	-	7	7	NED	2001
2.	Auckland Airport	6	-	5	6	ID & NED	2004
3.	Allied Farmers Limited	5	-	-	5	NED	2009
4.	Heritage Gold NZ Ltd. (HGD)	5	1	2	4	NED	1999
5.	Fletcher Building	9	-	9	9	ID & NED	2001
6.	Telecom Corp of NZ Ltd. (TEL)	7	1	5	6	ID & NED	2004
7.	Horizon Energy Dist Ltd. (HED)	4	1	1	2	ID & NED	NA
8.	NZ-Oil & Gas	7	2	5	-	ED	1981
9.	NZL Refining Comp Ltd. (NZR)						
10.	Warehouse	8	1	7	7	ID & NED	1994

Note: ED=Executive Director; NED=Non-Executive Director; ID=Independent Director.

Source: Refer 2009 Annual Report of Air New Zealand; Auckland Air Port, New Zealand; Allied Farmers Limited, New Zealand; Heritage Gold NZ Ltd. (HGD) New Zealand; Fletcher Building, New Zealand; Telecom Corp of NZ Ltd. (TEL) New Zealand; Horizon Energy Dist Ltd. (HED), New Zealand; NZ-Oil & Gas, New Zealand; NZL Refining Comp Ltd. (NZR), New Zealand; Warehouse, New Zealand.

3.9 Indian Context: Board Composition and Performance

3.9.1 Board Composition Listing Requirements: Indian SEBI Clause 49

SEBI guidelines: Based upon the recommendations of Kumar Mangalam Committee, SEBI included a new provision in Clause 49 of the listing agreement between the stock exchanges and the listed companies. These provisions are aimed at improving the standards of corporate governance in the listed companies in line with international best practices of good governance. First introduced on 21 February 2000, these provisions have been revised a number of times. Department of Public Enterprises, Government of India have directed all listed public enterprises to follow the provisions of SEBI guidelines as per Clause 49 of the listing agreement. The salient features of the provisions of the Clause 49 as issued on 29 March 2005 are listed below:-

Board composition: The board of directors of the company shall have an optimum combination of executive and non-executive directors with not less than 50 per cent of the Board comprising non-executive directors. Where the chairman of the board is non-executive director, at least one-third of the board should comprise independent directors and in case he is an executive director, at least half of the board should comprise independent directors.

Table 3.3 presents the board composition of top 10 Indian public listed companies. The companies are also in compliance with the listing relating to the outsider and insider mix in relevance to the chairman status. All the chairmen under the public sector company are executive directors and the proportion of the independent directors in the Board is either equal or more than half of the board size.

Table 3.4 presents board composition of top 10 Indian private listed companies. It is evident from the two tables that the Clause 49 of the listing requirement relating to the board composition is in practice in both the public and private listed companies. Majority (seven) of the chairmen under the top 10 private companies are non-executive directors and the chairmen of three companies are executive directors. However, under both the board mix they are in compliance with the 49 listing requirement.

Table 3.3

Board Composition Index of Top 10 Public Listed Companies for the Year 2008

No.	Companies	Board Size	NED	I-NED	ED	Women NED	FED/ FNED	Chairman
1	BHEL	16	10	8	0	0	6	ED
2	CIL	10	-	4	6	0	0	ED
3	GAIL	10	-	5	5	0	0	ED
4	HPCL	10	0	5	5	0	0	ED
5	NALCO	15	2	8	5	0	0	ED
6	MTNL	9	2	3	4	2	0	ED
7	NMDC	16	0	9	7	3	0	ED
8	NTPC	13	6	4	0	0	7	ED
9	ONGC	13	6	4	0	0	7	ED
10	SAIL	22	2	10	10	0	0	ED

Note: ED=Executive Director; NED=Non-Executive Director; ID=Independent Director.

Source: Refer 2010 Annual Report of BHEL, India; CIL, India; GAIL, India; HPCL, India; NALCO, India; MTNL, India; NMDC, India; NTPC, India ; ONGC, India; SAIL, India.

Table 3.4

Board Composition Index of Top 10 Private Listed Companies for the Year 2008

No.	Companies	Board Size	NED	I-NED	Women NED/ED	FED/ FNED	ED	Chairman
1	DRL	10	7	7	0	0	3	ED
2	Hindalco	10	9	6	1	0	1	NED
3	M&M Ltd.	12	9	8	0	1	3	NED
4	Maruti Suzuki India Ltd.	11	6	4	1 (NED)	1	5	NED
5	Ranbaxy Laboratories Ltd.	15	11	8	0	0	4	NED
6	Reliance Industries Ltd.	13	9	8	0	0	4	NED
7	Suzlon Energy	6	4	4	0	0	2	ED
8	Tata Motors Ltd.	10	8	4	0	0	2	NED
9	Tata Steel Ltd.	14	13	8	0	4	1	NED
10	Wipro	7	6	6	0	1	1	ED

Source: Refer 2010 Annual Report of DRL, India; Hindalco, India; M&M Ltd., India; Maruti Suzuki India Ltd., India; Ranbaxy Laboratories Ltd., India; Reliance Industries Ltd., India; Suzlon Energy, India; Tata Motors Ltd., India; Tata Steel Ltd., India; Wipro Ltd., India.

3.10 Board Leadership Structure

Agency theory, as well as stewardship theory, is also applicable to board leadership structure. Advocates of Agency theory favour the separation of the roles of CEO and chairman of the board. Splitting these roles dilutes the power of the CEO and reduces the potential for management to dominate the board. Conversely, stewardship theory suggests that if the CEO also serves as the chairman, this duality provides unified firm leadership, builds trust and stimulates the motivation to perform (Muth and Donaldson, 1998).

The results of academic research are inconclusive on the effects of leadership structure on performance. Coles *et al.* (2001) reported a positive relationship between a joint structure and economic value added, while the results for the meta-analysis by Dalton *et al.* (1998) show no relationship between board leadership structure and firm performance. However, a robust interaction effect is suggested between firm bankruptcy and board structures Firms that combine the CEO and chairman roles and that have lower representation of independent directors are associated with bankruptcy (Daily and Dalton, 1994a, 1994b).

3.11 Issues Relating to the Board Composition

It is understood from the extant literature that the board size can have both positive and negative effects on board performance. The following issues are worth considering:

- Does the positive effects on board performance outweigh the negative effects in case of the larger boards? or
- Does the positive effects outweigh the negative effects on board performance in case of the smaller boards?
- Are there any possibilities that one can strike a balance between the positives and negative effects?
- What are the organisations in which the larger boards are suitable? and why?
- What are the organisations in which the smaller boards are suitable? and why?

To conclude, in this chapter we presented the policies of board composition from the context of corporate governance, United Kingdom, New Zealand and India. We further observed the board composition practices of New Zealand and India. Further we examined the board composition practices of the top public and private listed companies. It is observed that the companies are in compliance with the listing relating to the outsider and insider mix in relevance to the Chairman status. All the chairmen under the public sector companies are executive directors and the proportion of the independent directors in the board is either equal or more than half of the board size. It is evident that the Indian public and private companies are in compliance with the Clause 49 of the listing requirement relating to the board composition.

References

Agrawal, A. and C.R. Knoeber (1996). "Firm Performance and Mechanisms to Control Agency Problems between Managers and Shareholders", *Journal of Financial Quantitative Analysis* 31: 377-397.

Baysinger, B.D. and H.N. Butler (1985). "Corporate Governance and the Boards of Directors; Performance Effects of changes in Board Composition", *Journal of Law, Economics and Organisation* 1: 101-124.

Baysinger, B. and R. Hoskisson (1990). "The Composition of Boards of Directors and Strategic Control: Effects on Corporate Strategy", *Academy of Management Review* 15(1): 72-87.

Barry, J. Reiter. (1999). "Independent Directors", *Ivey Business Journal*, May/June, 1999.

Conyon, M.J and S.I. Peck (1998). "Board Size and Corporate Performance: Evidence from European countries", *The European Journal of Finance* 4: 291-304.

Coles, J., V. McWilliams and N. Sen (2001). "An Examination of the Relationship between Governance Mechanisms to Performance", *Journal of Management* 27(1): 23-50.

Dalton, D.R., C.M. Daily, A.E. Ellstrand and J.L. Johnson (1998). "Meta-analytic Reviews of Board Composition, Leadership Structure and Financial Performance", *Strategic Management Journal* 19: 269-290.

Daily, C.M. and D.R. Dalton (1994a). "Bankruptcy and Corporate Governance: The Impact of Board Composition and Structure", *Academy of Management Journal* 37: 1603-1617.

———. (1994b). "Corporate Governance and the Bankrupt Firm: An Empirical Assessment", *Strategic Management Journal* 15: 643-654.

Eisenberg, T., S. Sundgren and M.T. Wells (1998). "Larger Board Size and Decreasing Firm Value in Small Firms", *Journal of Financial Economics* 48: 35-54.

Golden, B.R. and E.J. Zajac (2001). "When will Boards Influence Strategy? Inclination x Power = Strategic Change", *Strategic Management Journal* 15: 241-250.

Hermailin, B.E and M.S. Wiesbach (2000). "Boards of Directors as an Endogenously Determined Institutino: A Survey of Economic Literature", *NBER Working Paper* No.8161.

Judge, W. and C. Zeithaml (1992). "Institutional and Strategic Choice Perspectives on Board Involvement in the Strategic Decision Process", *Academy of Management Journal* 35 (4): 766-94.

Jensen, M.C. and W.H. Meckling (1976). "Theory of Firm, Managerial Behavior, Agency Costs and Ownership Structure", *Journal of Financial Economics* 3: 305-360.

Rosenstein, S. and J.G. Wyatt (1990). "Outside Directors, Board Independence, and Sharcholder Wealth", *Journal of Financial Economics* 26: 175-191.

Short, H., K. Keasey, M. Wright and A. Hull (1999). "Corporate Governance: From Accountability to Enterprise", *Accounting and Business Research* 29: 337-352.

Wagner, J.A., J.L Stimpaert and E.L. Fubara (1998). "Board Composition and Organization Performance: Two Studies of Insider/Outsider Effects", *Journal of Management Studies* 35: 655-677.

Yermack, D. (1996). "Higher Market Valuation of Companies with a Small Board of Directors", *Journal of Financial Economics* 40: 185-211.

4 | Board Committees
Principles and Practices

This chapter focusses on the board committees, principles and practices. The emergence of the concept of formalisation of the board committees in corporate governance is a significant contemporary phenomenon evidenced in recent times. Many codes also request that these committees are composed exclusively of independent directors or at least have a clear majority of independent members. The three principal board committees are the audit committee, the remuneration committee and the nominating committee. The other committees include the risk management committee and corporate governance committee.

4.1 Board Committees: Their Significance

Not every company organisation requires each of these committees. The board of directors should establish these committees where necessary for purposes of good corporate governance, or where it is necessary to have extra scrutiny of particular areas of the organisation. Infact, the board committees should have the functions and authority that match the activities and major risks of the organisations. In other words, the committee functions and authority must be tailored to the organisation's business activities and risk profile.

Boards' effectiveness and efficacy lie in how well they are managing board committees and other practical matters which include apart from the managing board committees; the managing meetings, agenda, and minutes; board information; the role of the company secretary; director induction, training and development; director remuneration; and director and officer insurance. Table 4.1 presents the board committees of top listed companies in New Zealand. Table 4.2 presents the board committees of top listed companies in India.

Table 4.1

Board Committees of Top Listed New Zealand Companies

S. No.	Company	No. of Board Committees	Board Committees		
1	Air New Zealand	3	Audit committee	Peoples' development and remuneration committee	Safety committee	-
2	Auckland Airport	3	Audit and risk committee	Remuneration committee	Nomination committee	-
3	Allied Farmers Limited	2	Audit committee	Remuneration committee	-	-
4	Heritage Gold NZ Ltd. (HGD)	3	Audit committee	Remuneration committee	Nomination committee	-
5	Fletcher Building	3	Audit committee	Remuneration committee	Nomination committee	-
6	Telecom Corporation of NZ Ltd. (TEL)	3	Audit and risk management committee	Human resources and compensation committee	Nomination and corporate governance committee	-
7	Horizon Energy Distribution Ltd. (HED)	2	Audit committee	-	Health and safety committee	
8	NZ-Oil & Gas Ltd.	3	Audit committee	Executive appointment and remuneration committee	Corporate governance and public affairs committee	-
9	NZL Refining Company Ltd. (NZR)	3	Audit committee	Remuneration committee		
10	Warehouse	4	Audit committee	Remuneration, talent and nomination committee	Corporate governance committee	Disclosure committee

Source: Annual Reports.

Table 4.2

Board Committees of Top Indian Public Listed Companies

S. No.	Company	No. of Board Committees	Board Committees
1	ONGC		Audit and ethics committee.
2	HPCL	5	Audit committee, committee of functional directors (CFD), investment committee, HR committee, investor grievance committee.
3	CIL	2	Audit committee, empowered sub-committee for evaluation of projects, sub-committee for reviewing DOP.
4	GAIL	3	Audit committee, shareholders/investors grievance committee, remuneration committee.
5	BHEL	6	Audit committee, shareholders/investors grievance and committee, remuneration committee and HR committee, project review committee, mergers and acquisitions committee.
6	Tata Steel	7	Audit committee, remuneration committee, shareholder's grievance committee, executive committee, nomination committee, committee of directors, ethics and compliance committee.
7	DRL	6	Audit committee, compensation committee, governance committee, shareholder's grievance committee, investment committee and management committee

Source: Annual Reports.

4.2 Board Committees: An International Perspective

The board committees, their policies and guidelines issued by regulatory bodies of India, New Zealand, USA and Australia are presented here. The Securities and Exchange Board of India (SEBI) has formulated guidelines for corporate governance by listed companies through the listing agreement. The relevant clause is Clause 49–Corporate Governance. These have and would continually evolve. Given below are the guidelines as enunciated by SEBI in October 2004.

4.2.1 The Audit Committee

It is the responsibility of the board of directors to provide the organisation with an efficient internal control system capable of constantly demonstrating its effectiveness and assets safeguard. Such a task is, however, entrusted to one standing committee of the board, called the audit committee. In fact, most if not all corporate governance guidelines recommend that all publicly traded organisations must have an audit committee, and this has brought new expectations of audit committee responsibilities and effectiveness (Vera-Munoz, 2005). The audit committee is defined as: a committee composed of independent, non-executive directors charged with the oversight functions of ensuring responsible corporate governance, a viable financial reporting process an effective internal control structure a credible audit function, an informed whistle blower complaint process and an appropriate code of business ethic with the purpose of creating long-term shareholder value while protecting the interest of other stakeholders (SOX, 2002).

Most of the stock exchanges entail the listed companies to have a minimum three-person audit committee composed entirely of directors that meet the independence standards and financial literacy, at least for some of them. The formal role of audit committee is to assist the board in carrying out its monitoring function within the organisation and the control over its operations, including its financial reporting and compliance with laws and regulations. This encompasses several areas such as:

- Monitoring the integrity of financial statements. The audit committee should monitor the integrity of the financial statements of the company, and this includes its annual and interim reports and other announcements relating to its financial performance.

- Monitoring external auditor activities. It is the responsibility of the audit committee to assess and make recommendations to the board, to be put to shareholders for approval at the general shareholders meeting, in relation to appointment, re-appointment, and their replacement in case of resignation.

- Monitoring internal audit activities: ensuring the independence of both the internal audit and external auditors and assessing their performance.

- Reviewing internal control and risk management systems. One of the most impacting roles of the audit committee is the monitoring of the internal control and the risk management, to ensure that key risks are identified and adequately managed, and to review and approve the statements to be included in the annual report concerning internal controls and risk management.

- Reporting: The audit committee has the responsibility of reporting the results to the boards. The reporting responsibilities include:
  - The chairman of the committee should formally report to the board after meeting its proceedings on all matters within its duties and responsibilities.
  - The audit committee should give recommendations to the board as it deems appropriate on any area within its scope where action or improvement is needed.
  - The committee reporting to the shareholders on its activities to be included in the company's annual report.

The audit committee will be empowered to effectively perform its functions, if the following authorities are given:

- It should have the power to require information from any employee or manager of the organisation.
- It should have the authority to obtain the required external legal assistance and professional advice, at the organisation's expenses.
- It should have the power to invite to its meetings every member of staff and to proceed to its interview.

The audit committee members are however, subject to certain restrictions. For instance, they can not receive any compensation except the reimbursement of the expenses engaged for doing their job, and the chairman of the committee must be an accountant or a financial expert. Recent legislations in corporate governance have conceded much more authority to the audit committee regarding, in particular, its relations with the external auditor. The audit committee must, in this regard:

- Make recommendations to the board for approval in general shareholder's meeting, the appointment of external auditors and their dismissal, as it must also approve their remuneration and employment conditions. The most recent corporate governance reforms require audit committees of listed companies, the annual assessing of external auditor qualifications and performance;
- The audit committee should be responsible for ensuring the external auditor independence and should carry permanent monitoring of the external auditor activities, ensure its independence and objectivity,

and should also take the necessary actions to guarantee the effectiveness of the complete auditing process, taking into account professional standards and regulatory requirements. This involves the development and the implementation of appropriate policies in respect to non-audit services that the external auditor can provide, as well as the safeguard of the ethical orientation of the organisation. The audit committee is also required to report to the board with regard to its activities and discuss annually, with the board, the performance of internal and external auditors in the implementing of audit plans;

- The audit committee must review the changes and amendments to be made to the accounting system and the financial disclosure policies. The audit committee must also examine the changes and amendments along with the desires and needs of the CEO and the internal auditor;

- The audit committee must meet at least twice a year, with internal and external auditors and without the presence of any officer or employee of the organisation, on the one hand, and with employees of the company without the presence of external auditors, on the other hand;

- The audit committee must have a written charter which should concentrate mainly on goal of the committee and should include the required help to be given to the board, to ensure the integrity of the organisation's financial statements, the compliance with the legal and regulatory requirements, the assurance of the external auditor independence, and the qualifications to monitor the internal audit function and external auditor performance;

- The audit committee must meet, on a regular basis, generally several times a year. The chairman, or any member of the audit committee, in consultation with the chairman, should be empowered to call a meeting of the committee. A notice of each meeting should be sent to all members, indicating the place, date, and time and should also be accompanied by the agenda of the issues to be discussed during the meeting.

In summary, the audit committee must ensure the implementation and maintenance of internal control, financial disclosure, and adequate risk management systems, including the prevention and the detection of fraud and errors. It must review and approve the appointment, the replacement, the transfer, or the dismissal of the internal and the external auditors. It should review the internal and external's auditors' mandate, the annual audit plan, and the required audit resources, and functions. Recent corporate governance reforms seem to have significantly increased audit committee roles and independence and contributed to auditor independence quality. (Hoitash *et al.*, 2008).

4.3 Satyam Computers Scandal and Role of Auditors

The Satyam fraud is not the sole brush with infamy for Pricewaterhouse, one of the world's top auditing firms. Pricewaterhouse is already in deep trouble in relation to its suspect auditing of the collapsed Global Trust Bank (GTB), for which it is being probed by the disciplinary committee of the Institute of Chartered Accountants of India (ICAI).

In the GTB case, Pricewaterhouse was hauled up for alleged negligence in auditing of books of the bank and failing to detect huge levels of non-performing assets (NPAs). The NPAs had accumulated due to massive exposure made by the erstwhile bank into the stock market, which Pricewaterhouse is alleged to have overlooked. In another instance, Lovelock & Lewes—another auditing entity of PricewaterhouseCoopers (PwC)—was the auditor of DSQ Software, which was found guilty of manipulating share prices and falsification of accounts by Serious Fraud Investigation Office (SFIO) of the Ministry of Corporate Affairs. Pricewaterhouse and Lovelock & Lewes are separate legal entities that handle audit functions for the umbrella outfit PwC.

Internationally, PwC was caught on the wrong foot when in 2006 it was ordered to pay nearly £1 million in fines and costs by the Joint Disciplinary Scheme (JDS), Britain's accountancy watchdog, for its work on three audits of Bank of Credit and Commerce International (BCCI) in the late 1980s. The bank had collapsed in 1991 under a debt load of over £1 billion and it was one of the largest banking scandals of the time. PwC, then known as PriceWaterhouse, was faulted for issuing inappropriate unqualified audits for 1987, 1988, and 1989 because it failed to properly disclose the related-party relationship between BCCI and another Cayman

Islands group, ICIC, as per media reports. The auditing firm though had maintained that it 'was deceived'.

On the Satyam fiasco, PwC issued a statement in the evening saying it would examine the issue. 'We have learnt of the disclosure made by the Chairman of Satyam Computer Services and are currently examining the contents of the statement. We are not commenting further on this subject due to issues of client confidentially.'

4.4 Spotlight on the Role of External Auditors

The Satyam fiasco has put the spotlight on the role of external auditors in a company. Industry experts say that the governing body of chartered accountants, Institute of Chartered Accountants of India (ICAI), should review the guidelines for audit firms. A council member of ICAI said that, 'There should be a rotation of auditors once in three years as this would restrict the association of a particular audit firm with a company for a long time.' Another independent chartered accountant said, 'Like in France and Denmark, in India too it should become mandatory for a joint audit, especially in listed companies, where the onus would be both the auditors rather than one like in the case of PricewaterhouseCoopers in Satyam. Currently in India, this requirement exists in financial services sector. One can make a mistake but two audit firms can't make it.' PwC, it is been reliably learnt, has been Satyam's auditor for almost nine years. A partner at a domestic chartered accountancy firm said that the underline problem is the basic relationship between auditors and management, where they trust the management too much and take things on face value. The satyam issue highlights that the auditor has not followed even the routine procedures and standards. Like the inflated cash balance on Satyam's books, if the auditor had physically verified the same, matters wouldn't have reached this extent. According to Dr. Suresh Surana, founder of RSM Astute Consulting group, 'this (developments at Satyam) is a major eye opener and would bring into renewed and critical focus on the role of auditors in Satyam. The extent of manipulation seen is blatant considering major gaps in most obvious assets like cash and bank balances and other items'.

Vishesh Chandiok, national managing partner of Grant Thornton said that, 'there is clear lack of focus on audit quality as the key issue by the

ICAI. All ICAI laws try and focus on dispersal of work amongst the 1.5 lakh CA's as opposed to audit quality, which is the focus globally, since Enron. Need to recognize that big (including the big four firms KPMG, E&Y, PWC and Deloitte) are not necessary the only upholders of audit quality and that big does not necessarily equal quality in the profession.' He added, 'the lack of an independent external audit review is a significant structural defect in our financial regulation and the still non functioning Quality Review Board despite being legislated some years ago. No requirement for audit firms to take out professional indemnity insurance is another big gap'. Hitesh Agrawal, Head (Research), Angel Broking, says, 'the role of the auditors has come under serious question. The biggest dent that the Satyam episode will make is in the "trust" factor of investors towards companies, the auditors, the reported numbers by companies.'

4.5 Listing Requirements

The Audit committee listing requirements of India and New Zealand are shown below.

4.5.1 Indian SEBI Clause 49 and Audit Committee

A qualified and independent audit committee shall be set up under the chairmanship of an independent director with minimum three directors as members of which two-third shall be independent. All members shall be financially literate with at least one member being a financial expert.

The audit committee shall meet at least four times a year and not more than four months shall elapse between two meetings.

The role of the audit committee to include: oversight of the company's financial reporting process, disclosure of its financial information, review of annual and quarterly financial statements, review of adequacy of internal control system, appointment of auditors, review of significant findings of internal and statutory auditors, compliance with listing and other legal requirements, review of defaults in payments and whistle blower mechanism etc. The audit committee shall also review all transactions with related parties and observance of accounting standards by the management.

4.5.2 New Zealand SEC Guidelines for Audit Committee

Each publicly owned company should establish an audit committee of the board with responsibilities to: recommend the appointment of external auditors; to oversee all aspects of the entity-audit firm relationship; and to promote integrity in financial reporting. The audit committee should comprise:

- all non-executive directors, a majority of whom are independent;
- at least one director who is a chartered accountant or has another recognised form of financial expertise; and
- a chairperson who is independent and who is not the chairperson of the board.

The Nomination Committee

Corporate governance reforms and exchange regulations also highlight the fundamental role of the nomination committee in the ethical functioning of organisations. The listing requirements usually require each listed company to have a nominating committee composed entirely of independent directors, and such committees is also a standing committee of the board and its role is crucial for the proper functioning of the board and the strengthening of its independence and the quality of board member candidates. The nomination should be mandated to play a leadership role in developing good governance within the organisation, mainly by ensuring the hiring of appropriate and efficient officers and managers. Figure 4.1 highlights the main functions of the nominating committee.

A precise nominating committee performs a number of specific functions:

- The nomination committee must formulate and design the appropriate governance structure of the organisation and must oversee its implementation;
- It must oversee and monitor all matters relating to the independence of directors that might involve any potential conflict of interest, just as it evaluates any change in status of a member of the board, and determine the propriety of his situation in light of this change;

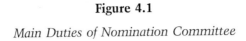

Figure 4.1

Main Duties of Nomination Committee

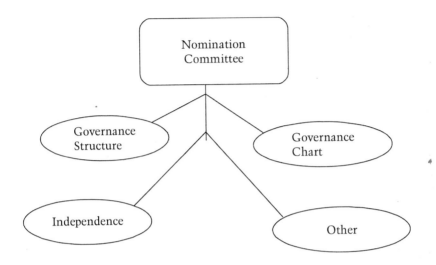

- It must carry out a detailed examination of the structure of corporate governance, at least once a year, and recommend to the board the necessary amendments, as it must review the structure of the board on the size, composition, and independence and make recommendations on changes deemed necessary;

- It must proceed in search of qualified candidates and recommend to the board candidates for election or appointment. It takes part in the appointment of chairman of various standing committees and determines the number of members who sit on the board of directors; and

- It should conduct the assessment of skills, knowledge, and experience already on the board of directors and, in the light of this assessment, a description of the role and capacity sought in candidates prior to identifying and recommending them.

4.5.3 UK Committees

The board delegates powers to its main committees and lays out formal terms and conditions for them, which it reviews annually. The

Combined Code and the Stock Exchange Listing Rules oblige a company to have three committees on board—the audit, remuneration and nomination committees—or explain why not.

Of the three committees the remuneration committee is the most universally adopted, followed closely by the audit committee, with the nomination committee lagging some way behind. According to Deloitte & Touche (2007) research findings, all but one FTSE 350 companies have established remuneration and audit committees.

The Audit Committee

The audit committee is intended to provide a link between auditor and board independent of the company executives, since the latter are responsible for the company's accounting rules and procedures that are the subject of the audit. The committee may thus help the board discharge its responsibility with regard to the validity of published statements. The Combined Code recommends that all members of the audit committee should be independent non-executive directors (NEDs). The audit committee frequently encompasses risk within its remit. Where it does not, companies tend to have a separate risk committee.

The Remuneration Committee

The remuneration committee plays a pivotal role in ensuring that the executive remuneration strategy is aligned with the company's strategy and that pay is linked to performance. It is vital that decisions on executive remuneration, benefits and bonuses are seen to be taken by those who do not stand to benefit directly from them. As a matter of good practice, executive directors should not be responsible for determining their own remuneration.

The Combined Code recommends that this should be the remit of a remuneration Committee made up wholly or mainly of NEDs. In listed companies and some larger private companies, therefore, policy on executive remuneration is usually decided by a committee of NEDs. The board retains ultimate responsibility for the setting of directors' pay and rewards and, in line with the Riggs guidance; the performance of members of the remuneration committee should be reviewed annually. Shareholders now have the right to an advisory vote on the remuneration report.

The Nomination Committee

One of the board's most crucial functions is to decide on new appointments to the board and to other senior positions in the company. As a matter of good practice the selection process of directors should be carried out by the nomination committee, which then makes recommendations to the full board. The committee should be composed of executive and non-executive directors (the latter should be in a majority), whose task is to ensure that appointments are made according to agreed specifications. Where implemented, the appraisal of directors is often tied directly into the selection and nomination process.

4.5.4 Other Committees

Depending on their size and nature, individual companies may also have other committees, either standing or ad hoc. In businesses with significant borrowings in multiple currencies there may be a case for a treasury committee. In some companies where health and safety risks and hazards are potentially high, such as airlines, railways and petrochemical businesses, there will be a separate health and safety committee.

Appraisal and Review

The Combined Code requires chairmen of all listed companies to meet with the NEDs separately each year, and the senior independent director to meet with the NEDs to appraise the chairman's performance each year. All directors will want to see that the board operates well, and the tool that most boards use to establish, is an annual board effectiveness review. The review is often 'outsourced' to a consultant or a professional body such as the Institute of Directors (IoD).

Public Enterprise Selection Board (PESB) Guidelines

The responsibilities of the nomination committee is discharged by the PESB.

Selection procedure: The PESB keeps a close and constant watch on the vacancies that are likely to arise and initiates the process of selection 12 months before the occurrence of the vacancies. The board initiates selection process by sending job description of the post to the concerned administrative ministry/department with a request to update the company profile and the job description within 10 days. In case, the ministries or departments do not respond within the aforesaid time frame the job description of the post is circulated *suo moto*. A period of 30 days is normally given to receive the applications after circulation of the vacancy.

Date of vacancy: The date of vacancy of a post is reckoned with reference to the date on which it will fall vacant or has fallen vacant. In respect of newly created post/posts or posts kept in abeyance, the date of the order creating the post/posts or reviving them will be the date of vacancy. In respect of a panel of PESB not approved by the competent authority, the date of order not approving the panel will be treated as the date of vacancy for fresh selection.

Circulation of the post: The post is circulated among all Central PSEs, Ministry of Defence (MoD), Establishment Officer (EO)-Department of Personnel & Training (DoPT), concerned administrative ministry/ department, and state chief secretaries. All the valid applications in the terms of the job description are required to be forwarded to PESB by respective organisations. Further no valid application should be withheld by the PSU or the sponsoring department.

Shortlist of candidates: After all the applications are received, including names taken from the data bank, wherever necessary, these are scrutinised in the light of the job description of the post and eligibility criteria, and thereafter a shortlist of persons to be called for selection meeting is finalised with the approval of the PESB.

Scheduling of selection date: Scheduling of selection meeting is done in consultation with the secretary of the administrative ministry/ department concerned.

Assistance by ministry representative and CMD/MD of the PSE: Secretary is invited to assist the PESB on behalf of the administrative ministry/department. However the concerned secretary may nominate an officer not below the rank of additional secretary to represent him for a board level post in schedules B, C and D. In the case of selection of functional directors, the concerned regular chief executive of the concerned enterprise is always invited to assist the PESB. However, in the case of subsidiaries, the chairman of the holding company is invited to assist the board.

Joint venture PSE: In the case of joint venture enterprises like Tehri Hydro Development Corporation (THDC) and Satluj Jal Vidyut Nigam Ltd. (SJVNL), which are joint ventures with the state governments, the chief secretaries of Uttar Pradesh and Himachal Pradesh respectively are also invited to assist the board. Similar procedure is followed in case of Mumbai Rail Vikas Nigam (MRVN) where the chief secretary of Maharashtra is invited.

Recirculation/constitution of search committee/press advertisement: After the first round of selection interview, in case no body is found suitable and the board wishes to see some more candidates, the post may be re-circulated. The board may also decide to convert itself into a search committee and follow the search committee mechanism for making selection. The board may also decide to advertise the post in prominent dailies in which case the eligibility pay scales for the post are in the next below schedule. Selection interviews are held on the basis of open advertisement.

Rule of immediate absorption: Officers from organised services will be considered only on 'immediate absorption basis', unless the posts have been exempted specifically from the rule of immediate absorption with the approval of the competent authority.

Exemption from the rule of immediate absorption: Provided if no suitable candidate is found and the administrative ministry so desires, the question of granting exemption from the rule of immediate absorption may be recommended by the board.

Vigilance clearance: The board while sending its recommendations to the concerned administrative ministry/department also conveys the recommendation to the Central Vigilance Commission to enable them to initiate advance action for processing vigilance clearance.

Internal candidate: Internal candidate is one, who is an employee of an enterprise who has put in a minimum of two years of continuous service in it, on the date of occurrence of vacancy, and who does not hold a lien in any other PSE/Government. An employee who holds a lien on a post in a central public sector enterprise (CPSE) can also be considered as an internal candidate of that enterprise, provided he/she has put in a minimum of two years of continuous service in that enterprise, on the date of acquiring the lien and the period for which he/she is away from the enterprise is not more than five years.

Age criteria: On the date of occurrence of vacancy:

Minimum age: For Schedule A & B posts—45 years; for Schedule C & D posts—40 years.

Maximum age:

(i)   Where the age of superannuation is 60 years, not more than 58 years for internal candidates and not more than 57 years for others.

(ii) Where the age of superannuation is 58 years, not more than 56 years for internal candidates and not more than 55 years for others.

There is no provision for relaxation in either minimum or maximum age in respect of post for which selection is made by PESB.

4.5.5 NYSE Listing Rules Concerning the Nominating/ Corporate Governance Committee

A nominating/corporate governance committee is central to the effective functioning of the board. New director and board committee nominations are among the board's most important functions. Placing this responsibility in the hands of an independent nominating/corporate governance committee can enhance the independence and quality of nominees. The committee is also responsible for taking a leadership role in shaping the corporate governance of a corporation.

If a listed company is legally required by contract or otherwise to provide third parties with the ability to nominate directors (for example, preferred stocks rights to elect directors upon a dividend default, shareholder agreements, and management agreements), the selection and nomination of such directors need not be subject to the nominating committee process.

The nominating/corporate governance committee charter should also address the following items: committee member qualifications; committee member appointment and removal; committee structure and operations (including authority to delegate to subcommittees); and committee reporting to the board. In addition, the charter should give the nominating/ corporate governance committee sole authority to retain and terminate any search firm to be used to identify director candidates, including sole authority to approve the search firm's fees and other retention terms.

Boards may allocate the responsibilities of the nominating/corporate governance committee to committees of their own denomination, provided that the committees are composed entirely of independent directors. Any such committee must have a published committee charter.

4.5.6 Australian Stock Exchange Listing Recommendations Relating to Nomination Committee

The board should establish a nomination committee.

Purpose of the Nomination Committee

A board nomination committee is an efficient mechanism for examination of the selection and appointment practices of the company. Ultimate responsibility for these practices, however, rests with the full board, whether or not a separate nomination committee exists. For smaller boards, the same efficiencies may not be derived from a formal committee structure. Companies without a nomination committee should have board processes in place which raise the issues that would otherwise be considered by the nomination committee.

Charter

The nomination committee should have a charter that clearly sets out its roles and responsibilities, composition, structure, membership requirements and the procedures for inviting non-committee members to attend meetings. The terms of reference of the nomination committee should allow it to have access to adequate internal and external resources, including access to advice from external consultants or specialists.

Composition of Nomination Committee

The nomination committee should be structured so that it:

- consists of a majority of independent directors;
- is chaired by an independent director;
- has at least three members.

Responsibilities

Responsibilities of the committee should include recommendations to the board about:

- the necessary and desirable competencies of directors;
- review of board succession plans;
- the development of a process for evaluation of the performance of the board, its committees and directors;
- the appointment and re-election of directors.

Selection and Appointment Process and Re-Election of Directors

A formal and transparent procedure for the selection, appointment and re-appointment of directors to the board helps promote investor understanding and confidence in that process.

Important issues to be considered as part of the process include:

- *Director competencies*: In order to be able to discharge its mandate effectively the board should comprise directors possessing an appropriate range of skills and expertise. The nomination committee should consider implementing a plan for identifying, assessing and enhancing director competencies. An evaluation of the range of skills, experience and expertise on the board is important when considering new candidates for nomination or appointment. Such an evaluation enables identification of the particular skills that will best increase board effectiveness.

- *Board renewal*: Board renewal is critical to performance, and directors should be conscious of the duration of each director's tenure in succession planning. The nomination committee should consider whether succession plans are in place to maintain an appropriate balance of skills, experience and expertise on the board.

- *Composition and commitment of the board*: The board should be of a size and composition that is conducive to making appropriate decisions. The board should be large enough to incorporate a variety of perspectives and skills, and to represent the best interests of the company as a whole rather than of individual shareholders or interest groups. It should not, however, be so large that effective decision-making is hindered. Individual board members should devote the necessary time to the tasks entrusted to them. All directors should consider the number and nature of their directorships and calls on their time from other commitments.

In support of their candidature for directorship or re-election, non-executive directors should provide the nomination committee with details of other commitments and an indication of time involved. Prior to appointment or being submitted for re-election, non-executive directors should specifically acknowledge to the company that they will have sufficient time to meet what is expected of them.

The nomination committee should regularly review the time required from a non-executive director, and whether directors are meeting that requirement. Non-executive directors should inform the chair and the chair of the nomination committee before accepting any new appointments as directors.

- *Election of directors*: The names of candidates submitted for election as directors should be accompanied by the following information to enable shareholders to make an informed decision on their election:
    - biographical details, including competencies and qualifications and information sufficient to enable an assessment of the independence of the candidate;
    - details of relationships between the candidate and the company, and the candidate and directors of the company directorships held;
    - particulars of other positions which involve significant time commitments;
    - the term of office currently served by any directors subject to re-election;
    - any other particulars required by law.

Non-executive directors should be appointed for specific terms subject to re-election and to the ASX Listing Rule and Corporations Act provisions concerning removal of a director. Re-appointment of directors should not be automatic.

4.6 New Zealand SEC Guidelines
Relating to Nomination Committee

It is important to recognise the contribution of executives: the skills and perspectives they have provide a sound basis for challenge by non-executive directors. Strong executive representation at board meetings or on boards promotes a constructive exchange between directors and executives that is necessary for boards to be effective. To maintain proper balance between executive and non-executive directors, it can be useful for the latter to meet regularly to share views and information without executives present.

Efficiency and accountability are improved if the respective roles of the board and executives are well understood by all. This can be assisted by the adoption of a board charter that sets out the responsibilities of the board and its directors and that includes details of any delegations given by the board to management. Directors are entitled to seek independent advice. This may be necessary to fully inform themselves about an issue before the board, and to effectively contribute to board decisions.

The chairperson is critical in director-executive relations. The chairperson's role includes promoting cooperation, mediating between perspectives, and leading informed debate and decision-making by the board. The chairperson also has a pivotal role between the CEO and the board. Balance in the relationship between management and the board is particularly important in entities with public shareholders. This balance is facilitated if the roles of chairperson and chief executive (or equivalent) are clearly separated and if the chairperson is an independent director. We agree with respondents to the consultation that in general, the chief executive should not move on to become chairperson. Only in special circumstances should the roles be combined, e.g., where an individual has skills, knowledge and experience not otherwise available to the entity (and where these circumstances are fully explained to investors).

The optimum number of directors for any entity will depend on its size and the nature and complexity of its activities, as well as its requirement for independent directors. If a board is too large, decision-making becomes unwieldy; if too small, it may not achieve the necessary balance of skills, knowledge and experience needed by the entity. This balance is most important for issuers.

The need to achieve the right mix, and to choose directors who can make an appropriate contribution, make director selection and nomination vitally important. Rigorous selection, nomination and appointment processes are needed to achieve this. A separate nomination committee can help to focus resources on this task, and also on succession planning.

Remuneration Committee

The remuneration committee will have the following functions:

- It will make proposals to the board of directors regarding the remuneration policy for the directors and senior officers; the individual remuneration of directors and the forms of contract the company should conclude with each executive director; hiring modalities for senior officers.

- It will oversee compliance with the remuneration policy set by the company.

- The remuneration committee will consult with the chairman or chief executive, especially on issues involving executive directors and senior officers.

Most organisations will want to have a remuneration policy that is competitive and motivational yet affordable. The incentive payments will be designed to support the behaviours required in driving forward the business strategy and within the values of the organisation. It is now considered best practice to include in the senior executives' contracts the basis of separation in the event of the company dismissing such a person.

4.7 Board Committee Practices

4.7.1 Warehouse, New Zealand: Responsibilities of Audit Committees

Financial Responsibilities

- To exercise oversight on the integrity and completeness of the financial statements (annual report and half-year financial report).

- The audit committee oversees the quality and integrity of external financial reporting including the accuracy, completeness and timeliness of financial statements.

- The audit committee relies on information provided by management and the external auditor. Management determines and makes representations to the board that the Warehouse financial statements and disclosures are complete and accurate.

- The audit committee reviews half-yearly and annual financial statements and makes recommendations to the board concerning accounting policies, areas of judgement, compliance with accounting standards, stock exchange and legal requirements and the results of the external and internal audit.

Responsibilities Relating to Appointment, Re-Appointment and Replacement

- The audit committee will recommend to the board the appointment, removal and remuneration of the external auditors.

- It reviews the terms of remuneration of the external auditors, and also reviews the terms of their engagement and the scope of non-audit services being provided by the external auditors.

Audit Committee and Monitoring the Internal Controls

- To assist the board to review the effectiveness of the organisation's internal control environment covering: effectiveness and efficiency of operations; reliability of financial reporting and compliance with applicable laws and regulations.

Audit Committee and Risk Management

- To oversee the effective operation of the risk management framework.

- The audit committee reviews the reports of management and the external and internal auditors on the effectiveness of systems for internal control, financial reporting and risk management.

- The reports includes quarterly reviews of store audit results, an annual strategic risk assessment of key risks and risk mitigation strategies and quarterly reports from Ernst & Young on internal audit findings.

Audit Committee and Monitoring Internal Audit Activities

- The audit committee receives regular reports from management and the internal and external auditors.

- The audit committee also held private session with the internal and external auditors during the year.

- The internal and external auditors have a clear line of direct communication at any time with either the chairman of the audit committee or the chairman of the board, both of whom are independent non-executive directors.

contd...

...contd...

Duties of Nomination Committee at Warehouse

- The committee is responsible for reviewing the structure, size and composition of the board.
- Identifying and nominating candidates for the approval of the board.
- Ensures that the succession planning framework is at place.

Duties of Remuneration Committee at Warehouse

- The remuneration committee is responsible for determining and reviewing compensation arrangements for the directors, CEO and the executive management team.
- Ensuring appropriate performance management.

4.7.2 Auckland International Airport Limited (AIAL)

Audit and Risk Committee: Charter

Objectives

1. To assist the board in performing its responsibilities, with particular reference to financial matters.

2. To review the financial reporting processes, the system of internal control and the internal and external audit process.

3. To review, the Company's process for identifying and managing risk, and for monitoring compliance with statutes and its own policies.

Structure and Composition

4. The committee shall comprise a minimum of three directors, with a quorum of two, all of whom shall be non-executive directors. The majority of the members shall be independent.

5. The chairman of the committee shall be an independent director and shall not be the chairman of the board. At least one member shall have an accounting or financial background and other members should have a working knowledge of finance and accounting practices, given the specialised function of the committee.

6. The committee will meet with the external auditor and internal auditor of the company at least once a year, and for at least part of that meeting, no executive directors or other employees of the company shall be present.

7. The auditor will be invited to attend those parts of any other meetings of the Committee that relate to its responsibilities and where the Committee considers it appropriate.

Functions of the Committee

8. Financial reporting:

   (i) Considering, and recommending for board approval, all major accounting policy issues, including any proposed changes to the company's accounting policies and practices which should be submitted to the committee by management for consideration.

   (ii) Considering, and recommending to the board, whether any changes to the company's accounting policies and practices are required as a result in changes to any generally accepted accounting principles or statutory requirements.

contd...

...contd...

(iii) Considering, and recommending to the board, adoption of both the interim (half-yearly) and final (year-end) financial statements (including the notes thereto) and all other financial statements prepared by the company (including the Disclosure Financial Statements required under the Airport Authorities (Airport Companies Information Disclosure) Regulations 1999.

(iv) Assessing the truth and fairness of annual and interim financial statements prepared by the company, and obtaining explanations from management and external (and any internal) auditors on whether:

- Actual financial results varied significantly from budgeted or projected results.- Any significant or unusual events or transactions are adequately disclosed.

- The company's financial and operating controls are functioning effectively.

- All annual and interim financial statements and announcements contain adequate and appropriate disclosures.

(v) Requiring from the chief executive officer and chief financial officer confirmation in writing that:

- The company's financial statements present a true and fair view, in all material respect, of the company's financial condition and operational results and are in accordance with relevant accounting standards.

- The statement given in the preceding paragraph is founded on a sound system of risk management and internal compliance and control which implements the policies adopted by the board.

- The company's risk management and internal compliance and control system is operating efficiently and effectively in all material respects.

(vi) Considering and recommending for board approval, the interim and final directors' report to shareholders.

(vii) Considering and recommending for board approval, releases relating to financial matters which are required to be made to the New Zealand Exchange Limited.

9   External audit: (i) Liaison with the external auditor, which will include:

- *Audit planning*: The Committee shall be the point-of-contact as representative of the board for the external auditor and should meet with the external auditor at the commencement of the planning phase of the audit so that areas of mutual interest and concern can be discussed. One aspect for specific consideration would be the levels of materiality to be adopted by the auditor in respect of the company.

- *Level of audit fee*: The proposed level of audit fee should be discussed and the committee shall recommend the level of audit fees to the board.

- *Areas of accounting difficulty*: Should areas of major difficulty or controversy arise during the course of the audit, then the committee will be available to meet with the auditors and work towards an acceptable resolution.

- *Audit opinion*: At the time the committee considers final financial statements bearing an audit opinion, it should consider the form and content of the opinion and confirm with the auditor that management has placed no restrictions on their audit.

- *Audit management letter*: At the time financial statements bearing an audit opinion are considered, the committee should receive and consider a report from the auditors on their audit, including the audit management letter. Any significant issues raised by the auditors should be discussed with them.

contd...

...contd...

     – *Audit appointment*: The committee will also:

        • Consider the independence of the external auditor (including reviewing the range of services provided by the auditors in the context of all consulting services bought by the company).

        • Review the performance of the external auditor.

        • Make recommendations to the board regarding the appointment of the external auditor and the rotation of the partner of the external auditor responsible for the audit.

10   Internal audit:

    (i) Liaison with the internal auditor, which will include:

     – *Audit planning*: The committee shall be the point-of-contact as representative of the board for the internal auditor and should meet with the internal auditor at the commencement of the planning phase of the audit so that areas of mutual interest and concern can be discussed. One aspect for specific consideration would be the levels of materiality to be adopted by the internal auditor in respect of the company.

     – *Level of internal audit expense*: The proposed level of expenses incurred in the conduct of the internal audit function should be discussed and the committee shall recommend an appropriate level to the board.

     – *Areas of accounting difficulty*: Should areas of major difficulty or controversy arise during the course of internal audit work, then the committee will be available to meet with the internal auditor and work towards an acceptable resolution.

     – *Reporting*: At the stages set out in the work plan approved by the committee for the conduct of the internal audit function, the internal auditor shall report to the committee and the committee shall consider the report and confirm with the auditor that management has placed no restrictions on its audit.

     – *Audit appointment*: The committee will also:

        * Consider the independence of the internal auditor (including reviewing the range of services provided by the internal auditor, if any, in the context of all consulting services bought by the company).

        * Review the performance of the internal auditor; and

        * Make recommendations to the board regarding the conduct of the internal audit function.

11   Treasury role:

    (i) Reviewing annually the company's treasury policies and practices and, when appropriate, recommending to the board any material changes to finance/funding arrangements, e.g., changes to promissory note facilities, new bond issues, and bank arrangements.

12   Risk management:

    (i) Reviewing the company's system for monitoring compliance with both statutes and the company's policies, and also obtaining regular updates from management and the company's legal counsel regarding such compliance.

    (ii) Evaluating the company's procedures for the management of its risk.

    (iii) Reviewing the effectiveness of the company's risk management activities.

contd...

...contd...

(iv) Ensuring that the company has prepared plans that would enable it to maintain business (operational and financial) continuity in the event of adverse circumstances.

13   General:

    (i) Undertaking a regular overview and assessment of the appropriateness of the functions of internal control and internal audit within the company.

    (ii) Reviewing the company's policies of insurance in place from time to time. No changes to any insurance policy shall occur without the approval of the board, as recommended by the committee.

    (iii) Recommending to the board dividends or other distributions to be made to the Company's shareholders, and the amount of those dividends or distributions

    (iv) Reviewing the findings of any examinations relating to the Company's financial matters by any regulatory or Government agency.

Meetings

14   The committee should meet formally at least three times per year for structured meetings, and at other appropriate times or if requested by the auditor. The proceedings of all meetings should be minuted.

15   (a) Meeting no.1: To be held six or seven months into the new calendar year. Business to include:

    (i) Review and approve proposed annual audit plan and scope as prepared and presented by the company's auditor.

    (ii) Review and recommend to the board the approval of the fees to be charged by the company's auditor.

    (iii) Review of the company's risk management procedures.

(b) Meeting no.2: Following preparation of the half-yearly financial statements. Business to include:

    (i) Approve any proposed changes in accounting policies or practices and review any major accounting problems.

    (ii) Review the half-yearly financial statements, including any proposed dividends.

    (iii) Review the draft director's report and review of operations in respect of the half-year.

    (iv) Recommend to the board approval of the financial statements and announcements to the Stock Exchanges.

(c) Meeting no.3: Following preparation of the annual financial statements and reports. Business to include:

    (i) Review accounting policies and practices and approve any proposed changes.

    (ii) Review draft annual financial statements including any proposed dividends.

    (iii) Review the draft director's report and review of operations.

    (iv) Discuss with the company's auditor:

       – Any restrictions placed on their audit.

       – Any areas of significant concerns.

       – Their proposed form of audit report.

contd...

...contd...

     – Compliance with all statutory reporting requirements.

     – The management review letter.

     – The appropriate application of the company's accounting practices.

  (v) Receive and consider the written confirmation from the chief executive officer (CEO) and chief financial officer (CFO) referred to in paragraph 4(a)(v) above.

  (vi) Recommend financial statements, reports and announcements to the Stock Exchanges to the board for approval.

Accountability and Reporting

16   The committee is accountable to the board. In this regard, the committee shall:

(a) Regularly update the board on the committee activities and make appropriate recommendations.

(b) Ensure that the board is made aware of any matters which may significantly impact on the financial condition or affairs of the company and its business; and

(c) Provide copies of minutes of all committee meetings to all members of the board at the next scheduled meeting of the board.

Nominations Committee: Charter

Objectives

1   The objectives of the committee are to:

(a) make recommendations to the board in respect of the criteria for the selection or nomination of new directors;

(b) provide assistance to the chairman of the board in respect of evaluating the performance of the board and individual directors;

(c) ensure letters of engagement are in place for all directors;

(d) ensure there is an appropriate induction programme in place for all new directors; and

(e) make annual determinations on the independence status of all directors in accordance with the company's independent director standards.

Structure and Composition

2   The committee shall comprise at least two directors appointed by the board who shall be independent non-executive directors, with a quorum of at least two members of the committee.

3   The committee shall be able to request at any time the retirement from the meeting of any person invited to attend the meeting.

Authority

4   The board authorises the committee, within the scope of its responsibilities, to:(a) liaise with the chief executive officer in respect of any ancillary information it requires from any employee of the company and/or any other external party; (b) obtain external legal or other professional advice; and (c) require the attendance of company officers at meetings as the committee deems appropriate.

contd...

...contd...

Functions of the Committee

5   In meeting the objectives of the committee the functions of the committee will include:
(a) reviewing the terms of engagement of board members other than remuneration; and
(b) developing a succession planning methodology and reviewing plans for board member development to ensure organisational safety with respect to succession planning.

Meetings

6   The committee shall meet formally at least once a year and at other times it considers necessary. The proceedings of all meetings should be minuted.

Accountability and Reporting

7   The committee shall:

(a) be accountable to the board;

(b) regularly update the board about the committee activities and make appropriate recommendations; and

(c) provide copies of minutes of all meetings of the committee to each member of the Board at the next scheduled meeting of the board.

Remuneration Committee: Charter

Objectives

1   The objectives of the Committee are to develop policies and make recommendations to the board in respect of:

2   (a) the organisational structure of the company to ensure adequate human resource development programmes are in place;

(b) the remuneration of senior executives of the company (and any subsidiaries) with a view to ensuring that:

(i) such staff are fairly and equitably remunerated relative to comparable positions within relevant New Zealand and Australian markets;

(ii) such staff are adequately rewarded for excellence in achievement and performance; and

(iii) the company is able to attract and retain people who are high performers and will ensure the achievement of company's objectives;

(c) the remuneration of non-executive directors to be submitted to shareholders for approval, with a view to attracting and retaining the non-executive directors required to ensure the achievement of the company's objectives;

(d) the operating framework for senior management remuneration delegated to the chief executive officer in respect of senior management positions;

(e) a robust succession planning system for the chief executive officer and general manager positions which identifies and targets individuals for development; and

(f) ensuring appropriate employment agreements are in place for the chief executive officer and the general manager positions.

3   The committee shall also:

(a) review the performance, and the terms and conditions of employment, of the chief executive officer and his/her reports annually;

---

contd...

...contd...

(b) authorise any annual allocation of options under any share scheme run by the company from time to time in accordance with authorities established by the board; and

(c) authorise any annual payments of short-term incentives in accordance with authorities established by the board.

Structure and Composition

4   The Committee shall comprise at least two directors who shall be independent non-executive directors, with a quorum of at least two members of the committee. Members will be appointed by the board and will hold office until changed by board resolution.

5   Management will not be represented on the committee, but the corporate secretary or the chief executive officer may be invited to act as secretary to the committee. The chief executive officer will provide recommendations to the committee in respect of his/her direct reports and will participate in the deliberations of the committee except in respect of matters relating to the chief executive officer on his/her remuneration.

6   The committee shall be able to request at any time the retirement from the meeting of any person invited to attend the meeting.

Authority

7   The board authorises the committee, within the scope of its responsibilities, to:

(a) liaise with the chief executive officer in respect of any ancillary information it requires from any employee of the company and/or any other external party;

(b) obtain external legal or other professional advice; and

(c) require the attendance of company officers at meetings as the committee deems appropriate.

Functions of the Committee

8   In meeting the objectives of the committee the functions of the committee will include: (a) over-viewing the company's remuneration policy and human resource practices as appropriate; (b) reviewing the remuneration of board members; (c) reviewing the terms and conditions of employment, and remuneration, of the chief executive officer and the chief executive officer's direct reports; and (d) making recommendations to the board in respect of succession planning methodology and reviewing plans for senior management team development to ensure organisational safety with respect to succession planning, including discussion with the chief executive officer on performance pertaining to his/her direct reports.

Meetings

9   The committee shall meet formally at least once a year and at other times as it thinks necessary. The proceedings of all meetings should be minuted.

Accountability and Reporting

10 The committee shall: (a) be accountable to the board; (b) regularly update the board about the committee activities and make appropriate recommendations; and (c) provide copies of minutes of all meetings of the committee to each member of the board at the next scheduled meeting of the board.

4.8 Conclusion

Thus, in this chapter we have made a review of the board committees, its policies and practices considering the international policies and practices.

References

Hoitash, R. and U. Hoitash (2008). "The Role of Audit Committees in Managing Relationships with External Auditors After SOX: Evidence from the US". Retrieved on June 23, 2008 from *http://ssm.com/abstract=1312024*

Vera-Munoz, S.C. (2005). "Corporate Governance Reforms: Redefined Expectations of Audit Committee Responsibilities and Effectiveness", *Journal of Business Ethics* 62(2): 115-27.

5 | Codes of Good Governance

This chapter focusses on the codes of good governance as the topic has become a central issue in policy and in academia. It is evident from the growing academic literature. An important debate in the international corporate governance world is whether countries should develop hard laws, such as the United States with the Sarbanes-Oxley Act of 2002, or whether soft regulation, such as codes of good governance, are sufficiently effective to improve existing corporate governance practices across countries, as well as to address the pressing issues of corporate accountability and disclosure.

Although the first country to issue a code of good governance was the United States in 1978 and the second country was Hong Kong in 1989, the pace of issuance has gathered speed ever since, particularly after 1992 when the United Kingdom's Cadbury Report was issued (Cuervo-Cazurra and Aguilera, 2004). By mid-2008, 64 countries had issued 196 distinct codes of good governance. Additionally, there is a large variety of issuers of codes, which include not only stock markets or its regulators, but also investor associations, employer associations, professional associations, and even governments. The explosion in the issuance of codes of good governance has been accompanied by an increase in the number of articles in academic publications. For example, since 1997, *Corporate Governance: An International Review* has published 14 papers that explicitly discuss the nature of codes in a given country and 59 papers that have the phrase 'governance code' in their abstract. Obviously, this shows that the topic of codes of good governance is central to the field and that there is plenty to take stock from. However, there is little systematic analysis of how codes of good governance have affected how corporations are structured or how managers behave across different corporate governance systems. For instance, a recent review of the literature on corporate governance published in the *Handbook of the Economics of Finance* (Becht, Bolton and Roell, 2003) briefly discusses codes of good governance and highlights how the existence of a 'striking schism between firmly held beliefs of business people and academic research calls for an explanation'.

Despite the importance and increasing interest in codes of good governance, there are no reviews of what we know and do not know about this topic, which is central to international corporate governance. In fact, the existing literature seems to have moved in two directions. One tends to focus on the influence that a particular code has on firms in a given country and the other tends to describe the existence and content of codes in multiple countries. However, the current state of knowledge appears to be at an impasse as there is some conflicting evidence on the effectiveness of codes of good governance, and there are few analytical, rather than descriptive, studies of codes across countries. All this is resulting in an apparent divergence in development between the real world, where codes continue to be developed and revised, and the academic world, where there is limited theoretical advancement on the topic (Aguilera and Cuervo-Cazurra, 2009).

5.1 Codes of Good Governance Worldwide

Codes of good governance have risen to prominence in the last decade as they have spread around the world. In the 30 years since the first code was issued in the US and the middle of 2008, codes of good governance have been created in 64 developed, transition, and developing countries. Although it was not until 1989 that Hong Kong issued a code of good governance, in the 1990s codes were quickly developed in many countries, partly inspired by the Cadbury Code that had been created in the United Kingdom in 1992. The spread of codes of good governance around the world was aided by the push from international entities, such as the World Bank and the Organisation for Economic Co-operation and Development (OECD), which started highlighting the need to improve institutions in general and corporate governance in particular to help countries grow and develop.

Codes of good governance have some key universal principles for effective corporate governance that are common to most countries. O'Shea (2005) shows that most codes have some recommendations on the following six governance practices, explicitly or implicitly: (1) a balance of executive and non-executive directors, such as independent non-executive directors; (2) a clear division of responsibilities between the chairman and the chief executive officer; (3) the need for timely and quality information provided to the board; (4) formal and transparent procedures for the appointment of new directors; (5) balanced and understandable financial reporting; and (6) maintenance of a sound system of internal control. Furthermore, detailed descriptions, as well as systematic summaries, of the content of codes have appeared in Gregory (1998; 1999), who reviews the content of codes in developed and developing countries, and in Van den Berghe and de Ridder (1999). Later, Gregory and Simmelkjaer (2002) integrate these studies on the content of codes in a report on codes of good governance that served as the base for the European Union's recommendation on codes of good governance for its member states.

The first code of good governance was issued in 1978 in the United States, but it was not until 1989 that a second country code of good governance appeared in another country, Hong Kong. Ireland was the third country to issue a code in 1991 and the United Kingdom was the fourth, in 1992, with the influential Cadbury Report. This report sparked a debate on good governance that resulted in the rapid introduction of codes in other countries. Additionally, the spread of codes around the world was encouraged by transnational institutions, such as the World Bank and the OECD. In the mid-1990s, these transnational institutions started to look at good governance as a condition necessary for the development of countries and suggested to their member countries to adopt best governance practices; these included not only good governance at the country level, in the form of control of corruption and efficient state bureaucracies (e.g. Cuervo-Cazurra, 2008), but also good governance at the firm level in the form of best practices for publicly traded firms. As a result, by the middle of 2008, 64 countries had issued at least one code of good governance.

Figure 5.1 illustrates the number of codes and countries that have issued codes. Some countries have had more than one code of good governance created since the first one, most notable are the United Kingdom and the United States with 25 codes each, while in others only one code has been issued, like in Argentina or Austria. The figure highlights the importance of the phenomenon, and how the creation of codes took some time to gain momentum. After the creation of the first

Figure 5.1

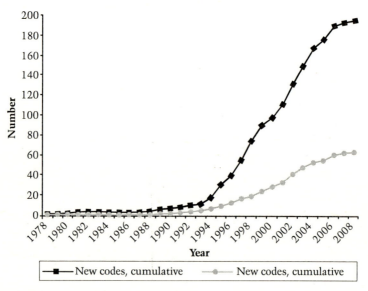

*Worldwide Creation of Codes of Good Governance
by Countries, 1978-Mid 2008*

code, very few new codes were created and very few new countries issued those. However, the Cadbury Report of 1992 accelerated the worldwide diffusion of codes, with a rapid number of new codes and new countries issuing codes after the mid-1990s and continuing into the 2000s.

Codes have also been created by transnational institutions to address the need for better corporate governance of multiple countries, not just the needs of a country in particular, as is generally the case with national codes of good governance. These codes of good governance issued by transnational institutions are important for two reasons. First, they signal the importance of corporate governance and help establish sets of best practices that address common corporate governance problems of firms around the world. Second, they serve, in some cases, as the basis for the creation of codes of good governance in individual countries. Figure 5.2 illustrates the development of such codes over time. They started in 1996 and were rapidly developed in the late 1990s, but slowed in the 2000s with no new codes being issued after 2005.

Figure 5.2

Worldwide Creation of Codes of Good Governance
by Transnational Institutions, 1995-Mid 2008

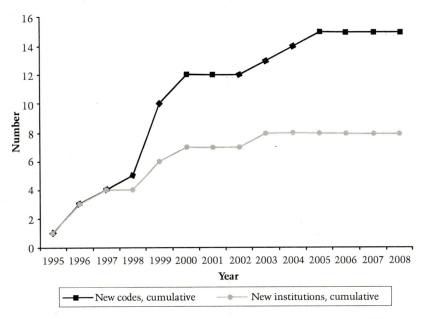

5.2 Creation of Codes by Countries

The worldwide diffusion of codes is impressive, but a more detailed explanation of the creation of codes in each country shows the wide differences across countries. First, countries vary in the year in which the first code were created. The United States was the country with the first code, followed by Hong Kong, Ireland, the United Kingdom, and Canada.

All these countries share in common a common-law, or English-based, legal system. This legal system, in contrast to the civil-law system, has a more flexible legislation, with common practices and previous judicial interpretations of laws and regulations having applicability in disputes. In the civil-law system, of which there are three types (French, Scandinavian, and Germanic), laws are issued by the national parliaments and assemblies and applied by judges with limited enforceability of accepted practices. It was not until 1994 that a country with a civil-law legal system, Sweden, created a code of good governance. That same year, the first developing country, South Africa, created a code of good governance. However, it was not until 1997 that other developing countries (e.g., Brazil, Thailand) and transition countries (e.g. Kyrgyz Republic) created codes.

Second, countries vary significantly in the number of codes that have been created. At one extreme are the United States and United Kingdom, where 25 distinct codes have been issued. After these two, the countries with the highest number of codes are Hong Kong with nine; Belgium and France with eight each; Canada with seven; Australia, Spain and Sweden with six each; and Denmark, Germany, Italy, Netherlands and Portugal with five each. The rest of the countries have four or fewer codes. There appears to be a connection between the development of capital markets and the number of codes issued. Countries with not only larger, but also deeper, capital markets have more codes of good governance; the need for good governance increases as the number of public firms grows because agency problems between disperse owners and managers, or between majority and minority shareholders emerge (Aguilera and Cuervo-Cazurra, 2009).

5.3 Creation of Codes by Transnational Institutions

Codes of good governance by transnational entities also vary. Figure 5.2 summarises the codes created by transnational institutions. These codes are designed to improve corporate governance of multiple countries and as such are more general than the codes developed in each country, which focus only on issues that need to be addressed there. Transnational institutions started issuing codes of good governance in 1996. Among them, the International Corporate Governance Network (ICGN) has become a repository of the texts of codes of good governance worldwide. Its website (*http: //www.icgn.org*) contains a list of recent codes of good governance. The OECD, on its part, issued its highly influential Principles of Corporate Governance in 1999, which has become the basis not only for the evaluation of corporate governance practices in developing countries by the World Bank, but also for the development of codes of good governance by countries.

In addition to these transnational institutions, the World Bank has taken an active role in promoting good corporate governance around the

Table 5.1

Creation of Codes of Good Governance by Countries

Country	Year of First Code	Number of Unique Codes Until the Middle of 2008	Country	Year of First Code	Number of Unique Codes Until the Middle of 2008
Argentina	2004	1	Luxembourg	2006	1
Australia	1995	6	Macedonia	2003	1
Austria	2002	1	Malaysia	2000	1
Bangladesh	2004	1	Malta	2001	1
Belgium	1995	8	Mexico	1999	2
Brazil	1997	2	Morocco	2008	1
Bulgaria	2007	1	Netherlands	1996	5
Canada	1993	7	New Zealand	2003	2
China	2001	2	Nigeria	2006	1
Cyprus	2002	1	Norway	2004	1
Czech Republic	2001	2	Pakistan	2002	1
Denmark	2000	5	Peru	2001	2
Estonia	2006	1	Philippines	2000	1
Finland	2003	2	Poland	2002	2
France	1995	8	Portugal	1999	5
Germany	1996	5	Romania	2000	1
Greece	1999	2	Russia	2002	1
Hong Kong	1989	9	Singapore	1998	3
Hungary	2002	1	Slovakia	2002	1
Iceland	2004	1	Slovenia	2004	1
India	1998	2	South Africa	1994	1
Indonesia	2000	1	Spain	1996	6
Ireland	1991	3	Sri Lanka	2006	1
Italy	1999	5	Sweden	1994	6
Jamaica	2005	1	Switzerland	2002	2
Japan	1997	4	Taiwan	2002	1
Kenya	2002	1	Thailand	1997	4
Korea	1999	1	Trinidad and Tobago	2006	1
Kyrgyz Republic	1997	1	Turkey	2003	1
Latvia	2005	1	UK	1992	25
Lebanon	2006	1	Ukraine	2003	1
Lithuania	2003	1	USA	1978	25

Source: Complied from Aguilera and Cuervo-Cazurra (2004).

world, helping developing and transition countries evaluate their current corporate governance practices and upgrade them to international levels. In collaboration with the International Monetary Fund on some occasions, the World Bank has issued a Corporate Governance Country Assessment or a Report on the Observance of Standards and Codes (ROSC) for 44 countries. These reports evaluate the corporate governance practices prevailing in the country against the benchmark of the OECD 'Principles for Corporate Governance'. However, the reports are not codes of good governance *per se*.

5.4 Extant Literature on Codes of Good Governance

The literature on codes of good governance has expanded a great deal since the issuance of the UK Cadbury Report in 1992, and particularly since the early 2000s. Codes have also become more relevant and have moved to the center stage of policy and business strategy. Companies, as well as countries, seek to make their corporate governance practices more effective, in part as a consequence of corporate governance scandals, but also to attract investors. Even though codes of good governance refer to the behaviour and structure of the board of directors, the area of study is broader, because directors are at the core of the firm and inevitably interact with other actors inside and outside the firm. Hence, codes of good governance include not only recommendation on the structure of the board, but also on the relationship of the board with executives in the firm and directors from other firms.

The emergence of codes of good governance around the world and by transnational organisations is noticeable. In addition to when codes emerge, it is also important to study the patterns of diffusion across countries and the reasons for such patterns. Aguilera and Cuervo-Cazurra (2004) was probably the first empirical study to examine the determinants of the diffusion of codes of good governance across countries. They argue that a combination of efficiency and legitimacy reasons trigger countries to issue codes of good governance. Their analysis of the adoption of codes of good governance in 49 countries reveals that codes are more likely to emerge in countries with a common-law legal system, a lack of strong shareholders' protection rights, high government liberalisation, and a strong presence of foreign institutional investors. Cuervo-Cazurra and

Aguilera (2004) also explored the speed of adoption of the codes, finding that codes are more likely to develop faster in countries with greater foreign investment exposure. Zattoni and Cuomo (2008) in a follow-up article examine the main drivers, such as efficiency and legitimacy, behind code adoption in different countries' legal systems. Using a sample of 60 countries, they conduct a comparative analysis of scope, coverage, and strictness of recommendations of codes in civil- and common-law systems. Their findings show that, for the most part, civil-law countries (such as France) issue codes of good governance later than common-law countries (such as the UK or the US), issue fewer codes, and state more lenient and ambiguous recommendations. Finally, Enrione, Mazza and Zerboni (2006) have looked at the stages of diffusion in the context of the institutionalisation process. They study 150 codes in 78 countries from 1978 to 2004 and relate the rate of code adoption to firm organisational structure. They discuss and empirically show the institutional life-cycle of codes from adoption to fully institutionalised (i.e., taken for granted) practices. For example, they indicate that the initial codes emerged as a reaction to the 1980s organisational shift from conglomerate strategies to core strategies in firms.

A critical debate in the variety of capitalism literature, as well as more generally in comparative political economy, is to what degree corporate governance systems and business systems in general are converging towards the Anglo-Saxon model of corporate governance, or the so called shareholder-value model (Hall and Soskice, 2001; Aguilera and Jackson, 2003; Morgan, Whitley and Moen, 2005; Yoshikawa, TsuiAuch and McGuire, 2007). This question arises also in the context of codes, because, despite a high level of difference in the adoption of corporate governance codes across countries, both Cuervo-Cazzura (2002) and Reid (2003) note that increasing external forces, such as globalisation, market liberalisation, emergence of powerful foreign investors, and recommendations on global best practices by transnational institutions such as the World Bank, appear to facilitate increasing confluence.

The second question in the convergence debate is to what degree codes of good governance are enabling mechanisms to facilitate further governance convergence across countries, or whether, on the contrary, codes are mechanisms to highlight and reinforce the unique national governance characteristics. Collier and Zaman's (2005) study of codes of good governance in 20 European countries address this question as to whether codes push convergence towards the Anglo-Saxon model in corporate governance systems. This convergence in governance practices is particularly salient, they find, in areas such as the audit committee, which is a strategic governance practice in the Anglo-Saxon corporate governance systems, but was rather uncommon within Continental Europe before the early 1990s (Birkett, 1986; Collier, 1996).

Convergence of governance practices is certainly encouraged by transnational institutions that seek to regulate markets and protect investors. Two illustrative examples are the European Commission (EC) and the OECD. The European unification has been an important trigger for governance convergence (Reid, 2003; Hermes, Postma and Zivkov, 2007), particularly through their Communication 284 (COM284) Report of 2003. This is an EC report that discusses how to enhance corporate governance in the European Union and provides specific governance recommendations, such as reinforcement of shareholder's rights, greater disclosure and accountability, and modernisation of the board of directors. There is some research evidence to suggest that the European-level governance guidelines are highly aligned with country codes (Cromme, 2005). Part of the explanation is that, in general, issues such as stakeholder rights and responsibilities are taken more seriously across Continental Europe, as their former weak capital markets are strengthened and institutional investors become more assertive in promoting more effective governance measures, such as higher accountability and better disclosure.

There have also been significant efforts by transnational institutions, such as the World Bank or the OECD, to encourage the adoption of global standards of governance practices, which are generally drafted more in line with the Anglo-Saxon model (Roberts, 2004). In particular, the attempts have been prominent in developing countries, as their firms are being privatised and seek to attract and retain foreign capital investments. To help developing economies to create and adopt codes of good governance, the OECD developed in 1999 the 'OECD Principles of Corporate Governance', which has been serving as a guiding rule for much of the corporate governance reforms (Coombes and Watson, 2001; Krambia-Kapardis and Psaros, 2006). For example, the new Russian code of good governance issued in 2002 is seen as an attempt to impose an Anglo-Saxon model of governance on Russian domestic businesses by emphasising the principle of shareholder protection (Roberts, 2004). Likewise, Krambia-Kapardis and Psaros (2006) argue that the code of good corporate governance in Cyprus, a developing country, largely draws on Anglo-Saxon principles of corporate governance. But even, Germany, a well-established country within the stakeholder model of corporate governance, has also included some governance practices in its codes that are more typical of the Anglo-Saxon corporate governance system, such as disclosure of individual executive compensation which was controversial given the two-tier system board system and co-determination legislation (Cromme, 2005; Chizema, 2008).

There is another side to this debate that argues that country characteristics are the main drivers of code adoption, as well as code content. For example, using the contents of codes in seven Eastern European countries, Hermes *et al.* (2007) assess whether external forces are the main drivers of the content of codes in these countries relative to the recommendations of the EC principles. Their findings show that Eastern European codes of good governance cover only about half of the recommendations of the EC principles. Hungary and Poland especially have greatly deviated form the EC recommendations. Hermes *et al.* (2007) study shows the influence of domestic forces in shaping the contents of codes of good governance. In fact, there are strong views among corporate governance scholars that, 'the one rule fits all' is flawed and that consequently a wide diversity of approaches to corporate governance should be expected due to the very different national contexts where firms are embedded (Sargent, 1997; Cuervo-Cazzura, 2002; Reid, 2003; Okike, 2007; Reaz and Hossain, 2007; Balgobin, 2008). From this perspective, Reaz and Hossain (2007) argue that more careful attention should be paid to the developing and transition economies, as they are less advanced in areas of corporate governance, Western models are difficult to implement by the latter, and instead some translation into a hybrid model is necessary. Also, this perspective claims that for a code of good governance to be effective it must capture the sociopolitical and economic environment in which firms operate (Cuervo-Cazzura, 2002; Roberts, 2004; Okike, 2007; Reaz and Hossain, 2007).

In sum, the dramatic diffusion of codes of good governance has generated a heated debate on its effects on the convergence of corporate governance systems, mostly towards the shareholder-oriented model. Examining the existing literature, we think that the outcomes are not as straightforward as one might think and hence it is important to move the debate beyond the convergence/divergence dichotomy and pay more attention to the dynamics of how firms apply certain aspects of the codes and not others, or how issuers follow the transnational code for one dimension of the specific practice, but not fully adopt the entire recommendation. For example, Yoshikawa *et al.* (2007) conduct a study using a sample of Japanese firms and discover intriguing results of the diffusion of governance innovation. According to their findings, Japan's corporate governance system neither fully converges to, nor completely diverges from the Anglo-Saxon model. Instead they argue that pressure from foreign capital and product markets may not always lead to convergence to international standards. It seems that when innovating governance practices, Japanese companies decoupled from the original context and customised their governance practices to their particular circumstances. Thus, well-governed firms exposed to foreign product and capital markets, such as Toyota, Honda and Canon, rejected the straight forward adoption of the Anglo-Saxon model, and eventually the government was forced to revise the Commercial Code to adjust to the Japanese reality and local demands. In this instance, the firm-level interaction with the code issuers and enforcers is a dimension that should not be overlooked. According to Yoshikawa *et al.* (2007), firm's financial performance, positioning in the business community and organisational culture play important roles in shaping corporate governance reforms. In sum, as codes diffuse around the world it is important to understand why and how they fit in the overall corporate governance system, as well as in the institutional environment.

5.5 Country-Level: Implementation of Codes of Good Governance

There are two mechanisms for code implementation—mandatory or voluntary regulation. The classic examples of the two alternative approaches to implement codes are legislation (e.g. the US Sarbanes-Oxley

Act of 2002) and a 'comply or explain' approach (e.g. the UK Combined Code of 2003) as suggested by Balgobin (2008). One mechanism to implement codes is through the development of stringent corporate legislation. However, such a compulsory approach is rarely found in codes of good governance and is more commonly associated with laws. The most well-known example is the 2002 Sarbanes-Oxley Act (SOX). After several accounting scandals rocked financial markets in the US, the Accounting Industry Reform Act of 2002, known as the Sarbanes-Oxley Act was enacted to prevent further corporate failure (Maassen, van den Bosch and Volberda, 2004). The federal SOX in 2002 and new listing requirements have a form of mandatory rules, and companies have no other alternative than to comply with them (MacNeil and Li, 2006). Under the New York Stock Exchange (NYSE) rules, chief executive officers (CEOs) and chief financial officers (CFOs) are required to certify quarterly and annual reports for their legal compliance (O'Shea, 2005; Balgobin, 2008). The underlying philosophy of SOX is that corporate governance practices need to be mandated, rather than be left to self-regulation of companies and markets, to prevent devastating corporate governance failures such as Enron (Taylor, 2003; MacNeil and Li, 2006).

Voluntary firm compliance is the other mechanism used to implement the codes, as it was originally done in the British Cadbury Report. It is based on the rule of 'comply or explain', where it is not required for listed companies to comply with all code recommendations, but companies are required to state how they have applied the principles in the code and in the cases of non-compliance, they must explain the reasons. According to MacNeil and Li (2006), this approach has two underlying considerations— flexibility to adjust the characteristics of different firms and an assumption that the capital markets will monitor and assess value to compliance. Maassen *et al.* (2004) claim that the voluntary self-regulation principle has had a significant impact on the development of corporate governance codes around the globe. They note that codes have been favoured by most international financial markets in adjusting to modern corporate governance standards.

There have however been some changes in the 'comply or explain' principle over time. Although the principle is based on self-regulation, O'Shea (2005) argues that as codes get revised, the requirements have become more prescriptive and stringent. Dewing and Russell (2004) show that code self-regulation had a characteristic of informal self-regulation during 1990s, but more recently the implementation of codes has progressed to formal and direct self-regulation in response to public concerns. For example, while the previous UK Cadbury Report in 1992 recommended the separation of the role of chairman and CEO, the revised Combined Code in 2003 requires that the CEO should not become chairman of the same company.

Despite the greater specificity of the governance recommendations in the codes, the debate on the need for regulation of corporate governance is still very much alive. Dewing and Russell (2004), MacNeil and Li (2006), and Maassen *et al.* (2004) note that some scholars and organisations have expressed their concerns about weak monitoring and enforcement mechanisms of corporate governance codes. As a monitor for effective voluntary disclosure, MacNeil and Li (2006) argue that the market does not seem to play its role. Originally, the market is supposed to penalise unjustified non-compliance with a lower share price. However, as indicated by the MacNeil and Li (2006) study, financial performance appears to excuse non-compliance, casting a doubt that compliance does not necessarily lead to positive financial performance. As a contribution to this debate on formal *versus* informal self-regulation, Dewing and Russell (2004) suggest that an appropriate structure of regulations of corporate governance may be better based on regulation of financial services. In addition, Cuervo-Cazurra (2002) proposes that, for countries characterised by a large shareholder-oriented system, it is necessary to expand formal market control mechanisms to compensate for deficiencies in the legal system, rather than developing codes of good governance.

Although most codes of good governance share similar issues, the specific content of the codes of good governance does vary significantly across countries, capturing the different needs across corporate governance systems. The implementation of the codes has increased over time, with country-level studies showing that firms tend to increasingly adopt a higher percentage of code recommendations despite their voluntary nature. This voluntary nature and the associated 'comply or explain' principle has given rise to a heated debate as to whether codes are an effective governance tool, or whether more stringent governance rules with mandatory implementation are needed to increase compliance, especially in countries that have weak institutions and underdeveloped governance systems.

5.6 Firm-Level: Compliance and Effectiveness

Although codes of good governance have been developed around the world for more than a decade, the degree to which firms adopt codes varies across countries, and the decision to adopt a given code does not automatically guarantee effective corporate governance.

The level of compliance with codes has varied significantly across countries. For example, in the UK, Conyon and Mallin (1997) and Weir and Laing (2000) show that British firms listed in the London Stock Exchange (LSE) to a large extent complied with the Cadbury Report's recommendations. MacNeil and Li (2006) note that the scale of compliance with the UK Combined Code has increased over time. Similarly, in terms of increasing compliance over time, O'Shea (2005) reports that only two-thirds of the top 100 UK listed companies had audit committees in 1992, prior to the Cadbury Report, while by June 1995, every single FTSE 100 company (the 100 most capitalised firms in the LSE) had an audit committee and almost 98 per cent of mid-250 UK companies also be counted with them. However, there is also evidence in the codes research for the other side of the story. For example, MacNeil and Li (2006) find significant evidence of non-compliance. They show that compliance is not properly monitored and argue that investors' tolerance of non-compliance is related to a great degree to superior financial performance. Investors seem to rely on financial performance as a proxy for non-compliance rather than engaging in the tedious task of evaluating merits of corporate provisions. MacNeil and Li's (2006) study clearly claims that financial performance has influence over excusing non-compliance in reverse.

There is also a fair amount of research around compliance surrounding the German code of good governance. This finds, for example, that company size is positively associated with a relatively higher level of compliance (Bebenroth, 2005; Werder, Talaulicar and Kolat, 2005), but assessments on the degree of compliance are mixed. On the one hand, Pellens, Hillebrandt and Ulmer (2001) survey companies in the DAX100 and find that 95.6 per cent of the firms comply with the provisions in the

German code of good governance and 48.5 per cent have already fully implemented the German code as a company guideline. Werder *et al.* (2005) examined the overall acceptance of the code recommendations, including critical recommendations that generated non-compliance. They nevertheless identify a high degree of acceptance of the code as well as willingness to comply in the future. On the other hand, the literature also reveals that the German code of good governance includes some controversial, and not so popular, recommendations that are not followed by the majority of companies, such as personal liability and compensation of the management and/or supervisory board (Bebenroth, 2005).

The institutional environment and, in particular, the development of the stock market determines a great deal the degree of monitoring of code compliance, even if it is simply informal and for legitimisation purposes. As it is to be expected, in developing countries, compliance with codes is scarce. For example, research on the Cyprus code of good governance by Krambia-Kapardis and Psaros (2006) finds a low level of compliance with all significant aspects of the code. This is in the context of Cyprus, which not only has weak capital markets and legal support, but also a low degree of free market controls, with highly concentrated ownership, and unreliable information flow. Their findings suggest that corporate governance codes in other developing economies might need to be strengthened by explicit institutional initiatives.

Thus, the 'comply or explain' approach allows for the possibility of non-compliance, with examples of market tolerance on non-compliance and of institutional resistance. Regarding non-compliance, it seems critical as research moves forward to study the link between a firm's governance structures and firm performance, mostly because research shows that financial performance can justify non-compliance. In emerging economies, on the other hand, it appears to be important that complementary institutions are strengthened in order to increase the effectiveness of codes.

The following literature examines the relationship between codes of good governance and firm performance. Since compliance with codes of good governance entails significant implementation costs (Aguilera, Filatotchev, Gospel and Jackson, 2008), it is reasonable for companies to expect benefits from compliance in the form of improved firm performance and eventually positive market reactions. Once again, the literature shows for the most part inconclusive results, suggesting the need for additional research. Thus a key puzzle that needs to be resolved in research on codes of good governance is whether they do have an impact on firm performance, or whether they merely serve to assuage investors' complaints. ·

The first step in reviewing the relationship between code compliance and firm performance is to differentiate how scholars conceptualise and measure performance. Below we describe the existing studies clustered by performance measures. The first group of studies reveal a positive relationship between code compliance and earnings management. For example, Benkel, Mather and Ramsay (2006) analyse whether independent directors on the board and audit committee are related to lower levels of earnings management. Using a sample of the top 300 Australian firms, they find that a higher proportion of independent directors on the board and in the audit committee is associated with reduced levels of earnings management. Their finding is consistent with those of previous US and UK research that illustrate the critical monitoring role of independent directors in corporate governance practices (Weir and Laing, 2000). Finally, based on a variety of earnings quality characteristics of Mexican firms, such as income smoothing, timely loss recognition, and abnormal accruals, Machuga and Teitel (2007) show that the quality of earnings improve after implementation of the codes.

Other studies find positive associations between codes of good governance and more traditional measures of performance, such as returns and market value. For example, Fernandez-Rodriguez, Gómez-Ansón and Cuervo-Garcia (2004) find abnormal positive returns associated with Spanish firms' announcements of compliance with the Olivencia Code; Del Brio, Maia Ramires and Perote (2006) indicate that the degree of compliance increases Spanish firms' value; and Alves and Mendes (2004) also uncover a positive relationship with equity returns among Portuguese firms. Moreover, codes of good governance also affect other performance variables more broadly defined. For example, Dahya, McConnell and Travlos (2002) illustrate that the adoption of the Cadbury report in 1992 increased CEO turnover in the UK, triggered by the need for the separation of chairman and CEO positions. At the same time, this UK code recommendation also heightened the sensitivity of the CEO turnover to poor performance.

However, many other studies show either an inconsistent or negative relationship between code compliance and firm performance. For example, Park and Shin (2001) do not find that compliance with the Toronto Stock Exchange's *Corporate Governance Guidelines* is associated with reductions in accruals management, and Nowak, Rott and Mahr (2004) find no association with the impact on the German capital market performance. There are also other studies that show, at a more general level, that universal code recommendations, such as board independence, is not systematically linked to financial performance (Dalton, Daily, Ellstrand and Johnson, 1998; Bhagat and Black, 2002).

Several factors might account for the mixed and inconclusive findings. First, other factors related to governance and broader than governance may affect the relationship between code compliance and firm performance. In other words, as pointed out by Mura (2007), many studies fail to control for the endogeneity of the explanatory variables due to unobserved firm heterogeneity. It indicates that if the studies have not controlled for this condition, the results may generate biased and inconsistent estimates. Second, firm-specific characteristics are very likely to influence this relationship. For example, Fernández-Rodriguez *et al.* (2004) find that the wealth effects are greater for firms with lower leverage rates and where managers dominate the board. Along similar lines, Benkel *et al.* (2006) also show that reduced levels of earnings management through the monitoring role of independent directors are mostly associated with large firms, but rarely with small firms. They suggest that it may be the result from higher public scrutiny of large firms that provide independent directors with more incentives to better monitor and from more resources to recruit more experienced and knowledgeable directors. These results illustrate that relative benefits and costs of compliance may rest on companies' pre-governance structures and firm-level characteristics. Third, an important issue is the concept of independent directors. Although most corporate governance codes underscore the independence of boards of directors, Maassen *et al.* (2004) question whether independent directors are truly independent enough to be effective monitors. This is particularly the case because the definition of director independence varies across countries and even firms. Moreover, depending on their expertise, experience, and given incentives, some boards may be more motivated to be more effective monitors. Although investors value positively firm's compliance with recommendations on board structure, there has been mixed results of the codes' impact on firm performance. Other factors and firm characteristics seem to affect the relationship, requiring more careful analyses to distill the value of codes of good governance on firms.

5.7 Areas for Future Research on Codes of Good Governance

Our review of the worldwide diffusion of codes of good governance and of the literature on codes highlights the importance of and interest in this governance topic. Codes of good governance have become a central issue in policy and in academia. This importance of the topic is highlighted in the growing academic literature, but there is still an apparent lag between advances in the creation of codes and the studies analysing them. Much progress has been made on our understanding of the diffusion of codes around the world, on the adoption of codes by firms, and on the impact of the codes on performance.

However, our review also reveals large lacunae in our understanding of the topic. Four areas are noticeable in terms of the lack of research being done—the systematic analysis of the content of codes of good governance and of the issuers of the codes, a better understanding of the consequences of codes issued by transnational institutions, and finally the evolution in the recommendations of codes (Aguilera and Cuervo-Cazurra, 2009).

First, many studies take the codes as a black box and focus on the diffusion of codes or the impact of codes on performance. These analyses assume that codes are equivalent across countries and therefore can be analysed as one common dependent variable or as a comparable independent variable. Although most of the codes tend to agree in the mechanisms that support more effective governance, such as a board of directors with independent members or the creation of committees, there are significant cross-national differences. For example, codes vary significantly because they are developed to address corporate governance issues that are specific to a given country. Moreover, the divergence in what is classified as a code across different studies, with some studies proposing different numbers of countries and codes that have been created, points to the need for a more careful examination of what each code contains to ensure their comparability and the soundness of the conclusions derived. Since the codes issued in different countries do in fact have different recommendations, the comparison of their adoption and effectiveness in improving corporate governance across countries faces serious limitations because the standards used differ.

Second, studies have identified that the nature of the issuer of the codes can differ significantly, with codes being issued by the country's stock exchange, director associations, employer associations, investors and investors associations, professional associations, or the government. However, the literature has not systematically studied how the nature of the issuer affects not only the code content, but also its enforceability. These different types of issuers have different objectives and as a result the codes they create will have distinct aims. Thus, recommendations on what are considered best practices regarding the behaviour of the board of directors are highly contingent on the issuer. However, once again, existing research has treated all codes as having similar underlying objectives, which a rigorous analysis by issuer may reveal as being a wrong assumption to hold. Additionally, the enforceability of the codes of good governance varies dramatically across issuers, speaking directly to the debate between the effectiveness of soft regulation *versus* hard legislation. The government and stock exchanges have the power to impose practices and penalties for non-compliance on all firms in the case of the former and publicly traded firms in the case of the latter. In contrast, investors and investor association only have the power to impose practices through activism in shareholder meetings, while other issuers director associations, professional associations, and employer associations have a limited ability to persuade firms to follow the recommendations of the codes. Although some studies touch upon the nature of the issuers, they do not analyse differences in the codes each type of issuer creates.

Third, the importance of transnational institutions in the creation and diffusion of codes of good governance has not been analysed properly. Transnational institutions like the World Bank and OECD have been actively promoting good governance, helping developing countries understand how to improve their corporate governance practices. However, studies on codes of good governance have focussed on the codes issued in each country rather than on codes issued by transnational institutions that have a wider applicability and speak to the important debate of global governance. These transnational issuers, by promoting a common set of practices regardless of country characteristics, may indirectly be contributing to the convergence of codes across national governance practices. In other words, they are not moving corporate governance toward a particular model (e.g., Anglo-Saxon or Continental), but toward a more general global governance model. This is a topic that has been rarely addressed in the academic literature of codes of good governance, despite its importance for understanding the drivers of the diffusion process.

Fourth, the recommendations contained in codes of good governance have evolved over time as some corporate governance problems are solved and others emerge, but there is limited research analysing how codes change over time. This evolution in the issues that codes tackle has been dealt with revisions of previous codes and with new codes that address new and different governance problems. Hence, there is need for a better understanding of how corporate governance problems co-evolve over time with best governance practices and how codes are developed to tackle these rapidly changing issues. This co-evolution in corporate governance issues and the content of codes highlights another source of differences across countries and the codes developed in each country. Countries with more sophisticated capital markets would require codes with more advanced recommendations, while countries with simpler capital markets are likely to require codes that tackle more basic issues. Hence, adopting the latest thinking in corporate governance in countries that have underdeveloped capital markets may not only be adequate but also counterproductive.

It is evident that the codes for good governance had grown over time. The developed and transitional countries are involved in developing the codes and also updating them. Codes of good governance are important in every corporate to meet their end results.

References

Aguilera, R.V. and A. Cuervo-Cazurra (2004). "Codes of Good Governance Worldwide: What's the Trigger?", *Organization Studies* 25: 417-46.

———. (2009). "Codes of Good Governance", *Corporate Governance: An International Review* 17(3): 376-87.

Aguilera, R.V. and G. Jackson (2003). "The Cross-national Diversity of Corporate Governance: Dimensions and Determinants", *Academy of Management Review* 28(3): 447-65.

Aguilera, R.V., I. Filatotchev, H. Gospel and G. Jackson (2008). "Contingencies, Complementarities, and Costs in Corporate Governance Models", *Organisation Science* 19(3): 475-92.

Alves, C. and V. Mendes (2004). "Corporate Governance Policy and Company Performance: The Portuguese Case", *Corporate Governance: An International Review* 12: 290-301.

Balgobin, R.N.S. (2008). "Global Governance Practice: The Impact of Measures Taken to Restore Trust in Corporate Governance Practice Internationally", *ICFAI Journal of Corporate Governance* 7: 7-21.

Bebenroth, R. (2005). "German Corporate Governance Code and Most Commonly Unaccepted Recommendations: Introduction and Some Explanation", *Corporate Ownership and Control* 3: 10-14.

Benkel, M., P. Mather and A. Ramsay (2006). "The Association between Corporate Governance and Earnings Management: The Role of Independent Directors", *Corporate Ownership and Control* 3: 65-75.

Bhagat, S. and B.S. Black (2002). "The Non-correlation between Board Independence and Long-term Firm Performance", *Journal of Corporation Law* 27: 1231-73.

Birkett, B.S. (1986). "The Recent History of Corporate Audit Committees", *Accounting Historians Journal* 13: 109-34.

Chizema, A. (2008). "Institutions and Voluntary Compliance: The Disclosure of Individual Executive Pay in Germany", 29 September.

Collier, P. (1996). "Audit Committees in UK Quoted Companies: A Curious Phenomenon?", *Accounting and Business History* 6: 121-40.

Collier, P. and M. Zaman (2005). "Convergence in European Corporate Governance: The Audit Committee Concept", *Corporate Governance: An International Review* 13: 753-68.

Conyon, M.J. and C. Mallin (1997). "A Review of Compliance with Cadbury", *Journal of General Management* 2: 24-37.

Coombes, P. and M. Watson (2001). "Corporate Reform in the Developing World", *The McKinsey Quarterly* 4: 89-92.

Cromme, G. (2005). "Corporate Governance in Germany and the German Corporate Governance Code", *Corporate Governance: An International Review* 13: 362-7.

Cuervo-Cazurra, A. (2002). "Corporate Governance Mechanisms: A Plea for Less Code of Good Governance and More Market Control", *Corporate Governance: An International Review* 10: 84.

———. (2008). "The Effectiveness of Laws Against Bribery Abroad", *Journal of International Business Studies* 39(4): 634-51.

Dahya, J., J.J. McConnell and N.G. Travios (2002). "The Cadbury Committee, Corporate Performance, and Top Management Turnover", *Journal of Finance:* 461-83.

Dalton, D.R., C.M. Daily, A.E. Elistrand and J.L. Johnson (1998). "Meta-analytic Reviews of Board Composition, Leadership Structure, and Financial Performance", *Strategic Management Journal* 19: 269.

Del Brio, E.B., E. Maia-Ramires and J. Perote (2006). "Corporate Governance Mechanisms and their Impact on Firm Value", *Corporate Ownership and Control* 4: 25-36.

Dewing, I.P. and P.O. Russell (2004). "Regulation of UK Corporate Governance: Lessons from Accounting, Audit, and Financial Services", *Corporate Governance: An International Review* 12: 107-15.

Enrione, A., C. Mazza and F. Zerboni (2006). "Institutionalizing Codes of Governance", *American Behavioral Scientist* 49: 961-73.

Fernandez-RodrIguez, E., S. Gómez-Anson and A. Cuervo-Garcia (2004). "The Stock Market Reaction to the Introduction of Best Practices Codes by Spanish Firms", *Corporate Governance: An International Review* 12: 29-46.

Gregory, H. and R. Simmelkjaer (2002). *Comparative Study of Corporate Governance Codes Relevant to the European Union and its Member States.* New York: Weil, Gotshal, and Manges LLP.

Gregory, H. J. (1998). "International Comparison of Board 'Best Practices': Investor Viewpoints".(*Mimeo*). Weil Goshtal and Manges LIP.

————. (1999). "Comparison of Board 'Best Practices' in Developing and Emerging Markets". (*Mimeo*). Weil Goshtal and Manges LLP.

Hall, P.A. and D. Soskice (2001). *Varieties of Capitalism: The Institutional Foundations of Comparative Advantage.* Oxford, UK: Oxford University Press.

Hermes, N., T.J.B.M. Postma and O. Zivkov (2007). "Corporate Governance Codes and their Contents: An Analysis of Eastern European Codes", *Journal for East European Management Studies* 12: 53-74.

Krambia-Kapardis, M. and J. Psaros (2006). "The Implementation of Corporate Governance Principles in an Emerging Economy: A Critique of the Situation in Cyprus", *Corporate Governance: An International Review* 14: 126-39.

Machuga, S. and K. Teitel (2007). "The Effects of the Mexican Corporate Governance Code on Quality of Earnings and its Components", *Journal of International Accounting Research* 6: 37-55.

Maassen, G.F., F.A.J. van den Bosch and H. Volberda (2004). "The Importance of Disclosure in Corporate Governance Self-regulation Across Europe: A Review of the Winter Report and the EU Action Plan", *International Journal of Disclosure and Governance* 1: 146- 59.

MacNeil, I. and X. Li (2006). "'Comply or Explain': Market Discipline and Non-compliance with the Combined Code", *Corporate Governance: An International Review* 14(5): 486-96.

Morgan, G., R. Whitley and E. Moen (eds.) (2005). *Changing Capitalisms? Internationalisation, Institutional Change, and Systems of Economic Organisation.* Oxford: Oxford University Press.

Mura, R. (2007). "Firm Performance: Do Non-executive Directors have Minds of their Own? Evidence from UK Panel Data", *Financial Management (2000)* 36: 81-112.

Nowak, E., R. Rott and G. Mahr (2004). "Rating Boersennotierter Unternehmen Auf Basis des Deutschen Corporate Governance Kodex-Eine Empirische Untersuchung zur Akzeptanz und Qualitaet Seiner Umsetzung in der Praxis", *Die Wirtschaftspruefung* 18: 998-1010.

Okike, E.N.M. (2007). "Corporate Governance in Nigeria: The Status Quo", *Corporate Governance: An International Review* 15: 173-93.

Park, Y.W. and H. Shin (2001). "Board Composition and Earnings Management in Canada", *Working Paper*. University of Lethbridge.

Pellens, B., F. Hillebrandt and B. Ulmer (2001). "Implementation of Corporate Governance Codes in German Practice: An Empirical Analysis of the DAX 100 Companies", *Betriebs-Berater* 56: 1243-50.

Reaz, M. and M. Hossain (2007). "Corporate Governance Around the World: An Investigation", *Journal of American Academy of Business* 11: 169-75. Cambridge.

Reid, A.S. (2003). "The Internationalisation of Corporate Governance Codes of Conduct", *Business Law Review* 24: 233-38.

Roberts, G.H. (2004). "Convergent Capitalisms? The Internationalisation of Financial Markets and the 2002 Russian Corporate Governance Code", *Europe-Asia Studies* 56: 1235-48.

Sargent, J. (1997). "Governance goes Global", *Global Finance* 11: 16.

Taylor, B. (2003). "Corporate Governance: The Crisis, Investors' Losses, and the Decline in Public Trust", *Corporate Governance* 11: 155-63.

Weir, C. and D. Laing (2000). "The Performance-governance Relationship: The Effects of Cadbury Compliance on UK Quoted Companies", *Journal of Management and Governance* 4: 265-81.

Werder, A., T. Talaulicar and G.L. Kolat (2005). "Compliance with the German Corporate Governance Code: An Empirical Analysis of the Compliance Statements by German Listed Companies", *Corporate Governance: An International Review* 13: 178-87.

Yoshikawa, T., L.S. Tsui-Auch and J. McGuire (2007). "Corporate Governance Reform as Institutional Innovation: The Case of Japan", *Organisation Science* 18: 973-88.

Zattoni, A. and F. Cuomo (2008). "Why Adopt Codes of Good Governance? A Comparison of Institutional and Efficiency Perspectives", *Corporate Governance: An International Review* 16: 1-15.

6 Corporate Governance

An International Perspective

This chapter presents the international perspectives in the area of corporate governance. The scope of this chapter has been restricted to studying corporate governance practices in China, France, Germany, UK and Italy.

6.1 China

Corporate governance in China has undergone significant change during the past three decades as the Chinese economy has liberalised and developed. Prior to the historic reforms initiated in 1978 the economy had been structured as a state-owned, centrally planned economy; practically all enterprises were government or commune-owned. Today, many companies are partially or wholly privately-owned, and that historic change has brought a enormous change in Chinese corporate governance, with securities policies well in place and governing boards well established.

The first significant changes in the company ownership came in the 1980s as small state-owned enterprises and collectively owned enterprises in rural areas began issuing shares to the public. As the reforms spread to the larger enterprises, the rapid increase in company-issued securities led the Chinese government to swiftly create a capital market from scratch. In 1990 it authorised the cities of Shanghai and Shenzhen to establish national stock exchanges.

The stock exchanges were tiny at the start: just 14 companies were listed at the outset, and in the early years state agencies and the listing companies kept some two-thirds of the shares out of the market. Company listing and trading volume rapidly increased in line with China's extraordinary economic growth, however, and the government created the China Securities Regulatory Commission (CSRC) in 1993 to provide regulatory oversight of the burgeoning listings and the fast-expanding capital market. China subsequently instituted the Company Law in 1994, which prohibited self-dealing by executives and directors and delegated merger approval shareholders, and the Securities Law of 1998, which strengthened the CSRC's supervision of the equity market and its power to penalise improper behaviour. China opened its equity market to foreign institutional investors in 2003, and in 2005 it initiated a programme to convert untraded state and company-held shares into tradable securities.

With China's market reforms and accelerating growth, the stock exchanges have come into their own over the past decade. By mid-2008 the Shenzhen Stock Exchange listed 540 companies with a total market value of RMB 1 trillion, and the Shanghai exchange listed 1,172 companies with a collective value of RMB 15 trillion. The combined 1,172 companies with a capitalisation of RMB 16 trillion (£1.3 trillion) remained modest by comparison with the New York Stock Exchange's 2,800 companies and £11.4 trillion ($20 trillion) capitalisation, and the London Stock Exchange's 3,000 companies and £3.5 trillion capitalisation. The Chinese exchanges were expanding rapidly, however, and the basic institutions of an activity traded public equity market had put in place.

In just two decades, China had created a capital market that measured up reasonably well by Western standards. Virtually, all 98 per cent of the state and company-held shares, for instance, had become tradable, eliminating the privileged ownership rights that had initially been reserved for state and company shareholders. The World Bank and the International Monetary Fund gave high marks to China's many reforms, and a study conducted in 2006 by Canada's Centre for International Governance Innovation (CIGI) concluded that China rated first among 10 Asian nations in adopting a set of governance principles put forward by the Organisation for the Economic Co-operation and Development (OECD). Much remained still to be done, however, with company compliance and public enforcement of the reforms far from complete. The same CIGI study rated China's actual governance practices ninth among 10 Asian countries.

6.1.1 Distinctive Features of Chinese Corporate Governance

Corporate governance practices in many countries have displayed some convergence towards Western standards in recent years (often emulating Britain's 1992 Cadbury Code and the United States's 2002

Sarbanes-Oxley Act), but countries generally retain a set of distinct practices. In building its own system, China has been no exception. Four distinctive features of Chinese corporate governance in the late 2000s are particularly notable: 1) highly concentrated ownership; 2) strong state ownership; 3) pyramid ownership structures; and 4) weak markets for corporate control.

Highly Concentrated Ownership

Company ownership is normally diffused in the United Kingdom, United States and other Western economies, with relatively few shareholders controlling more than a few per cent of the shares of any given firm. In contrast, ownership in China's listed firms is highly concentrated. Of the 1,602 companies listed on the Shanghai and Shenzhen stock exchanges in August 2008, the single largest owner held 36 per cent of an average company's shares, the top three owned 49 per cent and the biggest five controlled 52 per cent. The high degree of concentrated ownership has remained relatively to exercise more control over Chinese companies than is common among their Western counterparts.

Strong State Ownership

Despite a long-running process of privatisation of state-owned enterprises, government agencies have maintained a high level of ownership and thus strong influence over many of the country's publicly listed firms. State-owned or state-controlled enterprises were responsible for 31 per cent of China's GDP in 2007, but the Shanghai Stock Exchange reported that the government held 51 per cent of its listed shares. Government officials overseeing the state's ownership stakes are not immune to political considerations; members of the Communist Party are often appointed to company boards, and Chinese regulations require that publicly listed companies provide necessary support for the functioning of the Communist Party within their firms.

Pyramid Ownership Structures

Most major British and US publicly traded companies are owned and operated as stand-alone entities that work independently of one another to optimise investor returns. Many listed Chinese firms, by contrast are owned or controlled by an unlisted parent company, and many of the listed firms, by contrast are owned or contributed by an unlisted parent company, and many of the listed firms in turn control other listed companies. The resulting pyramid ownership structure has opened the way for the malfeasance of tunnelling, in which a controlling firm extracts resources from other firms in its pyramid whose minority owners would disapprove if the transfer came to light. A 2006 study by the Shanghai Stock Exchange revealed that such practices had become widespread: of the 1,377 firms studied, 35 per cent had misappropriated to their parent companies funds totalling RMB 48 billion. As a sign of the breadth of the problem, in 2006 China added pyramid misappropriation to its criminal code.

Weak Markets for Corporate Control

Because two-thirds of a typical firm's shares were held by the state and the companies themselves, and were untradeable before 2005, the market for corporate control in which companies and investors compete for control of other firms has been virtually non-existent. With formal movement of untraded shares on to the open market completed by 2007, active contests for control became more feasible. Yet even then, large blocks of a company's shares—often a third, half or even more—remained in the hands of public agencies. Unlike private investors, state organisations are concerned with a host of factors in addition to optimising shareholder value, and few of the newly 'tradable' shares were actually traded in any case. A CSRC Study in 2008 found that among the 10 largest market-cap companies on the exchanges, 8 of them had fewer than 10 per cent of their shares to active trading, and the other 2 had less than a third actively traded. As a result, mergers and acquisitions were achieved through negotiation, and most required state approval as well. A hostile takeover bid for a financially underperforming company—the most prominent weapon in the western arsenal for corporate control would rarely attract the shares required or win government approval. More entrenched management at poorly performing companies had been one result.

The Chinese Governing Board

As the Chinese public equity market matured, the organisation, composition and practices of boards of directors of some publicly listed companies in China came to acquire some features similar to those of Anglo-American firms. The personal computer maker Lenovo, for instance, brought several independent directors on to its boards after it acquired the IBM personal computer division in 2005. Chinese governing boards have nonetheless followed a distinctive path in the area of: 1) board structure, 2) shareholder rights, 3) disclosure and transparency, 4) corporate social responsibility, 5) the role of directors, and 6) executive compensation.

Board Structure

China has adopted a two-tier board structure similar to the German convention of having a supervisory board overseeing a board of directors. Chinese supervisory boards are required to have at least three members, and a third of the member must be employee representatives. In principle the supervisory board monitors the directors and the management, but in practice virtually all supervisory board members are from inside the firm, and the supervisory board largely rubber-stamps the decisions of directors and management.

The board of directors in the Anglo-American system sits at the hub of company governance, while in China the annual shareholders' meeting has emerged more to the front of the centre. Chinese Company Law endows the shareholders' meeting with power normally reserved for the board in the United Kingdom and United States. The board of directors in China, for instance, is required to 'develop and formulate' the company's annual budget and investment plan, but not approve the budget and plan, as is common in the Anglo-American world. Still, given that those attending the annual shareholders' meeting cannot effectively exercise discretionary authority in that venue, most of the real decision-making power remains in the hands of the directors and management.

Chinese regulations require a firm to designate one individual as 'legal person representative' to act on behalf of the firm. This position is normally assumed by the chairman of the board, and this rule has had the effect of investing greater power in the board chair than is common among British or American companies when the chair and CEO roles are separated.

Shareholder Rights

China's Company Law, revised in 2006, requires greater disclosure of information to stockholders than is common in the West. Shareholders elect directors and vote at shareholder meetings, but they also have access to company charters, shareholder lists and the minutes of meetings of both the supervisory boards and the board of directors.

To protect minority shareholders at companies where ownership is concentrated and pyramids prevail, companies are required to follow formal procedures for entering into related-party financial transactions. It is now mandatory for instance, that shareholders approve a company's transactions with a controlling company and the controlling company cannot vote its shares on such transactions. Minority shareholders have the right to introduce motions at, and to converge or even preside over, shareholders' meetings, and they can adopt a cumulative voting system for electing directors and supervisors.

Corporate Responsibility

China has placed formal emphasis on corporate social responsibility, more so than is common in many Western economies. The Company Law of 2006, for instance, has required that a company observe social norms and business ethics standards, operate honestly, accept monitoring by government and the general public, and assume its social responsibility.

The exchanges have gone even further, Shenzhen demands of its listed companies that in the process of maximising shareholders' value, they must also 'consider' the interests of their creditors, must not sacrifice creditors' interest for the sale of shareholder's value and must provide creditors with access to financial and operational data. Shenzhen companies must also 'commit themselves to social welfare services like environmental protection and community development in order to achieve social harmony'.

The Role of the Director

Prior to 2001, no law or regulation required that any directors be independent of management. China's CSRC now requires that a third of the seats on a publicly listed company board be held by independent directors, and many companies have reached that threshold. A 2004 study by the Shanghai Stock Exchange found that independent directors constitutes nearly a third of the board members, and on occasion have exercised a very independent role. In one widely publicised incident, for example, an independent director challenged related-party transaction by the board chair of a prominent food maker, and upon CSRC investigation the company ousted its chairman.

The 2006 Company Law strengthened the obligations of directors to include both 'duty of loyalty' and 'duty of care' though neither is defined very clearly. It did state that the loyalty obligations included forbidding the use of company funds for personal use, the making of loans to others without authorisation, the disclosure of proprietary information, self-dealing and bribes. It also held directors personally liable if director decisions violated state regulations or the company charter.

Executive Compensation

When compared to the West, the executive compensation has been substantially lower, though it has been substantially rising. According to the survey conducted by the Shanghai Stock Exchange the highest-paid executive of listed firms in 2003 was close to RMB 200,000 (£16,800), but just two years later the average had jumped to RMB 300,000 (£25,200). The highest-paid executive in 2005 received compensation of RMB 6 million (£500,000), but three years later the largest executive pay cheque had soared to RMB 66 million (£5.5 million). Not surprisingly, executive compensation in state-owned enterprises remained far below that in privately held corporations.

In spite, of the rapid rise of executive compensation, most pay remained fixed, rather than varying with performance. In many US and British listed firms the great majority of top executive compensation is variable, while in Chinese listed firms, according to a study in 2006, fully 97 per cent was still paid in the form of a fixed salary. Only a tenth of the firms used stock options at all. In 2006 the CSRC gave its blessing for more, though it declared that no more than 1 per cent of a company's shares can be used as options for the top executive, and no more than 10 per cent for all of the executives combined.

Chinese Governance

China has created one of the largest markets for publicly listed companies in the world. The total market capitalisation of the two Chinese stock exchanges ranked below only those of the United States, Japan, Europe and the United Kingdom in 2008, up from no market capitalisation at all less than three decades earlier.

China's regulatory regime has come to include everything from prohibitions against self-dealing and tunnelling to prescriptions for independent directors and contingent compensation. Though some features of Chinese corporate governance are akin to those found in most Western economies, several features remain distinctive, including highly concentrated ownership, much of it by the state, and a relatively weak market for corporate control. Likewise, though certain aspects of the governing boards of Chinese publicly traded companies are similar to those elsewhere, distinct features are evident here too, including less influential boards, weaker disclosure enforcement, greater social responsibility and less contingent compensation.

6.2 Germany

6.2.1 Corporate Governance in Germany

The Germany government realised the practical importance of better governance for Germany companies in the competitive international context, particularly after the Holzmann insolvency crisis in late 1999. In July 2000, the German chancellor convened the first official standards for German governance and to draft recommendations for future company law developments. In September 2001, a second Government commission was mandated to develop the official German Corporate Governance Code (GCGC). Its mission was to develop a code that would be broadly accepted and supported by all relevant interested groups. The members of commission were recruited from listed companies representing different industries, institutional and private investors, audit firms, academic experts on law and finance and union representatives. After five months of intensive work with a draft for public comment, the code was published in February 2002. The code is reviewed at least annually by the government commission, which acts as a standing commission.

The Underlying Corporate Governance Model

Considering the 'comply or explain' principle, as determined in the Stock Corporation Act (Article 161 of the AktG), German companies have to declare annually how they comply with the code and must explain any deviations from the code's 'shall recommendations'. The code comprises three layers of governance issues:

- The legal stipulations relating to key governance points;
- 'Shall recommendations', that do not comply with these recommendations have to say so in their annual report and on their website as well as explain the reasons for non-compliance;
- 'Should suggestions', which represent additional important elements of good governance. These 'suggestions' do not expressly require disclosure in case of non-compliance but it is a good-practice suggestion, and one that is increasingly followed.

Legal Framework

The key laws relating to corporate direction and control are as follows:

- Aktiengesetz (AktG) – the Stock Corporation Act;
- Bürgerliches Gesetzbuch (BGB) – the Civil Code;
- GmbH-Gesetz (GmbHG) – the Limited Liability Company Act;
- Handelsgesetzbuch (HGB) – the Commercial Code;
- Mitbestimmungsgesetz (SEAG) – the European Stock Corporation Act;
- Wertpapierhandelsgesetz (WpHG) – the Securities Trading Act;
- Wertpapiererwerbs- und Übernahmegesetz (WpÜG) – the Securities Acquisition and Takeover Act.

Board Structures and Roles

All German stock corporations have a two-tier board structure comprising a supervisory board and a management board.

The supervisory board appoints, supervises and advises the members of the management board and has to approve decisions of fundamental importance to the enterprise. The representatives of the shareholders are elected to the supervisory board by the general meeting. As specified by

The Co-determination Act, in companies with 500-2,000 employees one-third of members of the supervisory board must be employee representatives. In companies with more than 2,000 employees, the representatives elected by the shareholders and those of the employees must be equal in number, leading to supervisory boards with up to 20 members.

6.2.2 Supervisory Board of the German Corporate Governance Code

Key recommendations regarding the supervisory board in the German Corporate Governance Code (GCGC) are as follows:

- Essential requirements for supervisory board members are sufficient knowledge and industry experience (Article 5.4.1 GCGC).
- There is an age limit (Article 5.4.1 GCGC).
- They shall have sufficient independence (Article 5.4.2 GCGC).
- Election by the general meeting shall be on an individual basis (Article 5.4.3 GCGC).
- As a rule, a former CEO shall not become chairman of the supervisory board (Article 5.4.4 GCGC).
- Compensation must be appropriate (Article 5.4.6 GCGC).
- Efficient and regular cooperation between the management board and supervisory board shall take place (Article 3.4 GCGC).
- Resolution and review of an adequate management compensation system, including the main contract elements, shall take place. Appropriateness of management compensation shall be based on performance assessment (Article 4.2.2 and 4.2.3 GCGC).
- Conflicts of interest shall be dealt with properly (Article 5.5.2 and 5.5.3 GCGC).
- Committees shall be established (Article 5.3 GCGC), in particular,
  - The audit committee, which deals with issues relating to accounting, risk management and compliance, the necessary independence required of the auditor, the issuing of the audit mandate to the auditor, the determination of key audit points and fee agreement (Article 5.3.2 GCGC).

  − The nomination committee, which proposes qualified shareholder representatives to the supervisory board for its recommendation to the general meeting. It is composed exclusively of shareholder representatives (Article 5.3.3 GCGC).

- The efficiency of the supervisory board shall be evaluated regularly (Article 5.6 GCGC).

6.2.3 Structure and Role of the Management Board of German Corporate Governance Code

The management board is responsible for managing the business affairs of the enterprise. Management board of the large publicly listed companies is typically composed of three to eight members. In co-determined corporations with more than 2,000 employees the board must have a member responsible for all employee matters.

Key stipulations regarding the management board in the GCGC cover:

- Efficient and regular cooperation between management board and supervisory board.
- Individual disclosure of the remuneration of executives (including termination payments).
- Appropriateness of all compensation components, both individually and in total.
- A severance payment cap of two years' compensation in the case of a good leaver contract termination.
- Proper dealing with conflicts of interest.
- Proper dealing with third-party transactions.

6.2.4 Issues Relating to Shareholder Rights

There are two types of share in Germany; they are equity and preference shares:

- Ordinary shares with voting rights (the vast majority of all issued shares). Voting right restrictions for ordinary shares were legally banned in 1998. A one share, one vote therefore applies to all ordinary shares.

- Preferred shares without voting rights. In recent years the number of preferred shares with no voting power has declined substantially. Many of the outstanding preferred shares have been phased out since then. Important and relevant examples that remain include BMW, Metro and Volkswagen.

Current Issues Concerning Shareholder Rights

The lack of necessary shareholder consent for substantial takeovers or similar significant strategic moves remains a governance issue for Germany. A recent example: in a takeover of a major pharmaceutical company the acquiring company paid two-thirds of its own market capitalisation for a major strategic diversification without the consent of its shareholders.

The federal legislature in Germany has recently passed the Risk Limitation Act (2008). According to the new law, cooperation among shareholders constitutes acting in concert if only 'the shareholders enter binding agreements on exercise of voting rights or cooperate in other ways to influence a company's strategic orientation in a permanent and significant manner'. The interpretation of the later point is left to the jurisdiction. Issues that do not constitute acting in concert are:

- Agreements on single general meeting (GM) issues;
- Continuing cooperation on the same non-strategic issues over several GMs;
- Parallel, coordinated acquisition of shareholdings without further objectives concerning the issuer or target company;
- Standstill agreements, reciprocal rights of first refusal and options;
- Acting in concert to preserve the issuer's status quo.

Applicable disclosure rules are as follows:

- After reaching or passing the threshold of 10 per cent, detailed disclosures is obligatory within 20 trading days on the source of funds for the share purchases and the objectives of these purchases. (However, shareholders who reach or cross 10 per cent are not obliged to reveal whether they aim to gain control over the issuer.)
- Any change in the then stated objectives has to be disclosed within 20 trading days.

- Companies are allowed to waive (opt out of) these obligations by a change of their corporate statutes (with consent from GM).

- Such disclosures as well as failures to report are to be fully published by the issuer.

- Disclosure is also mandatory on voting rights emanating from financial instruments if they reach or cross a threshold of 5 per cent.

- The sanctions for violations of disclosure obligations have a six-month suspension of voting rights (but this applies to only international violations).

- All new disclosure obligations will only apply to future cases of acting in concert, or of crossing thresholds. The obligation to disclose holdings of financial instruments (derivatives etc.) was applicable from March 2009 onwards.

Disclosure and Transparency

Key governance-related stipulations are as follows:

- Companies shall annually publish a corporate governance report.
- All shareholders shall be informed equally (fair disclosure).
- Regular investor and stakeholder meetings to be held.
- Companies shall publish regularly a detailed analysis of deviations from major previously published performance and strategy targets.
- Companies that disclose information outside Germany must also disclose this information within the country.
- Actual shareholdings (including options and derivatives) by management and supervisory board members and any changes thereto shall be published without delay on individual basis and separately in the annual report or corporate governance report.

6.2.5 Governance-related Stipulations for Financial and Business Reporting and Accounting Practices

- Reports are to be prepared according to International Standards on Auditing (IAS).
- Special accounting standards and measures must always be made transparent.

- Consolidated financial statements are to contain information on stock option programmes and similar incentive systems, as well as information on their valuation and accounting treatment.

- Sufficient independence is to be an important criterion in the selection of auditors.

- The supervisory board must set an appropriate level for the auditing fee.

- Companies' business reporting is to be on non-financial key performance indicators.

6.2.6 Responsibility

Social responsibility issues have gained considerable momentum in the capital market. However, there is a strong need to find a uniform basis of application and for measurement through key performance indicators. Such key performance indicators should provide information about management systems, corporate governance, long-term viability, potential reputational risks and liability issues.

6.2.7 Current Governance Issues Relating to Non-Executive Directors

Some important supervisory board quality issues are as follows:

- Insufficient independence on the part of directors, including in committees;

- The impact of co-determination;

- The lack of diversity, such as international and gender representation;

- Too many past CEOs have become supervisory board chairmen.

Insufficient Independence

Independent non-executive directors comprise only 28 per cent of the German company boards compared to the European average of 54 per cent. Just 27 per cent of major companies have an independent chairman. The proportion of independent members of audit and remuneration committees in Germany is only 26 per cent and 23 per cent respectively. However, the eight EU Directives (auditor directive), implemented in 2008, could lead to a change of this proportion since it requires the audit committee to have an independent chairman. Improvement in board independence could also come from the recent recommendations of the German Government Code for a 'nomination committee' solely composed of shareholder representatives.

Co-Determination: The Special German Problem

The conceptually good solution of 'checks and balances' between the executive and the supervision of the German 'two-tier board' system is seriously affected by the German co-determination issues on board size, independence and international composition. With 20 board members for large companies, it is difficult to hold an engaging and serious discussion of complex issues. The employee representatives are by nature dependent.

Insufficient International Representation

Only 7 per cent of German supervisory boards are international board members compared to 31 per cent in the United Kingdom and 45 per cent in Switzerland. Given that the big German companies generate a major part of their income internationally, efforts to increase the international representation on the board do appear necessary. Again, this could change with increased usage of the European Company.

CEO Succession to Supervisory Board Chairman

A practice still prevalent in large German companies is the practice of former CEOs to become supervisory board chairman: at present, more than half of the chairmen of the supervisory boards of the 30 DAX (Deutsche Aktien Index 30) companies are former members of the management board (mostly former CEO). Conceptually, this requires that a CEO has the ability to change from a dynamic CEO to a balancing and controlling non-executive chairman with a truly independent mind. A good solution could be to make a previously successful CEO a normal supervisory board member without too much influence over decisions relating to his or her tenures as CEO.

6.2.8 Executive Pay and Performance

According to the German Corporate Code, appropriate compensation structures should take into account the following essential issues in order to avoid 'pay for failure':

- Compensation shall be linked to long-term profitability and to individual success.

- Share-based compensation shall depend on the longer-term share price and profit development, and be a substantial part of the compensation package.

- An appropriate length for employment contracts should also be established: a five-year term, still the norm in Germany, carries the risk of excessive pay-offs in the case of early termination. The German Code has included since June 2008 a 'shall recommendation' for a cap of two years (with an additional 50 per cent addition in 'change of control' cases).

- Recently the German Government Commission on Corporate Governance emphasised the appropriateness and long-term performance requirements. Executive compensation shall be linked to a manager's and company's long-term performance as well as external parameters such as the results of the company's peer group. A bonus/malus system shall be implemented and executives should be obliged to invest their own money as a precondition for participating in share based incentive schemes.

6.3 Australia

6.3.1 The Development of Corporate Governance in Australia

Australia is known for its significant growth and development among the OECD nations. It has mature corporate governance and regulatory institutions. The country also bears the legacy of colonial past, the origins of the industry in the vast resources of the country, and the dependence created by being relatively small country in terms of population and market capitalisation with high proportion of overseas ownership of Australian assets.

Australian corporate governance follows Anglo-American traditions, as a result of Australia's close economic relations with the United Kingdom and United States. However, the model of dispersed ownership is less applicable to Australia, where there is a higher proportion of concentrated holdings, whether due to foreign ownership or entrenched family ownership. Historically, Australian market cycles and corporate governance enjoyed an El Dorado aspect (Sykes, 1996); however, standards of market regulation and corporate governance have risen considerably.

6.3.2 Australian Laws, Codes and Models

Much of the Australian law originated from Great Britain during colonial times, but after independence and the establishment of the Constitution in 1901, Australian law-making followed its own peculiar path, because of the unique division of powers between federal and state governments. It was only very recently, in 2001, that the states reluctantly agreed to give up most of their powers in order to permit the creation of a national system of legislation set out in the Corporations Act, 2001.

Henry Bosch (who, like Adrian Cadbury in the United Kingdom, produced one of the first reports on corporate governance in Australia) commented, 'Before the crash of 1987 the term corporate was rarely used in Australia and few people gave much thought to concepts now covered by it' (2002: 273). As this suggests, reforming the Australian corporate law was a response to unethical behaviour and fear of economic downturn after several corporate scandals in the 1980s and 1990s. The hotch-potch of regulators at state level, all with different priorities and inadequate resources, was thought to have given free rein to Australia's corporate cowboys (Clarke, 2007: 146).

Corporations Act of 2001 created the Australian Securities & Investments Commission (ASIC), which is empowered to enforce both the Corporations Act 2001 and the Listing Rules of Australian Stock Exchange (ASX). Also, in recognition of the need for dynamic legislation, the Corporate Law Economic Reform Program (Audit Reform and Corporate Disclosure) or CLERP was commenced, involving regular policy reviews and legislative amendments to the Corporations Act 2001.

Corporate governance, both in practice and in theory, comprises more than just legal regulation. The first set of Australian corporate governance standards were developed by a working group made up of leading business organisations. After corporate collapses of 1980s it became difficult for companies to raise capital and it was the British Council, the Australian Institute of Company Directors (AICD), the ASX and professional accounting bodies that got together and published the document *Corporate Practices and Conduct* in 1991 (Bosch, 2002: 274). Commonly known as the Bosch Report, this document was revised and updated in 1993 following publication of the United Kingdom's Cadbury Report on the Financial Aspects of Corporate Governance in 1992 and again in 1995.

The ASX's *Corporate Governance Principles and Recommendations* (ASX Corporate Governance Council, 2007) is the guiding light of governance standards. This is a revised edition of the *Principles of Good Corporate Governance and Best Practice Recommendations*, launched in March 2003. The ASX principles were drafted by the ASX Corporate Governance Council (CGC), a body made up of representatives from 21 business organisations promoting the interests of a wide range of groups such as shareholders, directors, accountants and superannuation funds. The CGC reports to the ASX, which is a commercial entity licensed under the Corporation Act as a market operator. The ASX principles provide an extensive framework for good corporate governance by setting out eight broad principles together with more detailed recommendations for putting them into effect. They cover topics such as board composition, director independence, financial reporting, ethics, market disclosure, communication with shareholders, risk management and fair remuneration.

It is important to understand the regulatory context of the ASX principles. First, they apply only to ASX listed companies; and second, they do not have direct legal effect. The legal force behind them comes primarily from the ASX Listing Rules. Listing rule 4.10.3 requires companies to disclose the extent to which they have adopted the ASX principles and to explain any decision not to adopt particular recommendations. The adoption of the 'comply or explain' principle means that it is not necessary for all listed companies to apply all of the ASX principles. It is possible to comply fully by giving an explanation of why each recommendation has not been followed. (The only exception to this is in relation to audit committees, where an ASX listing rule requires mandatory compliance for larger companies).

Therefore, in general the ASX principles do not uniformly mandate or prescribe good governance and they do not restrictively prescribe which practices amount to good governance. By forcing disclosure, the system allows investors to decide how much importance to place on a company's governance practices. The impetus is on the companies—to either follow the ASX principles or explain why they have taken an alternative approach. In a strict legal sense, adoption of the ASX principles is entirely voluntary. The pressure to demonstrate that a company has good governance comes not from legal sanctions but from market forces. In principle it is possible to comply by giving an explanation of why an ASX recommendation has not been followed, and the market can decide whether this is an acceptable explanation or not. Yet there is considerable evidence that the benchmarking surveys of corporate governance conducted compliance reducing some of the flexibility that was intended for companies to develop models of corporate governance appropriate to their needs.

Australian law proposed various changes to the Corporations Act, 2001, focussing upon governance in the ninth policy paper in the legal reform programme (CLERP 9). Like the corporate governance developments of the early 1990s, these changes followed a period of international corporate disasters in 2001-02. The impact of the spectacular downfall of US companies such as Enron and WorldCom was heightened by the collapse of local Australian companies such as HIH Insurance and One. Tel Ltd. from similar causes.

CLERP 9 made amendments to the Corporations Act in four key areas: executive remuneration, financial reporting, continuous disclosure and shareholder participation. Therefore, the ASX principles and CLERP 9 are designed to increase the amount of information provided by companies to their investors and the public at large. The CLERP 9 provisions do not permit explanations of non-compliance but generally do not prescribe in detail how companies must arrange their internal affairs. The Australian approach overall is one of flexible regulation designed to leave much of the enforcement to the market. This follows the United Kingdom's Combined

Code approach rather than the more prescriptive nature of the Sarbanes-Oxley Act in the United States.

6.3.3 Board Structure and Roles

The board of an Australian listed company typically consists of six to eight directors of whom one or two would be executives and the rest non-executives. Increasingly, the non-executive directors meet the exacting ASX principles' definition of an independent director, although there has been some skepticism about the value of such independence. It is now unusual to find a CEO who also acts as chairman of the board. Nearly all listed companies will have an audit committee and most will also have a nomination and remuneration committee as recommended by the ASX principles.

Ownership structure tends to be more concentrated in Australia than in the United Kingdom or United States, with many companies having one or two influential shareholders owning a large proportion of shares. In 1999 only 11 of the 20 largest publicly quoted companies were widely held (Clarke, 2007: 144).

Nearly all listed companies now have a board charter in accordance with the ASX principles, which defines and separates the roles of board and management. The role of advisers, particularly accountants, has also been more carefully defined in recent years. CLERP 9 requires formal statements from directors regarding the integrity of the accounts, as well as disclosure of certain information related to auditor independence. Instead of prohibiting appointment of the auditor for consulting services, it requires disclosures of the amounts paid for such services and an explanation of why this does not compromise auditor independence.

Shareholder Rights

Under the Corporations Act 2001 the most significant rights of shareholders are: 1) the right to information and accounts; 2) the right to vote; 3) the right to requisition general meetings and propose resolutions; and 4) the right to appoint and remove directors (Farrar, 2005: 166).

A comply or explain system of corporate governance regulation relies on the market as arbiter of corporate behaviour, not the legislator. It is therefore vital that shareholders assess and act upon the information disclosed. Historically, however shareholder activism in Australia has not been strong. For this reason, CLERP 9 introduced various provisions aimed at encouraging shareholder participation in corporate governance. For example, annual general meeting (AGM) notices must be clear and concise, and the auditor must be available at the AGM to answer questions. However, it seems likely that technical advances such as the internet are likely to be most effective in promoting activism. Information is readily available on company websites, and some companies are now producing webcasts of their AGM and e-mail updates of ASX announcements.

Disclosure and Transparency

Australia has a continuous disclosure regime that requires prompt disclosure of price-sensitive information. The test is whether a reasonable person would expect the information to have a 'material effect' on the value of the securities of the entity. CLERP 9 strengthened this regime in two ways: 1) by imposing personal liability on individuals responsible for a failure to disclose; and 2) by giving ASIC the power to issue infringement notices.

The enforcement powers were deemed necessary to improve compliance with the continuous disclosure regime. They demonstrate a more traditional, legal approach to regulation through deterrence and sanctions for breach. If ASIC has a reasonable ground for believing that a disclosing entity has contravened the continuance of disclosure provisions (supported by prior investigation), it can issue a notice requiring payment of a penalty of up to A $100,000. Companies can choose to comply, request withdrawal of the notice or not comply. If they do not comply, ASIC can commence civil proceedings. The provisions aim to provide a method of enforcing minor breaches where costly court action would not be warranted at first instance.

Corporate Social Responsibility (CSR)

In Australia, there have been two inquiries into the issue of CSR. In March 2005, the Parliamentary Secretary to the Treasurer requested advice from the Corporations and Markets Advisory Committee (CAMAC) on 'the extent to which the duties of directors under the Corporations Act 2001 should include corporate social responsibility'. CAMAC released a discussion paper in November 2005 and then a final report in December 2006. In addition, in June 2005 Parliamentary Joint Committee on Corporations and Financial Services (PJC) initiated an inquiry into corporate responsibility. Its purpose was to examine 'the extent to which organisational decision-makers should have regard for the interest of the stakeholders other than shareholders, and the broader community'. Like the CAMAC inquiry, this involved an examination of the directors' duties and reporting requirements as well as broader policy issues. The PJC issued its final report in June 2006. Neither report recommended any change to the law. Thus, there is still no explicit legal requirement for directors to include social or environmental concerns in their general decision-making, nor is there any requirement to report on these issues. Nevertheless, both inquiry reports encouraged voluntary corporate reporting and suggested that there may be an implied duty on directors to take these factors into account on the basis that doing so is likely to be in the long-term interests of the company and its shareholders. The second edition of the ASX principles declined to recommend specific reporting on CSR. This leaves Australia some way behind the United Kingdom, the rest of Europe and Japan in corporate reporting.

Directors

The basic duties of Australian company directors are to act in good faith in the best interests of the company and for a proper purpose. These exist as fiduciary duties under the common law as well as being codified in Sections 180 and 181 of the Corporations Act, 2001. There is relatively little case law expanding on the detailed meaning of these duties, although it is generally understood that 'the interests of the company' equate to the interests of its shareholders as a general group rather than the company as a firm (Farrar, 2005: 109). This principle of 'shareholder primacy' has been much debated in recent years in the context of whether companies and their directors should be more widely accountable, not only to shareholders but to local communities and the environment. Certainly the job of the director has been said to have become more onerous in recent years. There is much more focus on the role of the board, the skills and experience of its directors as well as their independence or otherwise. The ASX principles recommend that companies have processes for evaluating the performance of their directors, and annual board evaluations are becoming more commonplace.

Executive Pay and Performance

CLERP 9 requires companies to include within their annual directors' report a remuneration report setting out details of executive and director remuneration. When the amendments were introduced, the Regulatory Impact Statement explained that the legislation 'does not seek to intervene in the market by pricing limits on the quantum of directors or executive remuneration'. Rather, it is aimed at ensuring transparency such that shareholders can make informed decisions about the remuneration policies of companies. Again shareholder activism on the issue in Australia is some way behind that in the United Kingdom. For example, at the 2008 AGM of Telstra, there was a majority shareholder vote against the remuneration report, which the Telstra board determined not to act upon.

The 2008 Financial Crisis

Australia has weathered out the global financial turmoil originating in the subprime mortgage crisis on the Wall Street better than most industrial countries. However, there have been still many casualties. Highly leveraged property trusts and financial companies witnessed their business models implode as asset prices fell, liquidity dried up and excessive debt levers were exposed. Not only were the companies highly leveraged, but executives and directors had often taken out large margin loans to fund share purchases, and as these margin loans were called in, company share prices hurtled into a spiral of decline, often hastened by predatory short-selling. Protracted and painful deleveraging caused the failure of a string of companies including MFS Ltd., Centro Properties Group, Allco Finance Group and Tricom, and severely damaged other companies including Babcock & Brown, Macquarie Bank and ABC Learning.

Conclusions

The IMF endorsed the high quality of regulation and corporate governance in Australia. A qualitative survey confirmed the view that Australian company boards across the ASX listed sector from ASX 100 to smaller companies have responded well to the challenge of reforming corporate governance policy and practice (UTS CCG, 2007). Yet an annual survey of adherence to governance standards completed by BDO Kendalls (2007) highlighted the lax standard of governance widespread in the burgeoning small-cap resources sector in Australia. This is a traditional problem of small resources companies being established in highly speculative industries, which have focussed on their operational and capital raising rather than their governance practices. It shows that even in well-regulated economies with high standards of corporate governance, problems can still occur.

6.4 New Zealand

6.4.1 Legal Framework: Laws, Models and Codes

The corporate governance legal framework in New Zealand is based upon common law, statutory laws and regulations and governance codes. Of central importance is the Companies Act 1993, along with a number of other acts such as the Securities Act 1978, the Securities Amendment Act 1988, the Financial Reporting Act 1993 and the Takeovers Act 1993. A board has responsibility for ensuring compliance with all legislation. In addition, directors may be personally liable for breaches by their companies.

Specific legislative requirements affect each organisation, industry or sector, such as the Dangerous Goods Act 1974 or the Machinery Act 1950, as well as more general legislative requirements such as the Commerce Act 1986, the Fair Trading Act 1986, the Contracts Enforcement Act 1956, the Insolvency Act 2006, the Consumer Guarantees Act 1993, the Privacy Act 1993, health and safety requirements, building codes, environmental legislation and so on.

Regulators and Supervisors

The Commerce Commission: The Commerce Commission enforces legislation that promotes competition in New Zealand markets and prohibits misleading and deceptive conduct by traders. It also enforces a number of pieces of legislation specific to the telecommunication, dairy and electricity.

The Securities Commission: The Securities Markets Act 1988 regulates activities on the securities markets, including registration of stock exchanges, regulation of insider trading, market manipulation, disclosure by listed companies and their directors, disclosure of changes to substantial securities holdings and dealings in futures contracts.

The Takeovers Panel: Established as a body corporate under the Takeovers Act 1993, the Takeovers Panel is responsible for both the operation of the Takeovers Code 2000 and promotion of public awareness of issues relating to takeovers. The code ensures that takeovers proceed in an orderly fashion. It establishes standards of proper disclosure and requires equal treatment of all shareholders.

6.4.2 New Zealand Stock Exchange (NZX)

NZX's functions include supervising listed issuers' compliance with Listing Rules, supervising market participants such as NZX firms and NZX advisers, and assisting the Securities Commission as a co-regulator as required under the Securities Markets Act 1988.

NZX is the only registered securities exchange in New Zealand. Conduct rules govern the relationship between registered exchange and entities and the rules that govern the conduct of business on the market, and persons who are authorised by the exchange to conduct trading activity. The Act also includes provisions relating to the imposition of a control limit (which is the highest percentage of voting rights in the body corporate that may be held or controlled by any person) on a registered exchange. NZX also has a 10 per cent control limit, which the board has included in NZX's constitution.

As a registered exchange, NZX also assumes a number of reporting obligations to the Securities Commission, which has monitoring powers conferred by the Securities Markets Act 1988. Under the act, NZX must:

- Notify the Securities Commission where it takes any disciplinary action for breach of its rules;
- Notify the Securities Commission where it knows or suspects that a person has committed, is committing or is likely to commit a significant contravention of NZX's conduct rules or certain laws;

- Pass on any material information disclosed to it under its Listing Rules to the Securities Commission; and

- Provide information, assistance and access to the Securities Commission or Takeovers Panel where such information, assistance and access is required to assist those bodies discharge their functions.

The act also confers on the Commission the power to give directions to NZX to suspend trading in a listed issuer's securities or a class of securities in certain limited circumstances. In recognition of the importance afforded to the continuous disclosure provisions in NZX's Listing Rules, NZX must consider any submissions that the Commission may make in considering Listing Rules. A memorandum of understanding (MoU) with the Securities Commission states that the shared goal of NZX and the Securities Commission is to ensure the optimum regulation of New Zealand's securities markets as fair, efficient, deep, well-informed and internationally competitive markets and to facilitate appropriate levels and quality disclosure. The MoU recognises NZX's role as the frontline regulator of its securities markets and details how NZX and the Commission will work together in overlapping areas of responsibilities.

6.4.3 Listing Criteria of Floatation

The New Zealand Stock Exchange (NZX) runs and regulates two equity markets:

- The NZX's stock market main board (NZSX);
- The NZX's alternative market (NZAX).

There is a diverse range of companies listed on the NZSX market, but majority of listed companies are large New Zealand enterprises and established businesses with solid track records of positive cash flow and earnings. Such companies generally have:

- Existing boards and governance procedures in place, independent directors and an audit committee;
- A history of audited accounts;
- Securities held by at least 500 members of the public holding with at least 25 per cent of the securities;

- Market capitalisation greater than NZ $5 million (NZX has discretion to refuse to consider an applicant for listing on the NZSX market if its capitalisation is below this level).

New Zealand Securities Act requirements apply in full to NZSX listing, including the requirement for a detailed prospectus and investment statement. There is also a diverse range of companies listed on the NZAX Market, but the majority are small to medium-sized businesses.

6.5 The United Kingdom

The United Kingdom always encouraged free trade, innovation and wealth creation. Historically, the country embraced a *laissezfaire* approach to business regulation—one based on principles rather than legislative rules. This approach encourages business practice instead of stifling it through detailed regulations, thus reducing compliance costs for UK and global businesses. As a result, the United Kingdom is consistently ahead of other countries in terms of corporate governance standards, while having lower compliance costs than countries with a more legislative approach (notably the United States). Justifiably, London remains the world's largest and most diverse international marketplace.

Although there is a strong basis of company legislation and regulation, at the heart of the United Kingdom's approach to corporate governance is self-regulation backed by codes and guidelines. Good corporate governance is seen as essential to the effective operation of a free market. It has become shorthand for the way an organisation is run, with particular emphasis on its accountability, integrity and risk management. The stronger its presence in daily business practices, the less the need for the government to intervene and legislate for the corporate sector.

The key aspects of corporate governance in the United Kingdom are based around the Combined Code on Corporate Governance, operating under the motto 'comply or explain'. In short, it promotes a unitary (or single) board with a collective responsibility for the company's success. It advocates the separation of the roles of chief executive and chairman and the importance of a balance between executive and independent non-executive directors; it recommends independent and transparent audit, remuneration and nomination committees and an annual evaluation by the board of its performance. Finally, it promotes effective rights for shareholders.

The 'comply or explain' regime allows companies to apply governance practices in a way that suits their particular circumstances, which can vary enormously from company to company depending on their size, ownership structure and the complexity of the business model.

6.5.1 Corporate Structure and Ownership

A company is a separate legal entity from those who manage it and those who have put up the capital. The key parties are the shareholders, the creditors and the directors. The directors must act in the best interests of the company at all times and not represent any special group of shareholders.

The United Kingdom has a plethora of company structures, including:

- companies limited by shares:
    - private companies;
    - public limited companies (plc);
- companies limited by guarantee;
- unlimited companies.

There are over 2.7 million active companies in the United Kingdom. Of these, 11,209 are public limited companies and some 2,100 are listed on the London Stock Exchange (LSE). This includes around 1,174 companies listed on the Alternative Investment Market (AIM), which is intended for new companies not eligible for the Official List. Given the numbers of registered companies, it is no surprise that a large majority of them are very small businesses. Their corporate structures are and will remain very different from those of the listed company (Burmajster, 2009).

The governance requirements should be tailor-made as per the company's size and structure. For each type of the company there are different governance requirements, with more stringent requirements for public limited companies. While the major principles of good corporate governance are of relevance to all companies, it would be a mistake to believe that every aspect of the detail of what is promulgated for large listed companies is relevant across the corporate spectrum. To achieve acceptance and, eventually, enthusiasm for corporate governance, the principles must be relevant to the size, structure and nature of the business entity.

Ownership patterns have changed radically over the past few decades. Direct shareholder involvement in the management of larger companies has diminished to a point where there is almost entire separation of the two. According to the National Statistics 2006 *Share Ownership Survey*, whereas 54 per cent of shares were owned by individuals in 1963, the figure had fallen to 12.8 per cent by the end of 2006. Overseas ownership has grown over the same period from 7 per cent to 40 per cent. This increase partly reflects international mergers where new companies are listed in the United Kingdom, flotation of UK subsidiaries of foreign companies, in which the parent has retained a significant stake, and companies moving their domicile to the United Kingdom.

Alongside this, the growing importance of share ownership in the hands of institutional investors has had a very real effect. Institutional shareholders accounted for 41.1 per cent of UK ordinary shares as of 31 December 2006, with a combined value of £762.8 billion. Of these, the largest holders were insurance companies (£272.8 billion) and pension funds (£235.8 billion). In recent times, institutional investors have increasingly turned to using their votes at annual general meetings. There are a number of reasons for this; one factor is probably the current state of the stock market, where many investors are holding stocks at a very large loss. Increasingly, it is seen as a role of corporate governance to attempt to align the interests of shareholders and boards. That said, it is noticeable that the average duration of institutional holding in the United Kingdom is no longer than two years. Companies find it hard to regard this as shareholders taking a long-term interest in the company (Burmajster, 2009).

6.5.2 Legal Framework

Two main areas are fundamental to the relationship between the director, the company, the shareholders and others: (i) the duty of care and skill, and (ii) the director's fiduciary duties. For over 250 years these two areas were governed by a common law system, which is the foundation of the legal framework of the United Kingdom.

The legal provisions relating to companies and their governance derive from a number of sources:

- statute and subsidiary legislation;
- directly applicable European Union law;
- regulation including accounting standards; Listing Rules applicable to quoted companies;
- takeover rules;
- specific legislation applying to companies operating in specific sectors (e.g. banking and insurance);
- decisions of the courts;
- extra-legislative codes.

The current basis of company legislation is the Companies Act 1985, the Companies Act 1989, the Companies Act 2006, the Company Directors Disqualification Act 1986, the Insolvency Act 1986, the Financial Services Act 1986, the Financial Services and Markets Act 2000 and the Corporate Manslaughter and Corporate Homicide Act 2007.

Company Law

European Union (EU) law has been the main source of amendment to UK company law since accession in 1973 and is expected to continue to be a significant factor. Because the EU Directives address specific subject areas and each has to be incorporated into the national law, there was, for a long period, no time for overall review and reform of company law to shape or even reflect modern corporate reality.

In 1997 the Company Law Review Steering Group was set up under the instructions of the Secretary of State for Trade and Industry with four key objectives:

- to enhance shareholder engagement and a long-term investment culture;
- to ensure better regulation and a 'think small first' approach;
- to make it easier to set up and run a company;
- to provide flexibility for the future.

After extensive consultation and investigations, the Steering Group issued its final report in 2001. In 2002 the government published a White Paper, 'Modernizing Company Law', suggesting some radical changes to the governance of UK companies. In 2005 there was a second White Paper, which included drafting for a number of provisions. The Company Law Reform Bill was introduced into the House of Lords later that year and finally received royal assent in November 2006.

The Companies Act 2006 is reputedly the longest piece of legislation ever to have been passed by the Westminster Parliament, or indeed any parliament anywhere in the world. However, it is better drafted and better organised than its predecessors. Its main provisions are as follows:

- The premise is that, unlike previously, the legislation was drafted from the viewpoint of the smallest companies, with additional requirements for larger companies. The new approach recognises the realities of the structure of companies.

- Probably the most radical changes are in the area of directors' duties. In the United Kingdom the law on directors' duties (both the duty of care and fiduciary duties) had previously been entirely based on common law. Now, for the first time in UK's legal history, many of these duties are codified. While there are no new duties or responsibilities as such, the act confirms and replaces in a single statement what has previously evolved in case law. The fundamentals of the current common law duties are retained; hence, the unitary board is recognised, with all directors being subject to the same general duties. Equally, the shareholder model is retained (that is, directors must act in a way that promotes the success of the company for the benefit of the members as a whole). In doing so, they need to have regard as necessary to long-term factors, the interests of other stakeholders such as employees, the community and the company's reputation.

- There will no longer be a statutory requirement for private companies to hold annual general meetings (AGMs). However, businesses can still hold AGMs if they wish.

- Shareholder meetings for private companies can now all be on a 14-day notice period, unless the company's articles specify different arrangements.

- Decisions by written resolution of a company's shareholders will be much easier to make. Written resolutions now need a signature from a majority of shareholders, not all of them, and special resolutions need a majority of 75 per cent.

- There will be a clearer way for shareholders to make a derivative claim to sue directors on behalf of the company—for instance, for fraud.

- Unless a company files small company accounts, its Directors' Report must contain a Business Review in its accounts.

Many of these changes do not apply to limited liability partnerships.

Competition Law

Companies can face civil penalties of up to 10 per cent of global turnover if they infringe Competition Law. Since 2003 it has also been possible for directors in the United Kingdom to be held personally liable for serious breaches of EU and UK Competition Law.

An individual who participates in a cartel can be found guilty of a criminal offence, and a director of a company that commits any breach of Competition Law can also be disqualified from acting as a director for up to 15 years.

Disqualification

A defaulting director not only may expect personal or criminal liabilities as a consequence of a breach of duty but also may receive a court order disqualifying him or her from acting as a director for up to 15 years. A person can be disqualified from acting as a director on a number of grounds, including persistent breach of company law legislation and conviction for fraud under the Company Directors Disqualification Act 1986.

The European Union

The European Union (EU) also significantly influences corporate governance in the United Kingdom. The European Union is very active in company law, and in 2001 appointed a High Level Group of Company Law Experts to make recommendations for a modern regulatory framework for company law in the European Union. Among the topics considered was corporate governance. In 2002 this Group published its final report (the Experts' Report) and in 2003 the EU Commission issued a communication to the EU Council and the European Parliament, Modernizing Company Law and Enhancing Corporate Governance in the European Union: A Plan to Move Forward (the Corporate Governance and Company Law Action Plan), proposing a mix of legislative and regulatory measures that will affect all member states.

Among the various EU member states there have been some 40 corporate governance codes over the past decade (with the United Kingdom acting as pioneer in this respect). A European Union-wide corporate governance code was not proposed; however, the report stated that 'some specific rules and principles need to be agreed at EU level'. The Plan targets for a legislative approach:

- disclosure requirements;
- exercise of voting rights;
- cross-border voting;
- enhanced disclosure by institutional investors;
- enhancing the responsibilities of board members.

Alongside the Company Law Action Plan (CLAP) sits the Financial Services Action Plan (FSAP). A number of measures with corporate governance implications fall within its remit. These include the draft Transparency Directive, which, among other provisions on disclosure requirements, introduces quarterly financial reporting. The EU Commission has moved to improve compliance across Europe with the 2003 Market Abuse Directive. This has led to the introduction of a new market regime abuse in the United Kingdom, which took effect in 2005. It encompasses both insider dealing and market manipulation, and classes seven types of behaviour as market abuse. Both insider dealing and market manipulation remain criminal offences.

The Sarbanes–Oxley Act

Examination of corporate governance in the United Kingdom would be incomplete without any reference to the US Sarbanes–Oxley Act of 2002 (SOX). SOX applies to all companies, whether incorporated in the United

States or elsewhere, that publicly issue securities in the United States and file reports with the US Securities and Exchange Commission (SEC), for example such UK companies as Cadbury Schweppes and British Airways, which trade on the New York Stock Exchange (NYSE).

It has no direct application to other companies. US and non-US subsidiaries outside the terms of the act may, however, be indirectly affected if their parents have to comply. For example, SEC rules require management to include a report on their internal controls and procedures for financial reporting in their annual reports filed with the SEC. Management must evaluate the effectiveness of those controls and procedures, and the company's auditors must issue a report on the assessment. These requirements are likely to have a knock-on effect on directors and managers in UK subsidiary companies, who may be asked to provide similar certificates and confirmations in respect of their own financial reporting and internal controls.

In 2002 Paul Sarbanes, a Democrat Senator, and Michael G. Oxley, a Republican Congressman, were responsible for a radical piece of corporate legislation, the Sarbanes–Oxley Act. This act of Congress is regarded by many commentators as the single most important piece of legislation affecting companies since the Securities Exchange Act of 1934. In the USA, corporate crisis associated with companies such as Enron, Tyco International and Global Crossing seem to have hastened the introduction of the Sarbanes–Oxley legislation. There is some evidence that the bankruptcy of WorldCom on 21 July 2002, and the public outrage that followed, encouraged President G.W. Bush to sign into law nine days later the Sarbanes–Oxley legislation (New York Times, 2 August 2002:1).

The Sarbanes–Oxley Act introduced sweeping corporate law changes relating to financial reporting, internal accounting controls, and personal loans from companies to their directors, whistle blowing and destruction of documents. In addition, Sarbanes–Oxley Act severely restricts the range of additional services that an audit firm can provide to a client. There are increased penalties for directors and professionals who have conspired to commit fraud. Some examples follow its provisions. Section 906 of the act requires that all periodic reports containing financial statements by the chief executive officer (CEO) and chief financial officer (CFO) of the company, certifying that the report fully complies with the Securities

Exchange Act and fairly present, in all material respects, the financial condition and results of operations. The penalties for knowingly certifying a statement, which does not comply with the requirements, can be severe: up to $1 million in fines and/or up to 10 years' imprisonment. Section 1102 provides that 'knowing and willful' destruction of any record or document with intent to impair an official proceeding carries fines and/or imprisonment up to 20 years. Section 806 provides protection for employees who provide evidence of fraud. There is also protection for 'whistle blowers' in publicly traded corporations. No company, officer or employee may threaten or harass an employee who reasonably believes that a criminal offence has been committed. Section 501 of the legislation also aimed to promote rules to address conflicts of interest where analysts recommend securities when their companies are involved in investment banking activities.

The Sarbanes–Oxley legislation also established a Public Company Accounting Oversight Board (PCAOB) to be responsible to the Securities and Exchange Commission (SEC) for the regulation of auditing in US companies, inspection of accounting firms and disciplinary proceedings. As a result of the Sarbanes–Oxley legislation, some companies felt that the burden of compliance was too heavy in relation to the perceived benefits. Companies were reported to be spending 'millions of dollars revamping their internal controls, updating compliance regimes, writing codes of ethics, setting up hotlines for internal complaints, writing governance principles and board committee charters. They are paying auditors and lawyers' greater fees, as well as directors' (Financial Times, 14 June 2004: 26). The chief executive of the New York Stock Exchange (NYSE), John Thain, argued that the additional burden of compliance was dissuading foreign companies from listing on the NYSE (Ibid).

Codes, Standards and Good Practice Guidelines

Although there is a strong basis of legislation and regulation, at the heart of the United Kingdom's approach to corporate governance is self-regulation backed by codes and guidelines. Widespread interest in the subject really took off in the early 1990s. There was increasing concern about the standards of corporate reporting and the accountability of boards in the wake of corporate scandals, including the Robert Maxwell pension funds scandal, the collapse of the BCCI bank, Coloroll and the collapse of Polly Peck, which all involved published accounts that did not give a true indication of the state of company finances. It was recognised that if published information could not be trusted, there would be serious consequences for the reputation of the United Kingdom as a business and financial centre. The UK business community recognised the need to put its house in order.

The Cadbury Report (1992)

Thus in May 1991 the Financial Aspects of Corporate Governance Committee was set up and sponsored by the London Stock Exchange, the Financial Reporting Council and the accountancy profession, under the chairmanship of Sir Adrian Cadbury. The resulting report, widely known as the Cadbury Report, was issued in December 1992 and included a Code of Best Practice, which was the first corporate governance code in the United Kingdom. Its recommendations were incorporated into the London Stock Exchange Listing Rules.

Key recommendations included the separation of the roles of chief executive and chairman, balanced composition of the board and selection processes for non-executive directors. The Cadbury committee was the first committee to be constituted to report on the financial aspects of corporate governance. The Cadbury Committee, acknowledged that the financial scandals and abuse of power as exposed in the Maxwell case were some of the reasons behind the setting up of the committee to report on corporate governance matters. Hence, the formation of the Cadbury Committee can be seen as reactive rather than proactive.

However, it is important to remember that Cadbury Report was compiled on the basic assumption that the existing implicit system of corporate governance in the UK was sound and that many of the recommendations were merely making explicit and a good implicit system (see Cadbury Report, 1982: 12, para 1.7). The Cadbury Code was not legally binding on board of the directors. Nevertheless, one of the rules in the Stock Exchange Yellow Book at the time of its publication was a statement of compliance with the Code. The result of this was that all companies publicly quoted on the Stock Exchange had to state in their annual reports whether or not they had implemented the Code in all respects. If they had not complied with the whole Code, then they were compelled to make a clear statement of the reasons why, detailing and explaining the points of non-compliance. The implications was that the companies' shareholders then had the opportunity of deciding whether or not they were satisfied with the companies' corporate governance systems.

The Cadbury Report and its accompanying Code covered three general areas, namely: the board of directors; auditing and shareholders. The Cadbury Report focussed attention on the board of directors as being the most important corporate governance mechanisms, requiring constant monitoring and assessment. However, the accounting and auditing functions were also shown to play an essential role in good corporate governance, emphasising the importance of the corporate transparency and communication with shareholders and other stakeholders. Lastly, Cadbury's focus on the importance of the institutional investors as the largest and most influential group of shareholders has had a lasting impact. This, more than any other initiative in corporate governance reform has led to the shift of directors' dialogue towards greater accountability and engagement with shareholders. Further, we consider that this move to greater shareholder engagement has generated a more significant metamorphosis of corporate responsibilities towards a range of stakeholders, encouraging greater corporate social responsibility in general. There is no denying the substantial impact that the Cadbury Code has had on corporate Britain and, indeed, on companies around the world. By the late 1990s there was strong evidence to show a high level of compliance with the Cadbury Code's recommendations (see Conyon and Mallin, 1997), partly due to the UK's 'comply or explain' approach.

Central to the final report's recommendations was that boards of all listed companies registered in the UK should comply with the Code of Best Practice as set out in the report. The code is given added weight by the disclosure requirement of the London Stock Exchange that companies must state in their annual report whether they are complying with the code and to give reasons for any aspects on non-compliance.

Code of Best Practice

At the time of publication of the Committee's final report Sir Adrian Cadbury said:

The planks on which the code is based are the need for disclosure and for checks and balances. Disclosure ensures that all those with a legitimate interest in a company have the information they need in order to exercise their rights and responsibilities toward it. In addition, openness by companies is the basis of public confidence in the corporate system. Checks and balances guard against undue concentrations of power and make certain that all the interests which boards have a duty to consider are properly taken into account.

The code recommendations consist of 19 points set out under: (1) the board of directors; (2) non-executive directors; (3) executive directors; and (4) reporting and controls. The main points are summarised as follows:

The Board of Directors

1) The board should meet regularly, retain full and effective control over the company and monitor the executive management.

2) There should be a clearly accepted division of responsibilities at the head of the company, which will ensure a balance of power and authority, such that no one individual has unfettered powers of decision. Ideally the roles of chairman and chief executive should be separated, although this may not always be practical, in which case there should be a strong and independent element on the board.

3) The board should include non-executive directors of sufficient caliber and number for their views to carry significant weight in the board's decisions.

Non-Executive Directors

1) Non-executive or 'outside' directors as the committee's chairman preferred to call them, should bring an independent judgment to bear on issues of strategy, performance, resources, including key appointments and standards of conduct.

2) The majority of non-executive directors should be 'independent' of management and free from any business or other relationship which could materially interfere with the exercise of their independent judgment, apart from their fees and shareholding.

3) Non-executive directors should be appointed by a formal process and their appointment should be a matter for the board as whole.

Appointments should be for specified terms and reappointment should not be automatic.

Executive Directors

1) Directors' service contracts should not exceed three years without shareholders' approval.

2) Directors' pay and emoluments, including pension contributions and stock options and the amount and the basis for any performance-related element, should be fully disclosed and subject to the recommendations of remuneration committees consisting mainly or wholly of non-executive directors and preferably chaired by a non-executive director.

Reporting and Controls

1) It is the board's duty to present a balanced and understandable assessment of the company's position.

2) The board should ensure that an objective and professional relationship is maintained with the auditors.

3) The board should establish an audit committee which should consist of at least three non-executive directors. Originally the committee referred to the annual audit as one of the cornerstones of corporate governance.

4) The directors should report on the effectiveness of the company's system of internal control.

5) The directors should report that the business is a growing concern, with supporting assumption or qualifications necessary.

The Greenbury Report (1995)

In 1995, following concerns about directors' pay and share options, the Confederation of British Industry (CBI) set up a group under the chairmanship of Sir Richard Greenbury to examine the remuneration of directors, particularly compensation packages, large pay increases and share options. The Greenbury Report put forward a code of best practice and established the remuneration committee composed of non-executive directors, which became responsible for executive director remuneration.

Again the majority of the recommendations were endorsed by the Listing Rules.

A particularly contentious aspect of corporate governance in recent years has been that of executive pay. In 1994/95 the seemingly endless escalation in executive pays, particularly in the newly privatised public, utilities such as British Gas, caused a public outcry in the UK. It forced the British Prime Minister at the time, John Major, to denounce 'unjustifiable' increases in company executive's pay in the House of Commons in November 1994. In response to such public concern, the CBI recruited a committee of 11 top managers (mainly chairmen) from UK's leading companies such as BP, BT, GKN, Boots and Marks & Spencer plc to conduct an inquiry into directors' remuneration. The committee was chaired by Sir Richard Greenbury executive chairman of Marks & Spencer and became known as the Greenbury Committee. Its brief was: 'To identify good practice in determining Directors' remuneration and prepare a Code of such practice for use by UK PLCs.'

The committee published its report on 17 July 1995 and its key themes were: 'accountability, responsibility, full disclosure, alignment of director and shareholder interests, and improved company performance' (Directors' Remuneration: Greenbury, 1995). The Greenbury Committee was formed after widespread public concern over what were seen as excessive amounts of remuneration paid to directors of quoted companies and newly privatised companies. 'Recent concerns about executive remuneration have centered above all on some large pay increases and large gains from share options in the recently privatized utility industries. These increases have sometimes coincided with staff reductions, pay restraints for other staff and price increases...there have also been concerns about the amounts of compensation paid to some departing directors' (Greenbury Report, 1995: 9). The Greenbury Committee were keen to ensure that directors' remuneration was linked to company performance, and the committee did not seem to see a problem with high levels of pay *per se*, as long as they were justified on the basis of the company's financial results.

A key concern should be to ensure, through the remuneration system, that directors share the interest of shareholders in making the company successful. Performance-related remuneration can be highly effective in aligning interest in this way. In many companies, therefore, there will be a case for a high gearing of performance-related remuneration to fixed pay. But there are two constraints on this. First, there will usually be a level of basic salary below which it will not be practicable to go. Second, the requirements and priorities of companies vary. The gearing, which suits one company, may be quite unsuitable for another (Greenbury Report, 1995: 38). The Greenbury Report also addressed the problem of departing directors whose performance had not been noticeably successful, but who still manage to leave the company with generous compensation for loss of office. Compensation payments to directors on loss of office have been a cause of public and shareholders' concern in recent times. Criticism has been directed at the scale of some of the payments made and at their apparent lack of justification in terms of performance. Some payments have been described as 'rewards for failure' (Greenbury Report, 1995: 45).

When the Greenbury Report was published in 1995 it dealt specifically with the question of directors 'remuneration and many of its recommendations were developed from the earlier Cadbury Report. The Greenbury Report recommended that the remuneration committee should consist exclusively of non-executive directors (the Cadbury Report had recommended wholly or mainly non-executive directors. These non-executive directors should have no personal financial interest, no potential conflicts of interest arising from cross-directorships and no day-to-day involvement in running the business. In all the Greenbury report contained some 20 recommendations, the key elements of which are summarised below:

1) Remuneration committees should consist only of non-executive directors. This should avoid pay being determined by directors with a direct financial interest. Remuneration committees should:

   - Publish an annual report giving full disclosure of all the elements (basic pay, bonuses, share options, pensions and so on);

   - Relate incentives to demanding performance targets, in order to 'align directors' and shareholders' interests';

   - Explain pay policy to shareholders and justify any unusual or exceptional awards;

- Have the committee chairman attend AGM to respond to shareholders questions.

2) Long-term incentive schemes to be approved by shareholders.

3) Discounted share options. No longer should directors be awarded share options at a discount to the prevailing market price.

The Hampel Report and Original Combined Code (1998)

Not long after the Greenbury Report had been published, a number of institutions: the London Stock Exchange (LSE), the Confederation of British Industry (CBI), the Institute of Directors (IoD), the Consultative Committee of Accountancy Bodies (CCAB), the National Association of Pension Funds (NAPF) and the Association of British Insurer (ABI) decided that the time was right to review the extent to which Cadbury Report and Greenbury Report had been implemented and whether their purposes were being achieved.

The Hampel Committee was created in 1995 to review implementation of the findings of the Cadbury and Greenbury Committees. Most of the recommendations in the earlier reports were then published in 1998 by the London Stock Exchange as *The Combined Code: Principles of Good Governance and Code of Best Practice*. The Combined Code (although redrafted since its original publication) is the currently applicable code of best corporate governance practice for UK listed companies. The recommendations of Hampel were along similar lines and on similar issues to Cadbury. An important contribution made by the Hampel Report was the emphasis attributed to avoiding a prescriptive approach to corporate governance improvements and recommendations. The Cadbury Report highlighted the importance of focussing on the spirit of corporate governance reform, and Hampel reinforced this by stipulating that companies and shareholders needed to avoid a 'box-ticking' approach to corporate governance. The Hampel Report emphasised the need to maintain principles-based, voluntary approach to corporate governance rather than a more regulated and possibly superficial one. This is typical of the UK approach to corporate governance and accounting as opposed to the US style of legislation, the rules-based approach. Indeed, the report stated: in some ways (such as the role of institutional investors in corporate governance) Hampel could be interpreted as being less demanding than

Cadbury. Indeed, there is a widely held perception that the report represented the interest of the company directors more than those of shareholders and that much of the positive impact from the Cadbury Report was diluted by the Hampel Report. Certainly, in the area of corporate social responsibility and corporate accountability to a broad range of stakeholders, there was a significant change in track between the Cadbury Report and the Hampel Report. The Hampel Report clearly felt the need to redress the balance between shareholders and stakeholders and made strong statements on these issues. For example, the Hampel Committee stated that:

> Good corporate governance is not just a matter of prescribing particular corporate structures and complying with a number of hard and fast rules. There is a need for broad principles. All concerned should then apply these flexibly and with common sense to the varying circumstances of individual companies. This is how the Cadbury and Greenbury Committees intended their recommendations to be implemented... Companies' experience of the Cadbury and the Greenbury Codes has been rather different. Too often they believe that the codes have been treated as sets of prescriptive rules. The shareholders or their advisors would be interested only in whether the letter of the rule had been complied with—yes or no. A 'yes' would receive a tick, hence the expression 'box ticking' for this approach. (The Hampel Report, 1998: 10, paras 1.11-1.12)

> The importance of corporate governance lies in its contribution both to business prosperity and to accountability. In the UK the later has pre- occupied much public debate over the past few years. We would wish to see the balance corrected. Public companies are now among the most accountable organizations in the society...which strongly endorse this accountability and we recognize the contribution made by the Cadbury and Greenbury Committees. But the emphasise on the accountability has tended obscure a board's first responsibility— to enhance the prosperity of the business over time. (The Hampel Report, 1998: 7, para.1.1)

An important contribution made by the Hampel Report related to pension fund trustees, as pension funds are the largest group of investors. Pension fund trustees were targetted by the report as a group who needed to take their corporate governance responsibilities more seriously. In particular, pension funds (and their trustees) were encouraged by the

Hampel Committee to adopt a more long-term approach to institutional investment, in order to avoid short-termism for which UK companies are notorious. Pension funds were highlighted as the main culprits in placing short-term pressure on their investing companies. This discussion in the Hampel Report has been instrumental in encouraging an overhaul in the pension fund trustee's role, culminating in the recent Myners Review of the trustee's role and responsibilities (Myners, 2001).

The impact of the Combined Code (and its predecessors) on UK company directors and institutional investors has been far-reaching, especially in the area of investor relations and shareholder activism. In a decade, corporate attitudes towards their core investors have been transformed from relative secrecy to greater transparency. Similarly, the attitudes of the institutional investors have been transformed from relative apathy towards their investee companies' activities to an active interest.

As was the case for Cadbury and Greenbury, the Hampel Report could also be seen as reactive rather than proactive, as further significant UK corporate failures arose from weak corporate governance structures between the publication of the Cadbury Report and the Hampel Report. One of these was a fall of the major UK bank, Barings, which created shockwaves through the corporate and financial communities throughout the UK and, indeed, across the world.

The Turnbull Report (1999)

This led to the establishment of a working group under the auspices of the Institute of Chartered Accountants in England and Wales (ICAEW), chaired by Nigel Turnbull.

The Combined Code (1998) dealt with internal control in Provisions D.2.1 and D.2.2. In these provisions the Code stated that company directors should conduct a review of the effectiveness of the internal control systems and should report this information to shareholders. The Turnbull Committee was established specifically to address the issue of internal control and to respond to these provisions in the Combined Code. The report provided an overview of the systems of internal control in existence in UK companies and made clear recommendations for improvements, without taking a prescriptive approach. The Turnbull Report was revolutionary in terms of corporate governance reform. It represented an attempt to formalise an explicit framework for internal control in companies. The aim was to provide companies with general guidance on how to develop and maintain their internal control systems and not to specify the details of such a system.

The resulting report, 'Internal Control: Guidance for Directors on the Combined Code', was issued in September 1999 and endorsed by the London Stock Exchange as consistent with the original Combined Code (1998).

The Myners Review (2001)

Paul Myners' review of institutional investment was commissioned by the government as a result of the investigation of possible distortions in institutional investment decision-making and concern over the reluctance of institutional investors to tackle corporate underperformance in companies in which they invest. It included suggestions for the improvement of communication between investors and companies, and encouraged institutional investors to consider their responsibilities as owners and how they should exercise their rights on behalf of beneficiaries.

The Directors' Remuneration Report Regulations (2002)

In 2002 the Directors' Remuneration Report Regulations were introduced to strengthen further the powers of shareholders in relation to directors' pay. The regulations increase the amount of information shareholders are given on directors' remuneration and certain disclosures, as well as performance graphs. Shareholders may vote in an advisory capacity to approve the directors' remuneration report.

The Higgs Report (2003)

In July 2002, following a review of Company Law, the Department of Trade and Industry (DTI) and the HM Treasury commenced a review of the Combined Code, which was conducted by Derek Higgs. The Higgs Report, 'The Role and Effectiveness of Non-Executive Directors', was published in 2003.

It raised the agenda of boardroom effectiveness and made a number of recommendations to give a more active role to independent directors. It gave a definition of 'independence' and stressed the importance of having the right proportion of independent non-executive directors on the board and its committees. The role of the senior independent director was to provide an alternative channel to shareholders and to lead evaluations of the chairman's performance. One of the recommendations highlighted the importance of the nomination process to the board and emphasised a transparent and rigorous process and evaluation of the performance of the board, its committees and individual directors.

Although the Cadbury Report and the Hampel Report stimulated substantial improvements in corporate governance in UK listed companies, certain areas have been highlighted for further examination. The fall of Enron spurred the UK and other countries into re-evaluating corporate governance issues, such as the role and effectiveness of non-executive directors. As evidenced from the Enron case, the non-executive directors were ineffective in performing their corporate governance role of monitoring the company's directors and were subject to conflicts of interest. Even though the emphasis on non-executive directors in the UK has represented an improvement in UK corporate governance, the UK government post-Enron felt obliged to set up an enquiry to examine their effectiveness.

One reason why non-executive directors are not fulfilling their potential is the difficulties of retaining their position. For example, one pension fund director suggested that: 'there is a feeling that somebody ought to exercise constraint on boards. I don't think the system of non-executive directors is terribly successful. It is very difficult being a non-executive director one actually has to let the chief executive run the show-while one cannot keep interfering, and that is the trouble. If one don't want to interfere—they will get themselves voted out.'

The Higgs Report dealt specifically with the role and effectiveness of non-executive directors, making recommendations for changes to the Combined Code. The general recommendations included a greater proportion of non-executive directors on boards (at least half of the board) and more apt remuneration for non-executive directors. The report also concluded that stronger links needed to be established between non-executive directors and companies' principal shareholders. This would help to foster more effective monitoring of the notorious agency problem, as it would enhance the abilities of non-executive directors to represent shareholder interest and align in the interest of shareholders and directors. One important recommendation of the Higgs Report was that one non-executive director should assume chief responsibility as a champion of shareholder interest.

The Smith Report (2003)

Some two months into Derek Higgs' review, the Financial Reporting Council (FRC) set up a group under the chairmanship of Sir Robert Smith to develop guidance on audit committees in the Combined Code. The ensuing Smith Report was published in January 2003. The UK Government in response to the Enron scandal commissioned this committee, *inter alia,* with the aim of examining the role of the audit committee in UK corporate governance. The main issue dealt with in the report concerned the relationship between the external auditor and the companies they audit, as well as the role and responsibilities of companies' audit committees.

The creation of audit committees was a recommendation of the Cadbury Report and represented a clear means of monitoring company directors' activities. In the case of Enron, the failure of the audit committee an internal audit function was one of the principal causes of the company's collapse. Improvements in this area represent one way of keeping a check on the production of reliable and honest accounts. Nevertheless, some have suggested that the report has not gone far enough; that a more prescriptive approach would have been preferable, which would, for example, prevent auditing companies from offering from other professional services, such as consultancy or IT services or to client companies that they audit. However, the Smith Report preserved the UK tradition of a principles-based approach, attempting not to create a 'once size fits all' set of rules for listed companies. This would be counterproductive as not all companies would be in a position to comply.

The Tyson Report (2003)

Following the publication of the Higgs and Smith Reports, the DTI commissioned the Tyson Task Force under the chairmanship of Prof. Laura D'Andrea Tyson, Dean of London Business School, which published 'The

Tyson Report on the Recruitment and Development of Non-Executive Directors' in 2003.

The Revised Combined Code (2003)

The recommendations made in these three reports (Higgs, Smith and Tyson) instigated changes to the Combined Code. The Financial Reporting Council (FRC), a body established by the government and comprising members from industry, commerce and the professions, issued the Revised Combined Code in July 2003. The FRC was appointed the guardian of the Combined Code and established a committee to keep it under review. The most recent update was issued in June 2008.

It was referred to as, 'the biggest shake-up of board room culture in more than a decade' (Tassel, 24 July 2003). Although the redrafted code was not as prescriptive as Higgs 'original recommendations, it retained much of the flavour of his concerns. Indeed, the redrafting was welcomed by both the corporate and institutional investment communities, despite their initial reactions to the Higgs' Report. The revised code in act retained almost all of the 50 recommendations contained in Higgs' original report. The language, not the message was altered. The main reforms of the new Code included the following:

- At least half the board of directors should comprise independent non-executive directors.
- A company's chief executive should not become chairman of the same company, except in exceptional circumstances.
- The board's chairman should be independent at appointment.
- A senior independent director should be appointed to be available to the company's shareholders, if they have unresolved concerns.
- Boards should undertake a formal and rigorous evaluation of their own performance, considering especially the performance and effectiveness of its committees and individual directors.
- Institutional investors should avoid box-ticking when assessing investee companies' corporate governance.
- Companies should adopt rigorous, formal and transparent procedures when recruiting new directors.

- Non-executive directors should only be reappointed after six years' service, following a particular rigorous review.

- Non-executive directors can only continue after nine years' service following annual re-elections and should be considered no longer independent.

- Boards should not agree to a full-time executive director accepting more than one non-executive directorship, or chairmanship, in a top 100 company.

One of the main targets of the redrafted Code was to re-address executive remuneration, as the new version of the code focussed on forcing companies to avoid excessive remuneration, which displayed little relation to corporate performance. The revised Code also placed an emphasis on shareholder activism as a means of furthering corporate accountability and transparency.

The Turnbull Review (2004)

In 2004 the FRC established the Turnbull Review Group to consider the impact of its original guidance for directors on internal control and to determine whether it needed to be updated. In 2005, 'Internal Control: Revised Guidance for Directors on the Combined Code' was published, reiterating the board of directors' responsibility for the company's system of internal control and risk management.

The Operating and Financial Review (OFR) and Business Review

In 1998 the UK government instigated a company law review and produced a White Paper in 2002, which put forward a number of proposals relating to company reporting. A significant development was the requirement for companies to produce a mandatory operating and financial review (OFR) to provide information on the company's current and prospective performance and strategy. This came into effect on 1 April 2005. However, on 28 November 2005, after reconsidering the matter, the government announced its intention to remove the statutory requirement for quoted companies to publish an OFR. Instead, all companies, public and private, with the exception of those private companies that fall under the definition of 'small companies', need to produce a business review as part of their directors' report. The Companies Act 2006 requires UK-quoted companies to follow the enhanced business review reporting.

The Revised Combined Code (2008)

The latest version of the Revised Combined Code was issued by the FRC in June 2008, following subsequent consultation on possible amendments to the Code. This Code supersedes and replaces the versions of the Combined Code issued in 2003 and 2006. The full text of the Code can be found on the FRC website, *www.frc.org.uk*. The FRC may be the custodian of the Code but compliance is a matter for the Listing Rules. Produced by the Financial Services Authority, these rules regulate companies with a full listing on the London Stock Exchange.

For a quoted company, reporting on its application of the Code is one of its continuing obligations under the Listing Rules published by the UK Listing Authority (UKLA). The Code does not form part of the UKLA Listing Rules, but is appended to them. It is a voluntary code, but since a statement of compliance with it is required by the Listing Rules to be included in each annual report, there is an element of compulsion.

The Code does not apply to companies whose shares are traded on the Alternative Investment Market (AIM) or other markets not covered by the Listing Rules, although companies listed on AIM are recommended to have regard to its provisions. Nor does the Code apply to listed companies incorporated outside the United Kingdom, though such companies do have a lesser reporting obligation. There is, though, nothing to stop such companies complying with the Code if they choose to do so. Shareholder pressure, or simply a wish to conform to 'best practice', may lead many 'exempt' companies to follow some or all of the Code's recommendations.

Most of the Code's principles, if not all the detailed provisions, provide a sound basis for the governance of many companies, and indeed it has had a noticeable wider impact on the governance of non-quoted companies. It has been the impetus for the development of a more formalised approach to governance among charities and other not-for-profit organizations and in the public sector. Universities have produced their own governance code; public sector bodies have guidance from the Independent Commission on Good Governance in Public Services. And mutual life companies are expected to follow guidelines on governance produced in the wake of the Equitable Life inquiry. All the UK reports and codes, including the latest revised 2008 version, have taken the 'comply or explain' approach.

The Code is divided into main principles, supporting principles and provisions. The main principles are general statements of corporate life. Supporting principles expand on the main principles and give more guidance. But it is the Code's provisions that state the detailed requirements necessary for upholding the principles.

For both main principles and supporting principles a company has to state how it applies those principles. There is deliberately no prescribed form, the intention being to allow companies a free hand to explain their governance policies. In relation to the Code provisions a company has to state whether it complies with the provisions or give an explanation where it does not. It is the Code provisions that contain the detail on matters such as separation of the roles of chairman and chief executive, the ratio of non-executive directors and the composition of the main board committees.

The 'comply or explain' basis of the Combined Code offers a degree of flexibility, but must be treated with care by both companies and investors. The expression has now become common parlance, but companies should not use it as an excuse to ignore the provisions. If they do this or provide unconvincing explanations they rightly run the risk of investors attacking their standards of governance. On the other hand, analysts and investors must get away from a 'box-ticking' approach and take seriously any proper explanations of 'non-compliance'.

The first principle of the Code states that 'every company should have an effective board.' The board's effectiveness is widely regarded as a prerequisite for sustained corporate success. The quality and effectiveness of directors determine the quality and effectiveness of the board. Formal processes for appointments induction and development should be adopted. Effectiveness of the board and its individual members has to be assessed. The Code states that no one individual should have unfettered powers of decision-making. It sets out how this can be avoided by splitting the roles of chairman and chief executive, and specifies what the role of the beginning chairman should be. The Code offers valuable guidance on the ratio of non-executive to executive directors and definitions of independence.

For the provisions, companies must either confirm that they have complied with them or, where they have not, provide an explanation.

Box 6.1

Main Principles of the Revised Combined Code (2008)

A. Directors

A.1 The Board

Every company should be headed by an effective board, which is collectively responsible for the success of the company.

A.2 Chairman and chief executive

There should be a clear division of responsibilities at the head of the company between the running of the board and the executive responsibility for the running of the company's business. No one individual should have unfettered powers of decision.

A.3 Board balance and independence

The board should include a balance of executive and non-executive directors (and in particular independent non-executive directors) such that no individual or small group of individuals can dominate the board's decision-taking.

A.4 Appointments to the board

There should be a formal, rigorous and transparent procedure for the appointment of new directors to the board.

A.5 Information and professional development

Tue board should be supplied in a timely manner with information in a form and of a quality appropriate to enable it to discharge its duties. All directors should receive induction on joining the board and should regularly update and refresh their skills and knowledge.

A.6 Performance evaluation

The board should undertake a formal and rigorous annual evaluation of its own performance and that of its committees and individual directors.

A.7 Re-election

All directors should be submitted for re-election at regular intervals, subject to continued satisfactory performance. The board should ensure planned and progressive refreshing of the board.

B. Remuneration

B.1 The level and make-up of remuneration

Levels of remuneration should be sufficient to attract, retain and motivate directors of the quality required to run the company successfully, but a company should avoid paying more than is necessary for this purpose. A significant proportion of directors' remuneration should be structured so as to link rewards to corporate and individual performance.

contd...

...contd...

B.2 Procedure

There should be a formal and transparent procedure for developing policy on executive remuneration and for fixing the remuneration packages of individual directors. No director should be involved in deciding his or her own remuneration.

C. Accountability and Audit

C.1 Financial reporting

The board should present a balanced and understandable assessment of the company's position and prospects.

C.2 Internal control

The board should maintain a sound system of internal control to safeguard shareholders' investment and the company's assets.

C.3 Audit committee and auditors

The board should establish formal and transparent arrangements for considering how they should apply the financial reporting and internal control principles and for maintaining an appropriate relationship with the company's auditors.

D. Relations with Shareholders

D.1 Dialogue with institutional shareholders

There should be a dialogue with shareholders based on the mutual understanding of objectives. The board as a whole has responsibility for ensuring that a satisfactory dialogue with shareholders takes place.

D.2 Constructive use of the ACM

The board should use the ACM to communicate with investors and to encourage their participation.

E. Institutional Shareholders

This section is not subject to any sanction, but it does stress the need for institutional shareholders to consider carefully explanations for departure from the Combined Code and make a reasoned judgment in each case.

E.1 Dialogue with companies

Institutional shareholders should enter into a dialogue with companies based on the mutual understanding of the objectives.

E.2 Evaluation of governance disclosures

When evaluating a company's governance arrangements, particularly those relating to board structure and composition, institutional shareholders should give due weight to all relevant factors drawn to their attention.

E.3 Shareholder voting

Institutional shareholders have a responsibility to make considered use of their votes.

Schedule A: Provisions on the design of performance related remuneration.

Schedule B: Guidance on liability of non-executive directors: care, skill and diligence.

Schedule C: Disclosure of corporate governance arrangements.

Source: *www.frc.org.uk*

6.6 France

6.6.1 Corporate Governance in France: Beyond Commonplaces

French capitalism has been through some profound changes since the mid-1980s, as have all Western countries, shifting from an international, managerial, Fordist form to a global, financial, share holder-driven form. This change has been particularly fast-moving since the law on financial deregulation in 1985, leading to a very high level of exposure to international financing and to an exceptionally high proportion of foreign investment: half of the capital of the companies in the SBF 250, and 40 per cent of that of the top 40, is now held by funds representing foreign investors (against 25 per cent in Germany and 22 per cent in the United Kingdom). This financing is due to the absence of pension funds in France.

At the same time, financial deregulation and highly conducive fiscal policies have brought about a large-scale shift of household saving towards investments in companies: while shares represented only 0.7 per cent of the assets of French households in 1974, they now represent 20 per cent and as much as 60 per cent if indirect investment products are taken into account. France ranks third in the world for investment fund management.

Lastly, the withdrawal of the state as a shareholder since the early 1990s has been considerable. While the state controlled 2,300 firms in 1996, it had majority holdings in just 845 companies in 2006. Just six of these, mainly in the energy sector (EDF, GDF, CEA), represent 75 per cent of the jobs in these corporations. Generally speaking, the past 15 years have seen a clear withdrawal of the public sector from all fields of economic activity, and a rise of company financing by individual investors at home and abroad. These ground shifts have transformed French capitalism, which is all too often interpreted, even today, in terms of commonplaces dating back to the 1970s (omnipresence of the state, poor minority shareholder protection etc.).

But the expansion and internationalisation of financing have also considerably increased the differences between companies in terms of size and shareholding structure. In all Western countries, recent developments have not concerned all companies to the same extent. The more open they are to international capital, the more they are affected by the consequences of shareholder power and financialisation. Conversely, the more they remain under the control of dominant shareholder groups, the more they have specific expectations, while still being affected by the consequences of general governance reforms. In a modest-sized country like France (and all European countries), no more than 100 or so corporations are genuinely confronted with the new rules of global shareholder capitalism: very diluted capital, short-term stock price sensitivity, international governance standards etc. The great majority of companies, because they have at least one reference shareholder (family, founder, etc.), do not obey this logic, although they are subject to the regulatory or legal requirements of the 'new governance standards'. In a study of more than 280,000 companies, carried out in 2000, the Banque de France showed that 72 per cent of these companies had a majority shareholder (either an individual or another company). Only 4 per cent of them had diluted shareholdings, meaning in this case that the biggest shareholder represented no more than 10 per cent of the capital. These figures have been confirmed by less extensive studies since then. In short, French capitalism is very much concentrated in the hands of entrepreneur shareholders, except for a small number of companies with a large number of shareholders.

A number of circles can be defined according to: 1) the varying levels of capital concentration; 2) the key role of an owner in corporate management; 3) the size of the company.

In the first circle can be found some 100 companies which are among the largest in France. The CAC 40, which is to say the 40 biggest market capitalisations on the Paris market, form a central core. Even among these companies very few are diluted to any great extent: half of them have a single reference shareholder exceeding 30 per cent of their capital. Their float is sufficiently large, however, for these companies to be subject to global governance rules.

The second circle contains the next 800 companies listed on the Paris market. For these 'Midcaps', the proportion of their float does not generally exceed 20 per cent. They have a market capitalisation of less than 1 billion euros, and represent only 4 per cent of the overall capitalisation of the Paris market and less than 2 per cent of transactions. So, even for listed companies the significance of their listing varies widely depending on their size. The third circle comprises 27,600 unlisted small and medium sized companies with over 50 employees, which essentially have one or several owners. Finally, in the fourth circle we find the 2,600,000 small companies (with from 0 to 50 employees) that make up the bulk of French firms in number.

In the first two categories we are seeing faster concentration of companies than in the other groups, and the creation of micro-groups. These have increased in number from 600 in 1980 to 5,300 in 1995 and to 32,000 in 2005. This restructuring of capitalism around small companies has been little studied, although it does have obvious implications for corporate governance.

So, when we are talking about corporate governance we must bear this capital structure in mind, not only to understand expectations in terms of governance which are not identical between different companies, but also to understand the tensions created by applying general rules without taking account of the specifics of companies.

6.6.2 Key Corporate Governance Trends: The Legal Framework Laws, Models and Codes

For large listed companies, changes in corporate governance have come mainly from two sources: codes of conduct and the law. As in all Western countries, these reforms have come in the wake of scandals that have forced either corporate leaders or the public authorities to step in to reform practices. Three codes have been decisive in defining good market conduct exclusively for listed companies: the Viénot I Report (1995), the Viénot II Report (1999) and the Bouton Report (2002). These reports were written under the supervision of the successive presidents of a bank (the Société Générale) by a commission composed exclusively of directors of large corporations. They adopted approaches very close to those of the OECD or of other reports of this type in Europe: inclusion of independent directors on company boards (at least 30 per cent), discussion of the separation of the powers of the CEO and the chairman, the importance of oversight by specialised committees, the independence of directors. To this effect, an independent director is one who 'has no relationship of any kind with the company or its group that might prevent them exercising their freedom of judgement' (Bouton Report, 2002: 9). These are only proposals and are in no way binding, although the vast majority of CAC 40 companies do refer to them, thereby creating a 'market culture'. For example, 92 per cent announce in their annual reports that they apply or draw inspiration from the Bouton Report, notably as regards the number of independent directors (one-third of board members). These texts are sufficiently general and flexible to be accepted by all, and there is no obligation to sign up to them or to take up a position on compliance in the official corporate documents.

In fact, they have been added to and discussed in a number of initiatives taken by associations or institutes seeking to improve governance practice in more specific ways: APIA, MiddleNext, AFGE, AFG, IFGE, JOD France, IFA etc. The VIGEO rating agency, set up by Nicole Notat, formerly the leader of one of the largest trade unions, takes account of 'good governance' standards in its ratings, thereby contributing to bringing about changes in practice. These multiple sources of thinking favour debate and an objective appraisal of 'good practice' by bringing a variety of points of view into play.

Another far from negligible form of indirect influence on governance is provided by the AMF (Autorité des Marches Financiers, the financial regulator), which enforces standards on disclosure of information to the public, among other things. For listed companies, as well as issuing an activity report, it requires the publication by the chairman of a report on internal control within the corporation, to ensure that all the provisions are applied to reduce exposure of companies to risk to the greatest extent possible. This report is obligatory for all listed companies according to the terms of the European 'Prospectus' Directive. It has given rise to ongoing debates, however, owing to the weight and cost of these procedures for smaller companies.

As far as public regulations are concerned, the laws of 2001 and 2003 tended to confirm the proposals of the Viénot and Bouton reports. These laws essentially provide a clearer distinction between internal and external directors, and qualify the independence of directors. On the whole, French law has sought to keep track with broader changes, rather than causing them. Under pressure from public opinion the law of 2002 required listed companies to publish an annual report on their social and environmental policy (Article 116). The law of 2003 mainly provided a framework for transparency on directors' pay, rendering disclosure in the annual report obligatory. The law has in fact been ahead of certain recent changes, however. For example, since 1967, French corporations have had the possibility of opting to separate the supervisory board from the board of directors, as in Germany, or to remain with a single board. Neither the reports nor the law require just one form, leaving the choice open to companies so that they can choose the one that is best suited to their culture or economic situation. In 2007, 26 per cent of the companies in the CAC 40 and 27 per cent of Midcaps had chosen this 'dual' form.

To summarise, reforms of practice have been largely due to the self-organisation of companies, with the backing of public intervention. They have been characterised by a very pragmatic approach and flexibility to adapt the rules to the different situations of listed companies. It is important to take this into account when we look at the French situation. Contrary to what people often think, the laws leave a lot of room for negotiation. In this respect, mention should be made, for non-listed companies, of the law of 1999 creating a new form of company, the SAS *(société anonyme simplifiée)*, the main feature of which is to leave companies free to establish the governance institutions to suit their needs. By 2008, over half of non-listed companies of more than 10 employees had chosen this form. Most have kept a single board of directors as the reference body.

6.6.3 Board Structure and Roles

France has seen the same changes as other Western countries, with a shift from somewhat inactive boards to institutional control by directors. Media coverage of certain scandals (Crédit Lyonnais in 1991, Vinci in 2006) has contributed much to transforming this role and increasing the responsibility of directors and the pressure on them. However, the role of the board still remains blurred. Article L 225—35 of the French Code Civil states that the board represents the interests both of the company and of the shareholder. In these times, when shareholding is diluted and global, the expectations of shareholders may vary, and getting their interests to coincide can be difficult. The codes have tried to limit this gap. Generally speaking, in the French tradition they give preference to the general interest of the company over that of the shareholders, considered as being an important stakeholder although not decisive. For example, the Viénot Report (1995) defines the board as follows: 'whatever the composition and organization of the board, it is and must remain a collegiate body representing all the shareholders collectively, and with the obligation of acting in all circumstances in the interests of the company' (page 2).

The legal term of office for directors is six years. In 2006 the average size of the boards of CAC 40 companies was 15 members, of whom 8.5 on average are independent. For Midcaps the figure was eight in total, three of them independents. The reports recommend creating three types of committees to help the board: a compensation committee, an appointments committee (with 50 per cent of independent directors) and an audit committee (with 66 per cent of independent directors). For the CAC 40, most companies have chosen to combine the audit and compensation committees. Eighty per cent apply the recommendations of the Bouton Report. More rarely, there are boards that set up a strategic committee or an ethics committee. For Midcaps the proportion is smaller: 43 per cent have an appointments committee, 40 per cent an audit committee, but just 20 per cent a strategic committee and 10 per cent a compensation committee.

Generally speaking, corporate boards have evolved to become more open. The 2003 law limited to five the number of board positions per director, thereby preventing directors from holding too many seats. Although this has not reduced the networking effect between directors, it has extended their networks and the interlocking between corporate boards. This is due essentially to the structure of capitalism, referred to earlier. While directors of large corporations are to be found in smaller companies, it does not work the other way round. The result of this is that the directors' market is structured by company size, thereby necessarily limiting the number of directors and increasing interlock within each of the 'circles' of companies that make up French capitalism.

6.6.4 Shareholder Rights

Minority shareholders are represented by associations and activists (ADAM, Deminor) or proxy consulting firms (Proxinvest), which benefit from a relatively high media profile and regularly take part in debates. In

France there are no class actions allowing certain shareholders to take legal action on behalf of all shareholders. Their approach generally involves ensuring media coverage before shareholders' meetings and then speaking in those meetings, in most cases on the subject of stock valuations in takeover bids. One particular case attracted much media attention in 2004, when shareholders in Eurotunnel joined forces to overthrow the management in place and impose a new one. This spectacular action remains the exception, however. In general, small shareholders are not very active and seem little interested in becoming so.

The law of 2003 requires that investment funds give a reason for not taking part in shareholders' meetings. This has led to greater participation by these funds, which on the whole, tend to vote in favour of management proposals.

Since the 1980s, the practice of issuing shares without voting rights (and shares with double or multiple voting rights) has developed. The use of non-voting preference shares, as allowed by Article L 225-126 of the French Code de Commerce, was extended in 2005 by the creation of preference shares, which enable companies to associate all sorts of rights with their shares in their by-laws, according to the expectations and interests of the owners and whether they wish to play a role in management or not.

Multiple voting shares are still widespread, especially in listed family companies such es Legrand or SEB. The law (Article L 225-123) authorises double or multiple voting rights to be associated with certain shares if the shareholder had their shares for at least two years—and as much as 10 years for Pernod Ricard, the spirits market leader. This practice is criticised by some, in the name of the 'one share, one vote' principle, and also because of the fact that it becomes obsolete as the capital becomes more diluted, as is the case for Danone or Total. But it is defended by others, who consider it normal to encourage shareholders' loyalty and their greater involvement in company management the longer they hold their shares.

In fact, if this type of share has been retained, it is due to the fact that French capitalism opened up suddenly and extensively to international financial markets in the mid-1980s. In a country where, as we have said, almost half the capital of large corporations belongs to foreign funds, the question is not merely one of ideology: multiple voting shares are a way for certain companies to ensure stability of their capital, especially in periods of intense speculation on markets. In many cases the founders of, or heirs to, companies have agreed to list their companies on stock markets only on condition that they could retain a certain amount of control over the strategy of companies in which they are investing over the very long term. If double or multiple voting shares were to be brought into question, this would probably lead some companies dominated by families or entrepreneurs to go private. However, debate on the subject in France has been far from intense, and has tended to lean in favour of the advocates of 'shareholder loyalty', notably during periods of stock market instability.

Finally, employee stock ownership has grown under the effect of a series of laws encouraging employee participation. Although it represents only 1 per cent of share ownership of all companies taken as a whole, it is very much concentrated in listed companies. It represents 2.5 per cent of the stock market capitalisation of listed companies. There are 38 firms in the SBF 250 in which employees hold over 3 per cent of the capital and the number of employees concerned is over 25 per cent of their total staff. Among CAC 40 companies, employee stock ownership exceeds 3 per cent of the capital in three of them, and 5 per cent in eight of them. As we can see, the further up we move into the large companies with diluted capital that are therefore the most closely concerned by new governance rules, the greater the employee stock ownership we find.

The Fédération des Associations d' Actionnaires Salariés (FAS), which comprises 30 employee shareholders' associations, has launched an index to show the relative performances of companies with more extensive employee shareholding. Questions have also emerged as to the rules on employee participation in corporate governance. The Giraud Law of 1994 on employee stock ownership required the presence of directors elected by the employees in privatised companies. The number of elected employee representatives on the board cannot exceed four and must remain lower than the number of shareholder representatives. Basing themselves on this, employee stockholders have sought admission to corporate boards, and have obtained it in 14 of the CAC 40 giants. By promoting more loyal (notably through the use of multiple voting shares), stable employee shareholding in capital that is otherwise increasingly diluted, on the one hand, and by enforcing rules of transparency and also of employee involvement in the economic life of corporations, this is much more likely to bring about profound changes in French corporate governance than might be achieved by changes in rules or laws.

On the whole, French corporate governance has evolved towards greater transparency and openness, in line with the general trend in the Western world. This shift towards global standards is also one of great pragmatism. The task now under way is to apply these changes to companies whose capital has not been diluted. In this respect, it would be absurd to apply the same costly transparency and control rules if their economic efficiency is not clear. Rather than demanding that the 'good conduct' rules of large listed corporations be generalised, what are now needed are governance rules that are compatible not only with the new financial situation, but also with the working of Midcaps and entrepreneurial companies.

6.7 Italy

Italian corporate governance is characterised by advanced regulations (equalling or exceeding the continental European average) but a low degree of enforcement. The ownership structure of listed companies is highly concentrated, and public companies with dispersed ownership are rare. Most of the time, a majority shareholder (a family, a company or the government) controls a relevant stake of voting rights and exercises full control of the company. Legal devices such as pyramidal groups, non-voting shares and voting agreements are relatively widespread and allow separation of ownership from control, especially in family groups. It follows that the typical agency conflict is not between managers and shareholders, as in the United States or the United Kingdom, but between majority and minority shareholders.

6.7.1 Regulatory Framework

Corporate governance regulations of Italian stock companies is mainly set out in the Italian Civil Code of 1942, as amended by a comprehensive corporate law that took effect on 1 January 2004 and supplemented by a few significant reforms enacted during the past decade. Unlike the US framework, the Italian Code fully regulates rights and duties of companies' main corporate bodies. These provisions are generally compelling and, except for some cases, they cannot be derogated by companies' by-laws. In the past 10 years, several law reforms have substantially modified the Italian corporate governance system (for thorough discussion of the topic, see Bianchi and Enriques, 2005; Ferrarini, Giudici and Stella Richter, 2005; Ferrarini, 2005) (see Figure 6.1).

The year 1998 represents a crucial stage in the Italian corporate governance reform process. The Consolidated Law on Financial Intermediation (Testo Unico della Finanza, TUF), also known as 'Draghi's law',' came into effect on 1 July of that year and strengthened minority shareholders' rights. In a nutshell, the interventions were in three key directions.

First, the Act increased minority shareholders' protection and 'voice', lowering the percentages of voting capital required to exercise some minority rights, such as the right to call an ordinary shareholders' meeting and the right to sue directors (from 20 per cent to 10 per cent, and from 10 per cent to 5 per cent, respectively). On the same lines, the statutory auditors' powers and responsibilities were enhanced, and stricter regulation of insider trading was established.

Figure 6.1

Events in the Reform of Italian Corporate Governance

1998	Corporate Governance Reforms
1999	Code of Conduct 1
2000	No Event
2001	No Event
2002	Code of Conduct 2
2003	No Event
2004	Corporate Law Reform
2005	Market Abuse
2006	Savings Law and Code of Conduct 3
2007	No Event
2008	Takeover Directive

Second, the reform was intended to improve market transparency through a wider set of disclosure requirements for listed firms: quarterly reports, a lower threshold (2 per cent) above which equity holdings have to be disclosed to the Italian market authority (the Commissione Nazionale per le Società e la Borsa, CONSOB) and full publicity regarding shareholders' agreements or voting pacts.

Third, a stricter discipline concerning takeovers was introduced, imposing equal treatment of shareholders (through a mandatory total tender offer on 100 per cent of the shares) when control is acquired by buying more than 30 per cent of voting shares of a listed firm (the so-called coat-tail provision). If evaluated on the basis of the index of La Porta *et al.* (1998), Draghi's law significantly improved the protection environment for Italian shareholders, increasing the Italian score for the index from 1 to 5 (out of 6) (Dyck and Zingales, 2004; Aganin and Volpin, 2005).

Another crucial step towards Italian corporate governance development is represented by 'Vietti's law', entitled 'Structural Reform of Corporations and Cooperatives', which took effect at the beginning of 2004. The innovations brought about by the reform greatly increased the degree of autonomy and flexibility achievable through companies' by-laws. The reform also introduced two new possible corporate governance structures: the 'dual' governance model, inspired by the German two-tier board structure, and a 'unitary' governance model in the classical Anglo-Saxon mould. These models will be discussed in more detail later in the chapter. Along with wider autonomy for the company charter provisions, minority shareholders' protection was increased through a wider application of the right to withdrawal. Finally, as a further element of flexibility the possibility of issuing financial instruments has been extended: a wide range of special classes of shares can now be created, including limited-voting shares, as can shares with economic rights tracked to a particular firm's business.

After some major financial scandals (such as Cirio, Parmalat and BPL-Antonveneta) the Italian government further toughened corporate regulation. Along the lines of the US Sarbanes–Oxley Act (SOX), the Italian Parliament approved the so-called Law on Savings (Legge sul Risparmio), which came into force on 12 January 2006. This new reform introduced a number of legislative changes aimed at protecting public savings and preventing corporate frauds. SOX certainly inspired some of the new provisions, such as the supervision of external auditing companies, the increased responsibility for companies' CFO and the increased transparency requirements for offshore companies and stock option plans, which must now be approved by the shareholders' meeting, disclosed and filed to the market regulator.

The Law on Savings also amended the 1998 TUF with regard to the appointment and composition of the board of directors of listed companies and potential actions against them. In particular, at least one director must be reserved for the minority shareholders' list that collected the greatest number of votes. Since the threshold for presenting a list varies from only 0.5 per cent to 2.5 per cent of the voting capital (depending on the company's size), the new provision attracted some activist funds (e.g. Hermes and Algebris), which bought small stakes in some Italian listed companies and tried to gain a seat on their board. However, ownership of 2.5 per cent of the shares is now sufficient to sue directors, as against the previous required level of 5 per cent.

Although a little later than required by the EU Commission, in 2005 the Italian Parliament transplanted the 'market abuse directive', which amended and partly replaced the 1998 TUF provisions on insider trading and other market abuses. Among the main interventions, this law carefully defines the notion of 'inside information' and the way in which price-sensitive news must be disclosed to the CONSOB and the public.

Recently, a law that came into effect at the end of December 2007 transplanted the EU 'Takeover Directive' 2004/25 IEC, aiming at harmonising member states' takeover regulations. The new Italian takeover law confirmed the existing 'passivity rule' and 'breakthrough rule', already in force since the 1998 TUF. As far as the 'squeeze-out'/'sell-out' provision is concerned, minorities are obligated or allowed to sell their shares once the bidder owns more than 95 per cent of total voting rights.

To conclude, we ought to mention that in the past few years the pressure towards better shareholder protection has by no means come exclusively at a mandatory level. In particular, in October 1999 a corporate governance committee appointed by the Italian Stock Exchange approved a code of conduct with the aim of consolidating best-practice principles and improving investors' confidence in the domestic financial market. Although compliance is on a voluntary basis, listed companies are required to disclose their level of adoption of the code and to justify why they are not fully compliant (the 'comply or explain' principle). After two thorough revisions (in 2002 and 2006), the third version of the code is now in place. It mainly regulates the role, composition, appointment and remuneration of the board of directors and the board of auditors, price-sensitive information and related party transactions. (Massimiliano, Marco and Stefano).

6.7.2 Shareholders' Meetings

Regardless of the specific corporate governance model chosen by the company, the general discipline of shareholders' meetings is largely the same. In Italy, two different types of shareholders' meetings exist: the ordinary meeting (or annual general meeting) and the extraordinary meeting. In traditional corporate governance the ordinary meeting takes the major decisions concerning the 'typical' activity of the company (such as the approval of the financial statements and the appointment of the other bodies), while an extraordinary meeting is convened to approve modifications of the company's charter or by-laws (resolutions concerning mergers, equity issue, etc.).

Depending on whether the meeting is ordinary or extraordinary, some specific rules governing its validity are in place. In fact, in order for the meeting to be valid, there is a minimum establishment quorum to be met. In the event that the required capital is not present at the first scheduled meeting, a second meeting has to be called. For ordinary meetings the quorum for the first call is set at 50 per cent of the voting capital, whereas no quorum is required for the second call. In both calls, resolutions are then adopted on the basis of a majority of the represented votes. For extraordinary meetings of unlisted firms, resolutions in the first call can be taken only if the votes of one-half of the voting capital (which is also the implicit minimum establishment quorum) are in favour, while in the second call, one-third of the capital must be present and resolutions are taken with a majority of two-thirds of the voting capital (the votes in favour must in any case exceed one-third of the capital for a given set of decisions). As far as listed firms are concerned, an extraordinary meeting needs an establishment quorum equal to one-half, one-third and one-fifth of the voting capital in the first, second and third call respectively while resolutions always have to be approved by a two-thirds majority of the voting capital represented at the meeting. For both unlisted and listed firms the company's charter is allowed to set higher establishment and deliberative quorums.

6.7.3 The Board of Directors

The 'traditional' Italian corporate governance system provides a board of directors (consiglio di amministrazione) and a separate board of statutory auditors (collegio sindaccile) with supervisory functions. As required by Italian law, an external auditor is in charge of auditing the financial statements of a listed company. The shareholders' meeting is the sovereign body, the expression of the will of the firm's owners. As a consequence, in the traditional system all the members of the board of directors and board of statutory auditors, as well as the external auditors, are appointed by the general shareholders' meeting.

However, the 2004 corporate law reform introduced two additional alternative structures of corporate governance: the two-tier system and the one-tier system. In line with the German governance model, in the two-tier (dualistic) system the shareholders' meeting appoints the members of the supervisory board (consiglio di sorveglianza), and this latter, in addition to its oversight and supervisory functions, has the power to appoint the management board (consiglio di gestione). As in the traditional model, the shareholders' meeting also nominates an external auditor. The second alternative model, reflecting the Anglo-Saxon practice, is 'unitary', or one-tier. Its main difference with respect to the traditional system regards the lack of a separate supervisory board. In fact, in the one-tier model the shareholders' meeting appoints the board of directors while a management control committee (comitato per il con trollo sulla gestione), composed only of independent directors, is endowed with the monitoring function. Despite some major banks having adopted the two-tier model, the most common corporate governance structure still remains the traditional one.

6.7.4 The Ownership Structure of Listed Companies and its Evolution

The Italian financial system can be seen as the archetypal one where publicly listed firms are characterised by the presence of 'a controlling ultimate shareholder' (often a family), whose limited capital exercises control on a wide amount of assets, thanks to pyramidal structures, non-voting shares and voting agreements. In this setting, controlling shareholders may extract a considerable amount of private benefits, as shown by the huge gap between the value of voting and non-voting shares and the high premium for control paid in controlling block transactions.

Italy has recently brought in relevant legal reforms, but these have not discouraged the ultimate owner from retaining full control of listed firms. However, the typical controlling block has gradually changed since 1998. In fact, the 1998 reform raised the quorum needed to deliberate in the shareholders' extraordinary meeting to two-thirds of the voting rights represented in the meeting. As a consequence, a block of 33.34 per cent of voting shares is now sufficient to prevent any hostile takeovers, as it can block any decision taken at an extraordinary shareholders' meeting. Moreover, since 1998 the takeover discipline has required that a bidder willing to take over a listed firm has to make a public offer to all minority shareholders once the bidder controls 30 per cent of the votes. The combined effect of such provisions is that many controlling stakes now comprise between 30 per cent and 40 per cent of voting rights (Mengoli, Pazzaglia and Sapienza, 2009).

6.7.5 Pyramiding, Dual-Class Shares and the Value of Voting Rights

Families typically use pyramidal groups, dual-class shares, voting agreements and cross-holdings in order to control large amounts of assets with limited capital. Recent studies (Mengoli, Pazzaglia and Sapienza, 2009) have shown that the percentage of firms that exhibit a pyramidal structure declined from 31 per cent in 1995 to 14 per cent in 2005 as a result of a change in corporate governance practices and disclosure regulation. Moreover, since 2008, 5 per cent of inter-corporate dividends are always double-taxed (they were completely tax-exempt till 2004 and 5 per cent were double-taxed in some circumstances after 2005).

About 44 per cent of listed firms had a dual-class equity structure in 1990 as against only about 10 per cent in 2008, thanks to many dual-class unifications made after 1998 (Bigelli, Mehrotra and Rau, 2007). The most common dual-class equity structure is made up of voting shares (carrying one vote) and non-voting shares (carrying no vote). Non-voting shares can be issued up to 50 per cent of equity capital and take precedence in the event of bankruptcy. They also have some dividend privileges, entitling their owner to a minimum dividend and to an extra dividend in respect of the voting share. Both dividend privileges are set by the company charter as percentages of the par value of the shares and are typically equal to 5 per cent and 2 per cent of par respectively. Notwithstanding the dividend privileges, non-voting shares were traded at a deep discount in the 1980s. The price difference between voting and non-voting shares (an underestimate of the value of a voting right) averaged about 82 per cent in the 1980s (Zingales, 1994) but decreased to about 20 per cent in recent years (Caprio and Croci, 2008). Thanks to stronger investor protection, the more international nature of investors, and expectations that in the future the dual classes will be unified.

References

Aganin, A. and P. Volpin (2005). "History of Corporate Ownership in Italy", in R. Morck (ed.), *The History of Corporate Ownership*. Chicago: University of Chicago Press.

ASX Corporate Governance Council (2007). *Corporate Governance Principles and Recommendations*. Second Edition.

Anna, Burmajster (2009). *The Handbook of International Corporate Governance: A Definitive Guide*. Second Edition. London and Philadelphia: Institute of Directors.

BDO Kendalls (2007). "Corporate Governance Report 2007", http//www.newcastle. edu.au/ Resources/Schools/Business%20and%20Management/Horwath%20Report/2007/2007-Mid-cap-Full-Report.pdf

Bianchi, M. and L. Enriques (2005). "Corporate Govemance in Italy after the 1998 Reform: What Role for Institutional Investors?", *Corporate Ownership and Control* 2: 11-31.

Bigelli, M., V. Mehrotra and P.R. Rau (2007). "Expropriation through Unification? Wealth Effects of Dual Class Share Unifications in Italy", *ECGI Finance Working Paper Series* No. 180.

Bosch, Henry (2002). "The Changing face of Corporate Governance", *University of New South Wales Law Journal* 25(2): 270-93.

Caprio, L. and E. Croci (2008). "The Determinants of the Voting Premium in Italy: The Evidence from 1974 to 2003", *Journal of Banking and Finance* 32: 2433-43.

Clarke, T. (2007). *International Corporate Governance: A Comparative Approach*. London: Routledge.

Dyck, A. and L. Zingales (2004). "Private Benefits of Control: An International Comparison", *Journal of Finance* 59: 537-600.

Farrar, J. (2005). *Corporate Governance: Theories, Principles and Practice*. Second Edition. South Melbourne, Victoria: Oxford University Press.

Ferrarini, C.A. (2005). "Corporate Governance Changes in the 20th Century: A View from Italy", *ECGI Law Working Paper Series* No. 29.

Ferrarini, G.A., G. Giudici and M. Stella Richter (2005). "Company Law Reform in Italy: Real Progress?", *Rabels Zeitschrift für Ausländisches und Internationales Privatrecht* 69: 658-97.

Greenbury, S.R. (1995). *Directors' Remuneration*. London: Gee & Co. Ltd.

La Porta, R., S.F. Lopez-de-Silafle, A. Shleifer and R. Vishny (1998). "Law and Finance", *Journal of Political Economy* 106: 1113-55.

Myners Report (2001). *Institutional Investment in the United Kingdom: A Review*. London: DTI.

Sykes, T. (1996). *The Bold Riders*. Sydney: Allen & Unwin.

UTS CCG (2007). *The Changing Roles and Responsibilities of Company Boards and Directors*. Final Report. Sydney: Centre for Corporate Governance, University of Technology. *http://www.ccg.uts.edu.au/PDF/Final Report.pdf*

Zingales, L. (1994) "The Value of the Voting Right: A Study of the Milan Stock Exchange Experience", *Review of Financial Studies* 7: 125-48.